Planet Golf

The aim of PLANET GOLF is to present readers with an authoritative reference to the great golf courses that exist beyond the borders of the United States of America.

During the research and selection process for this book we traveled over a quarter of a million miles, stopped off in more than forty countries and visited in excess of 600 golf courses in order to bring you the best golf from across the globe. The final reviewed list (overleaf) includes more than 130 golf courses, with the wonderful links of Britain and Ireland, the leading classics of Australia and Canada and the largely unheralded gems of Japan, France, New Zealand and South Africa most prominent.

While there is no doubt that the ancient Scottish game of golf has been most successfully exported to America, creating a 'world' book that does not focus on the USA's finest has allowed us to highlight a number of unknown international masterpieces. Courses like Augusta National, Pebble Beach, Pine Valley and Cypress Point have been covered exhaustively in prior publications, and what we hope PLANET GOLF will prove is just how many 'other' great courses there are on our great golf planet.

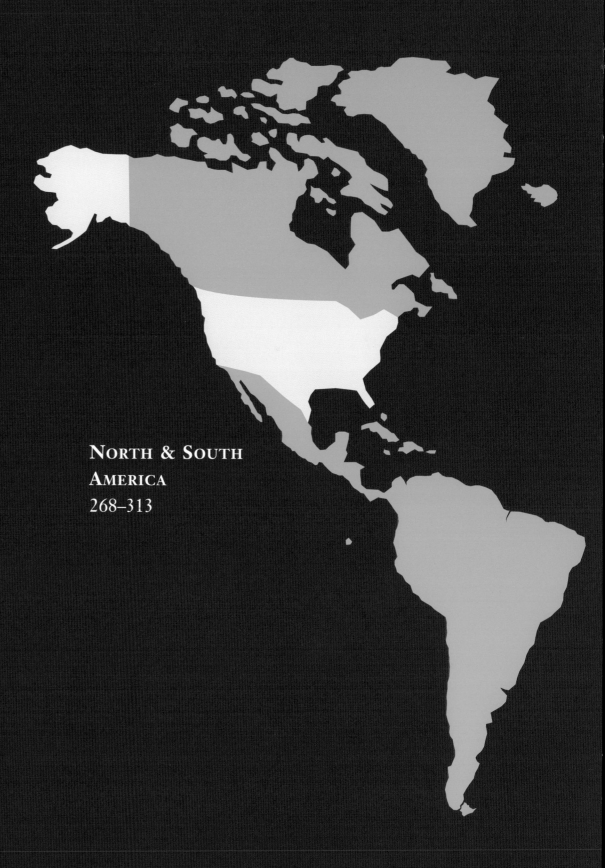

NORTH & SOUTH AMERICA
268–313

CONVERSIONS Throughout PLANET GOLF any reference to course length or hole length is consistent with the system of measurement used in that particular country. The golf courses of Great Britain & Ireland, Asia and North & South America typically use imperial measurements while European, Australasian and African courses generally use the metric system. As an approximate guide, to convert meters to yards simply add 10 per cent, or, for more accuracy, multiply the figure by 1.093.

PREVIOUS PAGES Kauri Cliffs, New Zealand – 17th hole.

PLANET GOLF

PLANET GOLF

The Definitive Reference to Great Golf Courses Outside the United States of America

BY DARIUS OLIVER | PHOTOGRAPHY BY DAVID SCALETTI

ABRAMS, NEW YORK

GREAT
BRITAIN &
IRELAND
1–147

EUROPE
218–267

ASIA
314–349

AFRICA
350–367

AUSTRALASIA
148–217

Quick Contents

Contents

Foreword

'PLANET GOLF is the finest, and most comprehensive, directory on golf courses I've ever seen.'

My obsession with the game of golf started as schoolboy curiosity back in Queensland in 1970, but has since grown into a lifelong passion that I share with millions of golfers worldwide. While the thrill of competition and the drive to continually improve were the factors behind my success as a player, it is the golf courses themselves which have most mesmerized me and have always been at the center of my love for the game. It is, after all, the courses that separate our sport from all others; in no other sport are the fields of play so glorious, so varied and so interesting as in golf.

From its modest roots along the Scottish coastline, golf has developed into a truly international game that is enjoyed by people in all corners of the globe and from all walks of life. I consider myself extremely fortunate to have been able to golf in so many countries over the past four decades, and to have played and studied most of the planet's premier courses. It has always been my belief that as elite sportspeople, PGA professionals have an obligation to help promote the sport worldwide wherever possible. Not only did I find it enlightening and educational to travel so much and to sample so many different golf courses, but there is no doubt that it helped me improve as a player, and now as a designer. It is a shame that some of today's stars no longer feel the same sense of responsibility to take their games onto the global stage.

Although America has become the dominant power in modern golf, there are hundreds of superb layouts in other parts of the world as well, including many that until now had been overlooked by the mainstream golf media. My own personal favorites include famous tournament venues such as Royal Melbourne, Augusta National, St Andrews and Shinnecock Hills as well as some of the game's lesser-known courses, including my own Doonbeg links and the ultra-private Ellerston. As a disciple of the design ideologies of golf's earliest course architects, I am continually inspired in my own design work by the wonderful old MacKenzie courses in my homeland, Australia, and the ancient links of Britain and Ireland. It is particularly pleasing, therefore, to see a number of courses that my company designed featured alongside these greats of yesteryear.

As an Australian who cut his teeth in Europe, settled in America and played golf all over the world, I am delighted to be associated with a publication that has a true international focus and so attractively highlights the very essence and quality that makes golf courses such fascinating and exciting creations. In my opinion, PLANET GOLF is the finest, and most comprehensive, directory on golf courses I've ever seen. I sincerely hope that you enjoy the book and that it encourages you to sample some of the great golf available outside the United States.

Greg Norman

OPPOSITE **The 14th hole at the Greg Norman-designed Ellerston Golf Course (page 182).**

Introduction

Despite the increasing popularity of our sport and the hundreds of books written on the subject of golf courses, until PLANET GOLF there remained a massive gap in the literary coverage of our playing fields. While numerous publications admirably document the leading golf courses of specific regions, none of those that purport to present a world view has, until now, been able to provide even close to a comprehensive guide to the globe's best golf.

Our unique concept from the very outset was to create a definitive reference to great golf courses, but to exclude the USA, golf's most prominent and powerful marketplace. This was done as a point of difference but also because the sheer size and nature of the American industry makes it difficult to cover with real accuracy or authority. The fact that as many new courses are built annually in the United States as the rest of the world combined means content is easily dated. Also, each previous 'world' publication has been written with a heavy American bias, and while not suggesting that the likes of Pine Valley, Pebble Beach, Augusta National and Cypress Point are not superb, they have been extensively covered in other books and their omission has allowed us to feature a number of the hidden international masterpieces so often denied their due publicity.

So, just what are the world's finest golf courses and how does one identify them and then separate the very good from the great and the great from the world-class?

Though golf course appreciation is a complex and subjective business, broadly speaking a course is made up of eighteen holes, with both the holes themselves and the greater layout essentially a composite of the fundamental elements of site, design, setting, construction and secondary issues like the greenness of its grass. As there is no such thing as a perfect golf course, ultimately it is the level of imperfection within these areas that determines the class of a course.

OPPOSITE **Par three 17th hole at the little-known Japanese gem Hirono.**

17th hole at the unheralded St Enodoc layout, its heaving dunes and subtle links undulation an example of why the 'Golden Age' produced so many wonderful courses.

The modern look of links golf, the 10th hole at South Africa's lush and symmetrical Fancourt Links.

OPPOSITE The rugged and more natural appearance of the classic British links, here Royal Birkdale's famous 12th hole.

Almost universally, the best layouts in golf remain those built prior to World War II, primarily because early architectural pioneers better understood the advantages of incorporating natural features into design and the land they used for their courses was usually more suitable to the game than the modern golf site. Originally a site was selected because of its golfing potential and the course was then hand-shaped. This is generally no longer the case, and despite some terrific advancements made in construction and turf technology, great golf on great land is still a winning combination.

The particular standout period was the so-called 'Golden Age' of design, which began in Britain around the turn of the 20th century, when the game spread inland and the first genuinely talented designers started to establish their reputations. Previous golf architects, mostly professional players and greenkeepers, had largely demonstrated an inability to fashion exciting golf away from the sea. As a result, golf had been almost exclusively played on links, those courses built on the rich coastal land left by the retreating seas. The breakthrough came with the 1901 opening of Willie Park Jr's Sunningdale course near London. Between this event and the Second World War, golf course architecture as a serious profession was born, and most of golf's worthwhile venues created.

The most successful and significant design career of this period belonged to Harry Colt. Initially alone, and then in partnership with Charles Alison, John Morrison and Dr Alister MacKenzie, Colt was responsible for more exceptional pieces of work than any other man in the industry. From Pine Valley (with George Crump) and Toronto in North America to Falkenstein, Kennemer, De Pan and Le Touquet on the mainland of Europe and the series of stunners in his native Britain, the scale and variety of Colt's body of work is astonishing and should still form the basis of most architectural educations.

MacKenzie also remains a giant of design's Golden Age and is probably the best known of all architects, thanks largely to his revered work at Augusta National, Cypress Point, Royal Melbourne and Lahinch. MacKenzie and Colt, along with Alison, Tom Simpson and others, like North American pioneers Charles B. Macdonald, Donald Ross and Stanley Thompson, shared a love of the old Scottish links and the design virtues these courses taught those able to appreciate their subtleties. Citing the great links as an inspiration remains a potent marketing tool for contemporary designers, though it is often little more than a promotional blurb rather than a legitimate statement of motivation. The difference between enjoying a course like St Andrews and understanding its relevant design concepts is huge, with many unable to distinguish between the features on the ground and the actual elements that really make the individual holes work.

Throughout the generations there have been disappointing golf courses. Unfortunately, in recent times the percentage of poor results in virtually every region has been increasing. A major reason for this has been the worldwide shift from the British philosophies employed by the early design pioneers to a modern marketplace dominated by an American style of design. While

Scotland's short and quirky Machrihanish links (8th hole) is proof that great golf does not need to be long, lush, green and mean.

The par three 13th (4 South) at Harry Colt's Hamilton Golf & County Club in Canada.

OPPOSITE 10th hole on the Jack Nicklaus-designed Ocean Course at Cabo del Sol in Mexico.

OVERLEAF Par three 2nd hole at the Kingsbarns Golf Links, Scotland.

American courses are usually visually appealing and exciting to play, the simple truth is that, with some very obvious exceptions, nobody does American golf quite like the Americans. Great golf land spoiled by low-budget Sawgrass-style design is particularly common throughout Asia, Africa and mainland Europe, where many new courses rely on gaud and green grass, rather than substance, to impress.

If one does detect a sentimental slant toward the classic courses featured in this book, that is because they have stood the test of time while, beyond the hype, many modern layouts, in reality, are formulaic, repetitive and disappointing. The blame for this does not rest entirely with the architect. A great portion must fall on the panels, professionals and high-profile magazines that hoodwink the average golfer and golf developer into believing that a course needs to be green, gruelling and tournament ready in order to be well regarded and highly ranked. This mindset is hurting golf badly, with the vast majority of new courses created with 'championship' length and built with an emphasis on difficulty, often at the expense of good golf holes.

The reality is that the difference between a championship venue and a quality course is considerable, and the fact that most golf tournaments these days are hosted by clubs that have paid for the privilege should not be forgotten. Nor should the fact that if quality golf really had to be tough and lush, then any scribble or sketch could be converted into a world-class venue by a grass guru and penal architect building the holes long, the fairways narrow, the roughs thick and the greens small. Compare the prospect of such a course with the charismatic classics of Britain or the strategic playability of the best from Colt, Braid, Simpson, Macdonald and MacKenzie, whose layouts actually provide a more diverse range of challenges than today's multiple tee box courses. The very shortfalls of modern golf, however, are what has made it even more rewarding to uncover gems like Carne, The National Moonah, Teeth of the Dog, Barnbougle Dunes, Doonbeg, Praia D'El Rey, Loch Lomond, Nirwana Bali, Cape Kidnappers, Prince de Provence, Ellerston, Cabo del Sol and Kingsbarns.

During the research process for this book we were fortunate to be able to visit more than six hundred golf courses worldwide. With more than five hundred missing out on being reviewed, there will no doubt be high-profile omissions that surprise some readers. Those that are featured, however, were the clear standouts in their region and each review aims to provide readers with an understanding of how the holes were created and what ultimately makes them so special. All critical remarks are made with due consideration and in the interests of providing balance to the reviews, while in a deliberate attempt to focus on the golf course rather than the golf experience, peripheral elements like exclusivity and championship history are largely ignored.

Written as a tribute to the world's best golf courses, and with a greater global perspective than any other publication, superb photography and leading designers providing interesting anecdotes on many of their layouts, it is our hope that you will find PLANET GOLF an insightful read and an indispensable guide to our mighty golf planet.

Great Britain & Ireland

OPPOSITE The birthplace of the game, Great Britain and Ireland are home to more high-quality courses than any other region in this book. From heathland and parkland golf to low-set links and big dune specials, there is no better place to golf than the British Isles. Right, Ireland's Ballybunion Old Course, 15th green.

Scotland

OPPOSITE The Old Course at St Andrews is a Scottish icon, as is the devilish Hell bunker on the par five 14th hole.

Although several countries and cultures have some historical claim on the development of golf, the genesis of the modern sport certainly stems from a simple game played with sticks and pebbles on the eastern coastal dunes of Scotland during the 15th century. This primitive game was popular enough in St Andrews by 1457 for King James II to issue a parliamentary decree forbidding it, worried that it might keep his subjects from the archery practice required to repel the frequent English incursions. Despite the decree, the game expanded beyond St Andrews and the Kingdom of Fife, and by 1650 there were a dozen links along the Scottish eastern seaboard, from Dornoch and Aberdeen in the north down through Montrose, Carnoustie, Leven and farther south around Edinburgh and East Lothian.

Between this period and the game's boom in the mid-to-late 19th century, golf was legalized and formalized, with clubs and rules established. The eighteen-hole course was standardized and its playing fields and hazards defined. Golf, however, remained prohibitively expensive owing to the cost of handcrafted equipment such as the individually stitched featherie balls. That all changed with the introduction of the mass-produced gutta-percha ball in 1848, which made the game more accessible and led to the most significant period of growth in its history.

As player numbers in Scotland increased, so too did golfing venues. Courses were created across the country with almost every seaside town, small or large, fuelling the national pastime by converting its suitable linksland into golfing fields. The influence of St Andrews on the greenkeepers and golf professionals who laid out Scotland's early links was considerable. The course continued to have a substantial impact on the work of the first professional golf architects, men like Colt, Braid, MacKenzie, Simpson, Park Jr and Fowler, who studied its every natural feature and then tried to copy its style and strategy in their designs.

Scottish golf has an antiquated charm all of its own. The links here are older, the clubs more traditional and the venues more naturally suited for the game than anywhere else in the world. Beyond the historic ambience and superb scenery, the beauty of Scotland is the number of genuine hidden gems situated in close proximity to the famous classics. Beyond those featured in the following pages you would do well to consider old-fashioned charmers like Elie and Crail outside of St Andrews, Monifieth and Panmure near Carnoustie, Western Gailes near Troon and Gullane's No. 1 Course next door to Muirfield. Also, on the remote island of Islay, the Machrie Golf Club is a wonderful destination and worth doubling with Machrihanish, while the championship quality of Nairn and the fun of Boat of Garten make both worthy of a side trip for those venturing into the Highlands for Royal Dornoch and Brora.

For many golfers a trip to Scotland is a rite of passage, and while its mighty Open championship venues are rightly revered throughout the world, to visit these shores and ignore ancient gems like North Berwick, Royal Dornoch, Machrihanish, Prestwick and those listed above is to miss as much as you see.

Royal Dornoch Golf Club – Championship Course

COURSE OPENED 1886
DESIGNERS Old Tom Morris,
John Sutherland,
George Duncan

'No golfer has completed his education until he has played and studied Royal Dornoch.'

HERBERT WARREN WIND

The historic Highlands village of Dornoch, in Scotland's far north, is home to some of the oldest linksland in the world, primitive golf starting on its seaside common ground prior to 1616. Like in most of the ancient golf towns, however, the game was a marginal sport here until the (Royal) Dornoch Golf Club was formed in 1877. Initially the club golfed on a basic nine-holer, with Old Tom Morris responsible for extending the course and rearranging the rudimentary layout into the links we now recognize as one of the game's greats. Although many of the Morris holes remain, his course was altered substantially by John Sutherland during his 50-year tenure as club secretary, and again by George Duncan after several holes were destroyed during World War II.

The present championship links is among the most attractive golfing venues on the planet. Occupying softly contoured dune ground that follows a curving coastline, the opening and closing holes are played along an upland plateau, with the rest heading back along the lower beachside area. The key features of Dornoch are its incredible green sites. Most are enormous and either built up on natural tables or sunken into small basins with a mix of cunning swales and knolls shrinking actual target areas and seriously complicating recovery play. In terms of your approach shots, the line between success and failure is finer at Dornoch than on any links. The key being not to push too hard when out of position, as the greens are tilted to accentuate mistakes and reject anything not coming in from a very precise line and with an ideal trajectory.

After an inviting opener, the core challenge of Dornoch becomes evident at the short 2nd. Its putting surface, like so many others, is elevated, with steep banks kicking stray balls into frightening recovery positions. The first glimpse of the course's beauty comes as you step through the whins onto the 3rd tee, which looks majestically down over the glorious lower ground and tumbles toward a left-to-right-sloping target tucked beyond a small ridge. The next two are an awesome double act, with the deceptively narrow 4th hole featuring a huge green set beyond a valley and cleverly angled to accept only the most perfectly struck irons. The 5th is then an outstanding mid-length par four that forces you to flirt with hazards from the tee in order to set up a decent shot into another brilliant plateau green. This heavily bunkered target is quite large but feels tiny when approached from the wrong side of the wide-open fairway.

Next is the six-hole Duncan loop, which begins with a wicked little par three across a swathe of gorse to a tabletop green cut into the side of a hill. Although each of the subsequent holes are excellent, the real standouts tend to reside either side of this solid central section. The 12th through 16th, for instance, remain largely unchanged from Morris's original plan

OPPOSITE Dornoch's gorgeous setting is enhanced with the golden gorse in full bloom, this the view from atop the par four 17th fairway.

and include Dornoch's world-famous Foxy hole, the 14th. This long, left-bending par four is totally bunkerless and features a broad green set on a natural ledge several feet above the fairway. A green in regulation here is an uncommon achievement, and from the surrounds your pitching, chipping and putting options are endless, though positive outcomes are again highly unlikely. The uphill 16th has fewer fans but is noteworthy as it brings you back up to the top shelf and the raw glamour of the 17th, which drops briefly before rising again around gorse and across a sandy ridge into its superb saucer-shaped green. The strong par four finishing hole is a magnificent end to proceedings, the partially hidden target wonderfully situated in a raised hollow beyond a small but significantly challenging gully.

Though your lasting impression of Royal Dornoch is likely to be dominated by the greens, all elements of the course are first-class, in particular the seemingly generous fairways, which actually play quite narrow and provide a stern examination of your driving skills. The remote and romantic village itself is steeped in history, and in many ways it is the tranquility of the experience here, as much as the quality of the links, which ensures that for golfers the longing to return to Dornoch is as strong as for anywhere on Earth.

ABOVE On a links full of great greens the fiercely bunkered 5th is one of the standouts.

OPPOSITE Your iron play needs to be precise from the start at Royal Dornoch, the short 2nd punishing anything hit left, right or long.

North Berwick – West Links

COURSE OPENED 1877
DESIGNERS Tom Anderson,
David Strath,
Ben Sayers

The 4th is the first in a set of strong par threes.

OPPOSITE The pleasure of playing at North Berwick is highlighted by the approach into the famous Pit hole.

Golf was first introduced to the sleepy seaside hamlet of North Berwick in East Lothian during the early 17th century, though it wasn't until players shifted from the Burgh Common onto what later became the West Links a century later that the game really started to flourish here. Confined at first to the land within its boundary walls, the town's initial six-hole course gradually expanded beyond its ancient borders until eighteen were in play by 1877. Created mostly by David Strath, the first full links, which included the famous Redan hole, was quite short but was lengthened substantially in 1895 by head greenkeeper Tom Anderson. Anderson is the man most responsible for shaping the modern North Berwick, although further expansion in 1932 allowed club professional Ben Sayers to add a new 10th hole and lengthen both the 9th and 11th. Aside from the odd moved or removed bunker and back tee, this cherished links has changed little since.

For aficionados and golf historians, North Berwick is almost as significant as St Andrews. Its ancient links are dotted with golfing monuments and traverse stone walls, snaking burns, yawning bunkers and house some of the most imitated holes in golf, as well as other gems impossible to replicate. Like St Andrews, the course starts and finishes within the town, the layout bumping its way along North Berwick's white sandy shoreline and enjoying commanding views over the Forth Estuary and its volcanic Bass Rock.

An unpredictable journey from beginning to end, the West Links opens with possibly the worst hole in Scotland but is followed by one of the best in the world, a brilliant par four that bends around the beach and proved the inspiration for the first of the thousands of subsequent Cape holes. The drive here is across the corner of the coast to a fairway that is relatively flat close to the sea but wildly undulating down its safer left side. The 3rd is also terrific and plays across the town's former boundary wall and into the newer links section. Following excellent short holes at the 4th and 6th and the two-shot Eli Burn 7th, the course then heads into the western dunes, where its three long holes, 8, 9 and 11, cleverly play into, across and then with the prevailing winds that follow the inward holes back toward town.

While the back nine tends to be dominated by the anticipation of playing the original Redan (15), the highlight is undoubtedly the Pit hole (13). A mid-length par four, the Pit is played along a diagonal stone wall to a sunken green resting in a natural hollow and squeezed between the wall and a beautiful beachside dune. A true original, this classic is just part of an extraordinary run of fine holes, from the superb simplicity and expert construction of the 11th and 12th through to audacious one-offs like the 14th and 16th. Named Perfection, the 14th hole initially hops along a wrinkled fairway ridge and is then blind over a crest toward a hidden green located a few yards from the

crashing surf. The 16th, by contrast, at first appears a fairly tame par four, but its flat fairway disguises one of the most memorable green formations anywhere, the putting surface actually two shallow shelves split by a swale several feet deep.

Sandwiched between these daring holes is Redan, said to be the most copied par three concept in golf. Played across an obscuring mound, this famous one-shotter features a heavily bunkered target that sits atop a plateau and is angled away from the tee. While the modern Redan holes tend to copy the bunker arrangement and shape of the green, it is really the slope of the large target and the variance each pin position brings that makes this hole so effective. Easily dismissed by the modern golfer as weak, the final two holes are also very good and provide ideal matchplay moments, particularly the drivable 18th, which heads back into town across a massive corrugated fairway to a green set close to an entrance road.

The embodiment of everything great about Scotland and the sport of golf, the unforgettable West Links at North Berwick is the quintessential quirky links and ought to be the first course confirmed on any Scottish golf itinerary. While St Andrews is the spiritual home of our game, it was links like this one that gave golf its soul.

ABOVE The unconventional fun of Perfection, North Berwick's 14th hole, which ends with this blind target.

OPPOSITE Hitting back toward town from the 18th tee.

St Andrews Links – The Old Course

COURSE OPENED prior to 1457
DESIGNERS Mother Nature
(with Allan Robertson and
Old Tom Morris)

St Andrews' iconic 18th green and the
Royal & Ancient clubhouse.

OPPOSITE Looking across the
tiny Road hole green and down the 18th
fairway toward town.

Whether golf evolved from a Dutch, Belgian, German, Roman or Chinese sport or is entirely indigenous to Scotland, St Andrews is unquestionably the birthplace of the modern game. The town's famous Old Course, the oldest golfing field continuously in existence, has been in action since at least 1457, when the game was banned from its common ground by King James II.

The evolution of these links, whose fairways were formed by grazing sheep and whose bunkers were created by animals sheltering from the wind, has had an enormous impact on golf as we know it. In 1764 the original 22-hole course was reduced to eighteen holes, creating the now standardized golf course configuration. In 1848 Allan Robertson doubled the width of the shared fairways, a move that laid the foundation for strategic design as it allowed golfers to take longer routes around hazards or continue with a direct but dangerous passage to the target. Around the same time the eight shared greens were also increased, while Old Tom Morris later rebuilt the stand-alone 18th green. He also split the 1st and 17th green, allowing the previously clockwise links to be played from the opposite direction, a change that became permanent after many years of alternating play.

Since then volumes have been written on St Andrews and the history of its links, and most readers won't need further flowing prose on the virtues and significance of a place they are already dying to visit. Instead, we really should ignore the history and heritage of the Old Course and concentrate on the strength of the holes in the ground and the canvas upon which they are laid in order to determine the real quality of this ancient links.

There are certainly more attractive pieces of golfing ground; the curving, crumpled linksland is quite grim and low-set, with several areas, such as around 9 and 10, unlikely to stir the emotions of even its most fervent fanatic. It may seem like blasphemy, but the outward stretch of golf here, though solid, is less impressive than many courses featured in this chapter. The real highlights are the generic features of the deep and at times hidden pot bunkers, the enormous and bizarrely contoured double green complexes and the fairways, which are massive but offer a genuine reward for those able to drive aggressively between the whins and the bunkers along the narrow right-side corridors. Throughout the round, finding one of the bottomless bunkers means a shot or more lost, but in avoiding them too cautiously you often leave your ball deep in three- or four-putt territory. This is the real joy of the Old Course – its playing areas are expansive yet the ideal corridors are quite thin, making the challenge as much about your management as your mechanics.

While the opening three holes are a fine start to the round and others such as 5 and 7 are also very good, the real strength of St Andrews

is the run home from the 11th. This is a stretch that rivals the outward half at Royal County Down for its long period of continued brilliance and includes several world-class moments. The 11th, for instance, is a wonderful short hole with the steepest green and deepest guarding bunkers imaginable, while the 14th is an amazing three-shot concept dominated by the huge Hell bunker. The 17th (Road hole) is arguably the most charismatic and exciting golf hole on the planet. Equally outstanding are the 12th, which can be driven only after dodging a collection of small hidden pots, and the obscured approach into the football-field-sized 13th green. The Principal's Nose bunkers on the 16th are also excellent, as they reward those squeezing a drive between the sand and the boundary fence with a significantly easier shot into its baffling green shape.

The biggest clichés in golf include the sentimental belief that St Andrews, as the home of the game, is the best course on earth, and the opposing assertion that beyond all the history she is overrated. It certainly seems a stretch to suggest that because the Old Course is the oldest in the world it cannot be compared to the rest, and in truth it does not belong near the top of ranking lists because of its vintage, but because it is an extraordinary piece of links with one of the longest stretches of great golf in Scotland.

OPPOSITE One of the most celebrated short holes in golf, the 11th on the Old Course features an enormous double green that is slanted steeply forward and protected by some of the deepest bunkers on earth.

Prestwick Golf Club

COURSE OPENED 1851
DESIGNER Old Tom Morris

'A man is less likely to be contradicted in lauding Prestwick than singing the praises of any other course in Christendom.'

BERNARD DARWIN

OPPOSITE Slicers beware! Prestwick's mid-iron, wedge opening hole is squeezed up against the railway fence and overlooks the local cemetery.

Birthplace of the Open Championship, the historic Prestwick Golf Club is one of the oldest along Scotland's golf-rich West Coast. It was formed in 1851 when founding members managed to poach Old Tom Morris from St Andrews to create its first course and then convinced him to remain on as clubmaker and head greenkeeper. Morris's course was a twelve-hole links on tight terrain, sandwiched between the club's present southern boundary and a stone wall beside its 3rd green. His holes zigzagged around dense dunes and crossed in and out of deep dells with most of the approach play blind and dangerous.

Despite its shortcomings, the course hosted the first twelve 'British' Opens and provided the framework for the full eighteen-hole layout, which was created in 1883. Though only the famous Alps hole resembles any of the original twelve, several iconic features were retained, including the massive Cardinal and Sahara bunkers as well as at least seven greens. Prestwick later fell from the Open Rota because of problems handling the championship's increasing crowds, but its full course was an immediate success and it remains one of the quirkiest and most enjoyable links in the world.

Although its appearance is somewhat unconventional, the course does provide a very conventional links examination. It has firm fescue fairways, deep revetted bunkers, thick, punishing rough areas and a number of blind shots played over large hills to mysterious target areas. These are often small and either set down in the original Morris hollows or built up on plateaus. Interestingly, some of the surviving 1851 greens, such as 13 and 15, were originally played from a different angle and, almost inconceivably, were left unaltered when the course expanded, meaning they now cruelly slant away as you play your approach.

For first-timers Prestwick can be a puzzling maze, as confusing to navigate around as it is difficult to master. There are almost too many highlights to mention, but several 'only in Scotland' type holes standout. The opening par four, for instance, is best tackled with a mid-iron from the tee, while the par three Himalayas (5) is totally blind over a huge sandhill. The Alps (17) hole has a thrilling approach first across another mountainous hill and then beyond the hidden Sahara bunker into a blind bowl. Most unusual, however, is the 15th, which heads into a narrow and heavily bunkered valley and then demands an impossibly delicate pitch across a crest to a green falling sharply away from play. More conventional is the strategic par four 4th, which bends around Pow Burn to a green tilted toward the water and favoring those driving close to the hazard. It is an excellent test, as is the Cardinal hole (3), notorious for its massive sleeper-faced bunker but with an underrated final third played over some of the humpiest turf in Scotland with all sorts of approach shot options.

Prestwick's great strength is not the quirkiness of its hidden bunkers or the one-off nature of holes like 1, 5 and 15, but instead the all-world quality of moments like the approach into 3, 4 and 17, the strong stretch of two-shot holes from the 6th and the crazed challenge of hitting into and then chipping around nasty targets like 7, 13 and 15. Aside from the blind shots and cruel greens, the most common gripe with Prestwick is its seemingly soft finish, though both the drivable 16th and 18th are pivotal swing holes in a close match with cleverly contoured greens that can punish those pushing too hard for closing birdies.

Though it is eccentric and at times confusing, if you can look past the odd spots and appreciate Prestwick for what it represents, then you may just walk away from a round here with a new perspective on your passion. Indeed, if I had to pick one course to play out my days on, this might well be it. Not because it is appealing and challenging to players of all ages and abilities, but because for even the longest serving member there remain at Prestwick more putts, pitches, stances and situations left unseen than on any other course I know. In every sense this is a links one could not possibly tire of playing.

ABOVE Deep bunkers guard a narrow entrance to the 12th green.

OPPOSITE The green and the enormous Sahara bunker are totally hidden from approaching golfers on Prestwick's famous Alps hole.

Royal Aberdeen Golf Club – Balgownie Links

COURSE OPENED 1887
DESIGNERS Robert Simpson,
Archie Simpson,
James Braid

Balgownie's par three 17th hole.

OPPOSITE The raw glamour of the opening holes at Royal Aberdeen, on display as you play the wild approach into the 4th green.

Although the formation of the (Royal) Aberdeen Golf Club in 1780 was the birth of organized golf in Scotland's North East, the genesis of the game in this region dates back much further. In fact, Aberdeen's initial layout, the Queen's Links, was the subject of the world's earliest recorded description of a golf hole in 1625 and many believe the game itself actually originated here. By 1887 the club had outgrown its increasingly popular links, however, and migrated across the River Don into the magnificent Balgownie linksland two miles north of town. There a new course was designed by Carnoustie golfers Archie and Robert Simpson, and later re-bunkered and lengthened by the great James Braid.

One of the oldest, finest and most underrated links in Britain, Balgownie has a classic out-and-back arrangement with holes laid out on lumpy links ground along the North Sea shoreline. The outward holes are the most celebrated, running beside the roaring ocean and following deep coastal dune formations. The less intimidating inward nine are set on a slightly elevated plateau but are equally demanding, as they are sensibly routed back into the prevailing winds.

The opening stretch of holes is among the strongest in Scotland and boast's the sort of scenery, design variety and visual excitement of golf's elite courses. The round begins with a terrific hole played from beneath the clubhouse, the drive needing to squeeze through bunkers before you play the memorable cross-valley approach into a steep plateau green. The next is a rugged par five through dunes and across a boldly contoured fairway, which is followed by a strong and semi-obscured par three that crosses small sandhills and completes an excellent opening trio. Also outstanding, the 4th features a fabulous approach across some of the site's wildest undulation, while the short 5th is a classic risk/reward par four with a well-bunkered but incredibly tempting away-sloping target. Concluding an extraordinary half of golf, the 9th bumps its way along a rippled ridge toward the northern corner of the property, where its green overlooks the terrific neighboring Murcar links.

Though the front nine occupies the prime coastal dunes and features most of the exciting terrain, the flatter and elevated back nine is still great fun, with the same clean-cut revetted bunkering, fascinating putting surfaces and first-rate links turf. Visually from the tee, the holes are slightly less impressive than the front nine, with the exception of a blind drive across a large ridge on the 10th. The golf remains fantastic, however, particularly the triple-tiered par three 17th and the rolling par four 18th, which heads into a raised and heavily bunkered green site.

Despite its out-and-back nature, Royal Aberdeen has tremendous variety and features plenty of subtle directional shifts. Though reluctant to make major changes to its layout, in recent times the club has added some sensible new back tees to ensure the links remains a relevant and strict test in today's terms. Given the discrepancy between nines, Balgownie is most often compared to other uneven big dune specials like Royal County Down and Machrihanish, though the disparity is probably less pronounced here than elsewhere. That said, the outward stretch is outstanding, the highlights coming thick and fast on a front nine that ranks among the finest in the world.

Carnoustie Golf Links – Championship Course

COURSE OPENED 1842
DESIGNERS James Braid,
Old Tom Morris,
Allan Robertson,
James Wright

Situated along the North Sea, across the Bay from St Andrews, lies the resort town of Carnoustie. Its spacious sandy linksland has been a venue for golf since the 1500s, though its current links were not formalized until 1842. Initially a ten-hole layout designed by Allan Robertson, the final eight holes were later completed by Old Tom Morris but revised substantially by James Braid who, in 1926, shaped the course into a genuine championship venue by lengthening holes, adding bunkers and shifting most of its green sites. The Braid course was well received and successfully hosted the 1931 Open, but it was felt that the finish proved an insufficient test. Prior to the 1937 Championship a local golfer, James Wright, redesigned 16, 17 and 18, wrapping them around the menacing Barry Burn and creating possibly the toughest closing stretch in the game. Aside from a few back tees, the course remains virtually unaltered to this day.

With the sea rarely in view and the grim industrial areas of the grey town prominent from several positions, Carnoustie is far from the prettiest links in Scotland but makes up for any aesthetic shortcomings with a strategic routing and a terrific collection of strong holes. The layout first heads out in a large clockwise arc before turning at the 11th to swing its way back toward the clubhouse. Unlike a traditional out-and-back routing, this unique arrangement ensures the wind quarters from every possible direction, never allowing the golfer to settle into any sort of rhythm.

One of the most relentless driving tests in golf, Braid's fairways are defended by native rough areas that can be grown out to frightening proportions, strong winds that whip across the site and deep, punitive bunkering. Most of the hazards are strategically positioned and often protrude up from dead flat ground to confuse depth perception and obscure the green sites. The links landscape itself is quite stark here, but the number of high-quality holes constructed on featureless ground is remarkable. The likes of 7, 9, 10 and 12 are unlikely to stimulate the senses but have stern driving challenges and well-bunkered greens that force those seeking out pins to take substantial gambles.

All eighteen holes are capable of hurting the unsuspecting golfer. After an attractive but relatively soft opener, the first real test is the terrific 2nd, played through a narrow valley and into a long, tiered green pinched in by greenside bunkers. The pitch across Jockie's Burn into the heavily contoured 3rd green is another gem, as is Hogan's Alley (6), a brilliantly conceived three-shotter along an out-of-bounds fence with central bunkers splitting the fairway and squeezing the aggressive driving line. For a relatively flat five this hole is almost perfect, with each shot becoming progressively more difficult the more conservatively one has played and each bold decision carrying a significant risk but genuine reward. The 7th is then the archetypal Carnoustie hole, a well-bunkered but bleak par four that forces those looking for birdie to either drive

OPPOSITE The par four 15th at Carnoustie marks the start of one of golf's hardest closing runs.

close to the boundary fence or to a couple of hungry bunkers, according to the pin position.

As for the rest of the course, both the 8th and 13th are outstanding short holes with great green sites, while the 14th is the most intimidating from the tee, and the start of Carnoustie's famous finish that includes one of golf's hardest par threes (16) and three of its strongest fours (15, 17 and 18). The final two holes both use the naturally snaking Barry Burn to tremendous effect. Splitting their fairways several times, the burn creates strategic golf holes that are relatively simple to bogey but can prove quite an ordeal for those searching for better.

Forget what you may have read about Carnoustie, for although it is tough, it is far from the unplayable monster that many make it out to be, especially when the rough areas are robust without being ridiculous. The course is a great challenge and an absolute pleasure to play. Though it lacks the obvious sex appeal of a Royal Dornoch or a Turnberry, Carnoustie has as many outstanding holes as either and remains one of Scotland's must-see layouts.

ABOVE The testing pitch shot into the small 3rd green.

OPPOSITE Barry Burn and an out-of-bounds fence are just two of the obstacles on Carnoustie's fierce finishing hole.

Gleneagles – Kings Course

COURSE OPENED 1919
DESIGNER James Braid

Approaching the par four 7th green.

OPPOSITE Nowhere to miss on the gorgeous par three 5th with its steep plateau green.

OVERLEAF Braid's best, the mighty 13th on the Kings Course.

Nestled at the foot of the Highlands and surrounded by some of the prettiest countryside in all of Scotland, Gleneagles is a luxury hotel and golf resort situated on the windswept moorlands of Perthshire. It was built by the Caledonian Railway Company during the 1910s and was most likely inspired by the success of other rail and resort destinations such as Turnberry and Cruden Bay. James Braid designed the first two courses on the vast estate, both his Queens and Kings layouts opening in 1919 with the magnificent chateau-style hotel completed five years later.

The Kings Course was created out of a dramatic wilderness cleared mostly by horse and cart, its holes built over an undulating sandy heath and the springy fairways lined with punishing gorse areas, heather patches and frequent copse's of pine and birch. Most of the golf falls naturally across ridges and deep glades or through small, secluded valleys and attractive glens. With sweeping views of mountains to the north and rolling green hills to the south, the scenery throughout the journey is as rich and impressive as the resort's luxurious lodgings.

The starting stretch is particularly solid and, although the opening hole seems an unlikely design highlight, its fairway is so wide and the steeply elevated green so clearly the major obstacle that sleepy golfers are often lulled into a sloppy approach with dire consequences. Snaking its way downhill, the 2nd is then an excellent driving hole while the Silver Tassie 3rd heads back up into a hidden fairway and an outrageously hidden green site. The round doesn't get any easier from here,

but thankfully the highlights continue. The short 5th, with its cruel tabletop target, and the doglegging 7th across a blind rise are further standouts on a front nine that ends with a dangerous par four heading toward the distant hills. The inward run then heads out to the farthest point on the property before turning and snaking back toward the hotel. Aside from being a nine of great balance with a variety of hole lengths and challenges, the real star of the back nine is Braid's beloved 13th, a wild ride across tumbling ridges and through gorse, bracken and deep, devious bunkers into its superbly tilted green.

Beyond great golf, Gleneagles can also provide design enthusiasts with a valuable insight into the shift in design philosophies through the decades. The newer Centenary Course, designed by Jack Nicklaus, may be a Ryder Cup venue and occupy an attractive piece of ground, but it is indistinguishable from many of his other projects and disappointing when compared to the mighty Kings and its under-appreciated little sister. Shots into the 9th, 12th and 17th on the Queens Course, for instance, are among the most enjoyable on the entire property.

There is also much to admire about the tremendously original and consistent Kings layout, especially its best few holes, which are absolutely outstanding. Though Woodhall Spa and Ganton are both more difficult, and Sunningdale, Swinley Forest and Loch Lomond more exclusive, Gleneagles Kings is the equal of them all and unquestionably one of the premier inland courses in Britain.

The Honourable Company of Edinburgh Golfers – Muirfield

COURSE OPENED 1891
DESIGNERS Harry S. Colt,
Tom Simpson,
Old Tom Morris

Muirfield's distinctive 18th green
and bunker.

OPPOSITE The approach into the par five
9th is played through an out-of-bounds wall
and this collection of deep bunkers.

The oldest golf club in existence, the Honourable Company of Edinburgh Golfers was formed in 1744 and golfed in both Leith and Musselburgh prior to moving to the messy, medium-sized dunes of Muirfield in Gullane in 1891. Overlooking the Firth of Forth, the Muirfield links was first designed by Old Tom Morris but was altered substantially in 1928 when the club purchased additional land and employed Harry Colt to rearrange the links into its current form.

Rather than a traditional strip of linksland, at Muirfield Colt was presented with a squarer paddock of ground, which famously enabled him to devise his much-copied two loops arrangement with a counter-clockwise back nine laid within a larger clockwise front nine loop. This ensures that the golfer experiences the wind from every possible direction. To complicate play, Colt lined his holes with some of the most brutal bunkers in Britain. His original plans had in excess of two hundred traps, although more than one hundred were removed a few years later at the suggestion of Tom Simpson.

Like most championship links, Muirfield is a beast in high wind, when the otherwise generous driving areas shrink and avoiding the deep hay and punishing pot bunkers turn it into a test of survival. The course begins with a right-bending par four that in every way sets the tone for the round: thread the eye of a needle off the tee or approach the green with your third. Better holes to follow include strategically bunkered par fours at the 6th and 8th, the long 9th which heads along an out-of-bounds stone wall, the gorgeous short 13th and one of the sternest closing runs in the game. The real highlight of Muirfield, though, is the bunkering and the contouring of the green surrounds. The 3rd green, set attractively between the dunes, is a stunning example, as are beautifully protected targets at 4, 5, 11, 12, 13, 15 and 16.

Far from the most attractive links on the Scottish East Coast, Muirfield works owing to the logic of its structure and the consistent and intelligent quality of its holes. There are few here that really stand out as exceptional, but none, aside from perhaps the 10th, which golfers might look upon with displeasure. One common gripe with the links is that it cramps you from the opening tee shot right through to the final approach, tempting you to make a mistake and punishing you severely when you do. The chances of playing the sort of brave recovery shots or risky wrong-angle approaches that you can elsewhere in Scotland are reduced by the fact that a slight spray here often means a sideways chip or sand blast.

Muirfield polarizes popular opinion, with some critical of its bleak landscape and penal severity and others convinced that, by virtue of its difficulty, it is the greatest links in the world. While there is little doubt that most of Colt's best holes exist elsewhere, this is undeniably his most difficult course and most suitable tournament venue. The ruthless routing is also the most effective at exposing deficiencies in your game, and if this really is the hallmark of great golf then Muirfield may well be, as often rated, among the best ten tracks on the planet.

Machrihanish Golf Club

COURSE OPENED 1879
DESIGNERS Old Tom Morris,
Sir Guy Campbell,
J.H. Taylor

'Specifically designed by the Almighty for playing golf.'

OLD TOM MORRIS ON THE
LINKSLAND AT MACHRIHANISH

OPPOSITE Welcome to Machrihanish!
This the view from the tee on arguably
the finest opening hole in the game.

Situated at the southern tip of Scotland's romantic Kintyre Peninsula, the Machrihanish Golf Club is one of the most remote courses in golf and started life in 1876 on a ten-hole links laid out on farming ground adjacent to the Atlantic Ocean. The club soon flourished, and in 1879 Old Tom Morris arrived from St Andrews to extend the links out to eighteen holes. The course was then redesigned by J.H. Taylor in 1914 and again 30 years later by Sir Guy Campbell, though the efforts of each man are barely visible upon what is one of the game's most natural landforms.

Machrihanish is an old-fashioned links with a very traditional out-and-back layout that first follows the humps and hollows of the sand dunes bordering the Atlantic and then heads home inland toward the Kintyre hills. The most significant features of the links are the incredibly natural greens, which are among the coolest target areas on earth. Many are merely a conclusion of its rollicking fairways, with some set down in bowls and others on top of steep ridges or built through fairway valleys. The memorable greens are almost too numerous to mention, but there is little to compare with the pleasure of pitching or putting into targets like the hidden 2nd, set beyond a hill in a fractured punchbowl, or the away-sloping 13th green with its massive false front.

The round begins with a cracking hole, regularly rated the best opener in golf. Built by Morris, this bruising par four is played across the corner of Machrihanish Bay, and often into the wind, to a fairway set diagonally across the tee. The course itself is much more than a one-hole wonder. In fact, the entire front nine are exceptional, with wild moments like the approach into the sunken 3rd green, the terrifying short par three 4th and the partly obscured 7th hole, just as impressive as the intimidating opening drive. The 6th is a great short par four, as is the 8th with its frightening target sitting atop a flattened hill. Most outstanding of all, however, is the 5th, with a fairway that narrows as it turns hard-left into a remarkably undulating green site that falls away from play. The longer one drives on this mid-length par four, the more palatable the approach, as those coming from too far back have to cross a sharp left-to-right slope.

As with a number of other renowned out-and-back links, the inland holes here are inferior, though aside from a couple of flat holes at the finish, the remainder are full of real quality. The par five 10th and small tabletop par three 15th, for instance, are very fine, while both the 12th and 13th are moderate holes worth seeing for their incredible green complexes. The 12th is a three-shot hole on relatively dull ground that ends with a bumpy basin-shaped green, which is raised above deep bunkers, set beyond a slight dip and slopes noticeably from front to back. The second of consecutive par threes, the long 16th is another

excellent test, though somewhat disappointingly a dune ridge was shaved down in the 1990s to allow a view of its previously hidden target. From here the journey back to the clubhouse takes you across two flat fairways, with avoiding a burn on the 17th and an out-of-bounds area on the 18th the key to finishing your round well.

There is no doubt that part of Machrihanish's attraction lies in the remoteness of its setting and the escapism that playing here provides, but to dismiss the golf as simply remote is to overlook a front nine of real quality and the most imaginative set of greens to be found anywhere. Indeed, there are few more enjoyable places to golf than Machrihanish, especially on those rare mornings where the sun is shining, the wind is blowing and the ball is still flying straight.

OPPOSITE The semi-sunken 3rd is a classic Machrihanish green with endless options of attack.

The Westin Turnberry Resort – Ailsa Course

COURSE OPENED 1950

DESIGNER Mackenzie Ross

The dangerous 16th hole with its built-up green and deep burn.

OPPOSITE The most attractive of Britain's Open Championship venues, the Ailsa Course gets right down by the sea and overlooks Turnberry's famous lighthouse.

One of golf's earliest resort destinations, Turnberry's origins date back to 1901 when the Marquess of Ailsa commissioned Willie Fernie from Royal Troon to lay out a course beside the spectacular West Ayrshire coastline. The Marquess then used his directorship of a local railway company to extend the rail line into Turnberry to service the course and a new luxury hotel he had helped build.

In 1909 Fernie added a second course, later becoming the Ailsa, but Turnberry was requisitioned by the British government during the first and second World Wars, its hotel used as a hospital and the fairways converted into concrete runways. Following World War II, the site was left dilapidated and seemingly useless until Scottish architect Mackenzie Ross undertook the enormous task of demolishing the aircraft hangars, removing the concrete and tarmac, and recreating the course on what was left of the linksland. Damaged considerably, much of the original golf land was devoid of the natural contours that had existed prior to the runways, so Ross shrewdly pushed the Ailsa Course closer to the sea and into the heavier coastal dunes untouched by the armed forces. There he was able to create a grand-scale links that complemented the dramatic nature of the site, building a series of testing holes and an exceptional set of greens that he had first sculpted in plasticine prior to construction.

Enjoying sweeping views across the Irish Sea to the peaks of Arran and the famous Ailsa Craig rock, the Ailsa Course actually begins quite tamely but,

following an excellent 3rd hole, it settles into a memorable out-and-back rhythm, first along the shoreline and then back along the flattened portion of the property. The strength of the links is the impressive stretch of front nine holes, the 4th through 8th, that head along the high dune ridges shielding the layout from the sea. Its most notorious, however, are 9, 10 and 11, which touch the coast and overlook the iconic Turnberry lighthouse.

The 9th is a unique hole with a blind drive played from a rocky promontory to a hog's-back fairway that is almost impossible to hold. The approach must then find a green which falls away sharply on both sides. The next two are good holes on great real estate down by the surf, and as you turn to head back toward the clubhouse, the rest of the layout is an interesting, if somewhat mixed, collection of holes. The first few along the flattened ground are a little dull but the finish, from the short 15th, is terrific. It includes a deep snaking burn abutting the built-up back-to-front-sloping 16th green and a penultimate par five that is reachable, but cleverly positioned at a pivotal point in the round to bite those pushing too hard for birdie.

Thanks to Mackenzie Ross and its Open Championship status, Turnberry is now a legend in this part of the world and the Ailsa Course is one of the first links selected on the itinerary of most traveling golfers. Although the early holes on each nine are a little soft, the six or seven great holes and the sheer beauty of the setting combine to make this one of Scotland's most satisfying golf experiences.

Kingsbarns Golf Links

COURSE OPENED 2000

DESIGNER Kyle Phillips

'From my first visit to the site I could see the potential for a great course.'

KYLE PHILLIPS

Opening in 2000 to unprecedented levels of international acclaim, Kingsbarns is a remarkable links achievement that stretches along one-and-a-half miles of Fife coastline just outside St Andrews. Covered in a sublime dunescape and with outlooks across the North Sea from every hole, the site appears ideal for golf, yet the virgin land here was devoid of any natural feature, clay-based and mostly unsuitable for the game.

Golf on this particular property actually dates back as far as the 1790s when the Kingsbarns Golfing Society was formed, though the land had been used as agricultural ground ever since the Second World War. When American designer Kyle Phillips first saw the property during the 1990s he immediately recognized its potential, and dreamed of converting the flat site into a big dune links complete with high hills, rolling fairways and constant sea views. His concept was sold to Californian developer Mark Parsinen, who helped finance a project that required a considerable amount of earthmoving to complete.

The key to making the Phillips vision effective was building a realistic dune system. Drawing upon previous experiences in the field and extensive studies in terrain analysis, Phillips first created an immense artificial landscape and then spent weeks roughing up the hills to make them look natural. The result is the most authentic-looking set of dunes constructed for golf, with a series of attractive parallel ridges built along the thin strip of coastal land and the fairways then cut into staggered sand shelves to ensure panoramic and uninterrupted

views of the water. Complementing the gorgeous playing corridors are highly contoured target areas that are generally angled to offer the bold driver a range of approach shot options.

The round begins with a terrific starter that tumbles toward the sea and immediately introduces golfers to the views and the layout's classic links characteristics. The rest of the journey is rock solid, with great design variety and a routing full of visually appealing holes that are exciting to play. The best stretch of golf comes through the middle of the round, with the short par four 6th a particular favorite. Its green is simple and open for golfers able to drive onto the narrow right shelf, but blind and treacherous for those bailing down the safer left side. Also excellent are short holes at 2 and 13 and the dramatic par five 12th that sweeps around the shoreline. The closing stretch, from the beachside par three 15th, is especially strong and ends with a fine par four that demands a bold approach across a burn into its steeply tilted green.

Kingsbarns was a massive opportunity for Kyle Phillips and came shortly after he left Robert Trent Jones Jr to start his own design business. Although he did an exceptional job, in many ways the links is a triumph of vision and construction rather than design, with the experience more about the authenticity of its appearance than a large number of standout moments. There is no denying that Kingsbarns is scenic, challenging, well built and kept in super condition. Were there just a couple more outstanding golf holes, however, it would unquestionably rank among Scotland's finest few.

OPPOSITE The 5th fairway showcases Kyle Phillips's remarkable shaping at Kingbarns.

Cruden Bay Golf Club

COURSE OPENED 1899
DESIGNERS Old Tom Morris,
Tom Simpson

'Never was a links more adapted by nature for a golf course than that fine stretch of ground lying round the Bay of Cruden.'

GOLF MAGAZINE, 1899

OPPOSITE A magnificent view of Cruden Bay's sunken 14th green as well as its sweeping coastline. Note the ruins of Slains Castle in the distance.

Occupying some of the mightiest duneland in Scotland, Cruden Bay is a cult classic situated 20 miles north of Aberdeen. Golf was first played in this small village as far back as 1791, although the present links were created by Old Tom Morris in 1899 for the Great North of Scotland Railway Company to complement its newly completed Cruden Bay Hotel. Erected on cliffs overlooking the sea, this grand hotel was reminiscent in scale and splendor of the famous Turnberry Hotel but was demolished after falling into a state of disrepair during the Great Depression. Fortunately the links was saved a similar fate by a group of local businessman who purchased the site and established the Cruden Bay Golf Club.

Set amid glorious coastal dunes and along the white sandy beaches of the curving bay, the links of today differs considerably from the 1899 version, with Tom Simpson redesigning the layout in 1926 and responsible for its current configuration. Simpson was generally critical of Morris's design work, but at Cruden Bay he found much to admire and kept the basic routing and several green sites, including the 6th, which he believed was one of the finest in Britain. Despite almost a thousand yards being added since the 1920s, Cruden Bay remains very much as Simpson and Morris had conceived.

The ancient ruins of Slains Castle, the inspiration for Bram Stoker's *Dracula*, provides a striking backdrop to early holes that head east toward the historic fishing village of Port Erroll. The first standout hole is Simpson's drivable par four 3rd, with its sunken green hidden from the tee and pushed into a hollow immediately above the village's tidal river. The long par three 4th then heads along the river and toward the sea and is another mighty Simpson hole of considerable quality. From here the course turns to follow the shoreline and onto the strongest stretch of golf on the links. Both the 5th and 7th are fine two-shotters through big dunes, while the 6th is one of the sportiest par fives in Scotland, where attempting to hit the green in two requires the boldest of strokes across wild rough areas to a narrow tiered shelf of green set beyond a burn.

The character of the links changes briefly at the 8th as you head through a large grassy amphitheatre and onto the hilltop 9th hole, with its stunning views across the site and out over the ocean. From an elevated tee, the 10th crashes back onto the lower linksland where both Simpson's short 11th and the par four 17th are among the notable remaining holes. The tee shot on the 17th is dominated by a large central mound, said to be a burial ground for some of the ten thousand soldiers slain on the site during a bloody 1012 battle between the Scots and Danes. The real talking point, however, is the bizarre stretch from 14 to 16, which features back-to-back blind greens and consecutive par threes. Played into a narrow valley between the beach and huge dunes,

the 14th is a terrific hole that rises into a dell green located in a hidden hollow. Next up are the two par threes, the first a brutal long shot across the corner of a large hill and the second, a shorter hole, typically played into the headwinds to an obscured target that slopes away from play.

Largely unheralded for many decades, Cruden Bay was recently 'discovered' by several prominent writers and golf professionals and its popularity has since exploded. While there is much to admire about this unusual links, in some ways the course suffers from its own success, as it seems to sit more comfortably within the hidden gem category than as a stand-alone, must-play destination like Royal Dornoch, St Andrews or the nearby Royal Aberdeen. There are some very odd moments here, a bland start, an out-of-context central section and successive blind par threes that many are bound to dislike. There is also some exceptional and unconventional golf, however, which combined with the charming, laid-back ambience of the small village and its wonderful duneland make Cruden Bay a hugely enjoyable experience.

OPPOSITE In the shadows of the charming village of Port Erroll, Tom Simpson's strong par three 4th is played across a deep hollow and along a tidal river to an elevated green cut into the facing sandhill.

Loch Lomond Golf Club

COURSE OPENED 1993
DESIGNERS Tom Weiskopf,
Jay Morrish

*'I consider Loch Lomond my
lasting memorial to golf.'*

TOM WEISKOPF

Set along the bonnie banks of the magnificent Loch Lomond and enjoying startling vistas across its glassy waters to the surrounding Ben Lomond Mountain, the Loch Lomond Golf Club is one of the most sumptuous golfing experiences in all of Europe. Built on land that is sacred to the Scots, it took ten years to convince authorities to grant the necessary permission to build a golf course on the site. When finally approved, the original investor offered the design job to former Open champion Tom Weiskopf after being frustrated that other 'signature' designers had indicated they would only send associates to the site to do the work. Being a very 'hands on' designer, Weiskopf, by contrast, was able to devote the time necessary for a project of such significance.

When Weiskopf arrived in Scotland there hadn't been a course built for almost 20 years and to his great surprise, aside from resting beside one of the most beautiful lochs in the country, his property was blessed with a collection of huge old trees, natural wetlands, marshes, trout streams and enough elevation change to create interesting holes. Unlike many designers, he and partner Jay Morrish spent a great deal of time on site, recognizing the rare opportunity they had been given to create something quite remarkable and pouring their energies into the course. Weiskopf even relocated his family to the area for two summers while he worked on shaping its every feature.

With a distracting setting and a course maintained in mint condition, the quality of the design on the ground is at times overlooked here. While its overtly American character upsets some, the site did not lend itself to links style golf, as parts lie below the level of the lake and the soil is heavy and damp. The variety of holes and shotmaking challenges is impressive, however, and the actual design elements employed are first rate, particularly the interesting use of hazards like the low stone wall that crosses the 3rd green, clever central traps at the 6th, 7th and 9th and the burns and lakes dotted strategically through the back nine.

Arranged in two loops, the first eight holes run through pine forests and along the banks of the Loch and the final ten, cut by several burns and streams, end alongside a small cove. Front nine highlights include the par three 5th, which heads toward the Loch, and the two subsequent long holes that follow its shoreline. Turning away from the water, the short par four 9th is an interesting hole on flat land while the 10th is a downhill two-shotter along a pond that provides a demanding start to an inward half full of outstanding features. These include the fall-away green on the 12th and the intriguing par five 13th, with a creek set well back from the green and either flown in two or three depending on the strength and accuracy of the drive. The 14th is then an excellent short par four that is reachable for long hitters who can carry the wetlands and chase the ball onto the green via a narrow frontal apron. The finishing

stretch is particularly difficult and starts with an impossibly long side-hill par four at the 16th followed by a stunning long shot over wetlands to an attractively bunkered green at the 17th. Concluding the round is a wonderful Cape-style hole around the Loch to a fairway leaning toward the water. Its three-tiered green is set up to favor those driving bravely down the left side and rests beneath the ruins of the 15th century Rossdhu Castle.

Though unashamedly American, the design at Loch Lomond has more substance than is sometimes apparent. Tom Weiskopf was so passionate about his work on this extraordinary property that he literally worked himself into the ground, very nearly dying early one morning when he sank up to his chin in a quicksand bog beside the 13th hole. Had he not been six foot-three he might never have seen the completion of a course which is one of the most impressive modern creations in the British Isles, and clearly the best of any built away from the sea.

ABOVE Facing the water, the short 5th is the first of Loch Lomond's glamour holes.

OPPOSITE Weiskopf's wonderful closing Cape hole, which bends around a small inlet.

Royal Troon Golf Club – Old Course

COURSE OPENED 1885
DESIGNERS George Strath,
Willie Fernie,
James Braid

A speeding train passes the difficult
11th green.

OPPOSITE Golf's ultimate par three,
Troon's world-famous Postage Stamp hole.

The Royal Troon Golf Club was formed in 1878 on a five-hole links created by the head greenkeeper at the neighboring Prestwick Golf Club. This initial layout was extended to eighteen holes within a few years by club professional George Strath and then altered by his successor, Willie Fernie, and again by James Braid prior to the 1923 Open Championship. Though little structural change has taken place since, as a regular championship venue its holes have been stretched considerably through the years, to the point where today's links is among the longest, and certainly the most difficult, in the British Isles.

In many ways Troon is the archetypal Scottish links and an ideal Open venue, its classic routing running out-and-back along bouncy low-set links terrain and dominated by deep rough areas and punishing revetted pot bunkers. While its landscape is a little bleak by comparison to others along the Ayrshire Coast, the links does feature pockets of quirkiness and the occasional exciting blind element, especially through a memorable cross-country central section.

Very much a tale of two parts, the round starts with a series of gentle holes running out along the sea and typically played with a helping wind, before turning inland and then onto a furious back nine which is much longer, has a lower par and plays into the stiff winds. The best stretch of golf comes through the middle of the round, which links the tamer start to the tougher close and enjoys the only significant elevation change on the property. The first to turn inland is the 7th, a medium-length par four of considerable intrigue with a fine green site and endless options of attack. The next is the highlight, Troon's world-famous Postage Stamp hole, which plays little more than 120 yards but features one of the greatest target areas in golf. Its tiny green is cut into the side of a sandhill and falls sharply away to deep, sheer-faced bunkers. With the penalties for any miss severe, the only way to avoid catastrophe here is to find the putting surface from the tee.

For those struggling to come down from the euphoria of the Postage Stamp, the 9th is a dangerous little sleeper and from here things only get more difficult as you turn for home and face the headwinds for the first time. The back nine challenge starts immediately with a blind drive over a gorse-covered hill and a perilous approach into a plateau green followed by an even fiercer test on the 11th, with its hidden fairway nestled between a railway line and thick gorse. The remaining stretch provides little respite. The only hole running back downwind, the 12th is a tricky par four with a tiered green, while the short 14th and 17th are both very fine, testing shots into tight targets. The 18th is then a classic finishing hole played through sand and fescues toward a green set beneath the clubhouse.

Royal Troon is a good links but a great tournament venue. It may not be the most exhilarating place to golf, but there is a nice flow to the layout and the final nine is certainly proficient at separating the pretenders from the contenders. Plus, in the Postage Stamp Troon boasts one of those rare holes that alone are worth traveling long distances to experience.

Murcar Golf Club

COURSE OPENED 1909
DESIGNER Archie Simpson

Occupying an impressive stretch of coastal dunes along Scotland's North Coast, Murcar is an unassuming golf club located beside the famous Balgownie links of Royal Aberdeen. Designed in 1909 by Royal Aberdeen's head professional Archie Simpson, the links was slightly altered during the 1930s by James Braid and George Smith but remains very true to Simpson's original form.

The front nine, set mostly within the heaviest dunes, is the standout. After a couple of solid narrow holes it explodes at the brilliant 3rd, with its crashing fairway partly obscured and tumbling down to a gorgeous bowl green that abuts the 10th at Royal Aberdeen. The left side of the fairway falls away heavily, while the right side is lined by thick gorse and provides the preferred angle but does mean an approach with only limited visibility. Other cracking holes include the short but deadly 5th and the mighty par four 7th, which is squeezed between a gorse-covered dune and marshy bog land, its oblique fairway cut by a burn and rewarding those who bravely drive close to the hazard. The 8th through 10th, 15th and short 16th are also very good.

Murcar may be a little short and a rung down from the quality of its illustrious neighbor, but a stack of great driving holes, nice green complexes and narrow, bumpy fairways make it a very interesting challenge and tremendous fun to play.

Brora Golf Club

COURSE OPENED 1923
DESIGNER James Braid

Located in the northern Scottish highlands, the unpretentious links of Brora occupy an ancient tract of farming land alongside the North Sea and enjoy spectacular views across the water to the distant purple hills. Old Tom Morris first laid out a course on the site in 1891, though it was totally overhauled when James Braid built a new eighteen-hole layout in 1923, his modest design remaining remarkably well preserved ever since.

Exposed to fierce sea winds, Braid's course heads out-and-back along the shore in a classic single loop and features a memorable array of green sites and naturally undulating fairway structures. There are also a number of genuinely outstanding golf holes to feast on, such as the drivable opener, the 5th, 11th and treacherous short threes at the 6th and 9th. The real highlights, though, come within a closing stretch of considerable dramatic merit. The monstrous uphill par three 18th and approach into the 16th, which plays from a narrow valley up into a fall-away green sitting atop a large ridge, are particularly impressive, while the 17th is a tremendous hole that sweeps down, splits in two and then rises into its tight, sloping target.

Like stepping back in time, Brora is totally wild, with electric fences around its greens to protect them from roaming livestock. Rabbit holes, cattle dung and barren fescue fairways are among its effective hazards. The course does struggle with conditioning and has a number of ordinary holes, but it is nevertheless an unforgettable experience and able to charm most of those who golf here.

OPPOSITE Approach into the
16th green at Brora.

England

OPPOSITE Oozing old English charm,
Sunningdale helped popularize heathland golf
and is a significant club in the history of the
sport. Pictured is the 7th hole, Old Course.

Although golf in England doesn't quite have the history of Scotland, it does share a similar lineage, with Scottish King and avid golfer James VI responsible for the increasing popularity of the sport in his homeland, and its later spread south when he succeeded to the English throne in 1603. Though the oldest recorded golf club here, Royal Blackheath, dates back to 1766, there are suggestions that the King and his courtiers had golfed on Blackheath as early as 1608, and certainly his highness did introduce the sport to the English nobility around this time.

As in Scotland, the game only really expanded in England following the arrival of the gutta-percha ball. The oldest surviving links, at Westward Ho! in Devon (1864), was the first of a string of links formed around a fertile coastline that provided early golfers with the same ideal contours and easy-draining sandy base of the famous northern links. Initial attempts, in the late 19th century, to bring golf inland toward the major population bases were largely unsuccessful, the early layouts servicing a demand but offering little in terms of genuine quality. That would change, however, when the sandy heathlands of Surrey and Berkshire, outside of London, were discovered, allowing Britons to experience quality golf away from the sea for the first time and leading to the English game developing its own unique identity.

The growth and success of the heathland was a significant part of the history of 20th century golf, primarily because it was here that talented architects elevated the art of golf course design into a serious profession. Men like Willie Park Jr, Herbert Fowler, Harry Colt, and later Tom Simpson and Dr Alister MacKenzie, were the first to successfully manipulate wooded terrain into strategic, exciting and aesthetically pleasing golf courses, the legacy of their early work living on in the well-preserved classics featured within this chapter.

There are fine golf courses in every corner of England, and its small size and the ease with which one can get around makes it possible to see a substantial number of the best courses in a short space of time. Sandwich, Deal (Royal Cinque Ports), Rye, West Sussex, Brancaster, Hunstanton, The Grove and the wonderful nine-hole Royal Worlington and Newmarket course are all easily accessible from a London base, while the likes of Ganton, Alwoodley, Woodhall Spa, Notts and the fine Lancashire links are reasonably close to major northern centers such as Leeds and Liverpool.

English golf does not seem to have quite the aura of Ireland or the mystique of Scotland, yet its best courses are the equal of any in the British Isles and the tremendous variety of golf styles available is unmatched anywhere in the world. With an abundance of outstanding big and small dune links, championship challenges and quirky charmers as well as premier parkland layouts and the subtle splendor of its heathland classics, England is able to please the fancy of every single traveling golfer.

St George's Hill Golf Club

COURSE OPENED 1913

DESIGNER Harry S. Colt

Famous for his short holes, Colt built some gems at St George's Hill, including the cross-valley 8th.

OPPOSITE The superb opening hole, with the abundant heather adding visual definition to the stunning landscape.

The prettiest and possibly the best of all heathland courses in Great Britain, St George's Hill was the vision of a builder, George Tarrant, who in 1911 purchased almost 1,000 acres on St George's Hill in Weybridge and then conceived of one of the world's earliest golf and residential developments.

From a golfing perspective, Tarrant's decision to include a course within his estate was a godsend. The sandy property was covered in a rich carpet of the purple heather and stands of the stately pines that around this time came to characterize quality inland golf. More important, it was full of the sort of dramatic natural contours that most courses in this part of the world show only glimpses of. His choice of Harry Colt as architect was also inspired and following almost two years of substantial tree clearing, the master designer set about constructing his holes through the dense woodland.

Full of outstanding moments, Colt's classy routing rolls up and over steep hills, ridges and ravines with hard-running, rumpled fairways and cleverly conceived greens that are quite large, yet often seem to have small target areas when approached from the wrong angle. Rising up through an attractive valley, the first hole is a magnificent start to the round and features a fabulous green saddled atop a crest. The 2nd is even stronger. Its drive is blind over the brow of a hill, and from a hanging lie the approach crosses a stream and heads toward an elevated target. The start of the back nine is just as impressive. The short 11th and wonderfully natural 12th are both excellent holes but dwarfed by the brilliant 10th, an

all-world par four with a touch of County Down. First played blind across a heather-covered hill, the approach is then semi-blind over a sandy ridge, cunningly positioned back from the green to kick the poorly struck shots into hungry gathering bunkers or leave them on the green's higher level. The 17th also occupies prime golfing real estate and, like the 10th, has a partially obscured green with a parallel tier that makes it either tighter or more forgiving depending on your angle of approach.

Typical of Colt's best work, the course has a great set of par threes, though it is really the two-shot holes that set St George's Hill apart from its Surrey neighbors. There isn't quite the difficulty of a Walton Heath or the variety of a Woking, as holes tend to fall predominantly right-to-left across the landscape, but the individual quality of the par fours is truly outstanding. Of the short holes, the Redan-style 3rd is a terrific test, as is the 11th, which features a tiny target unsympathetic to those unable to strike a precise wedge. The 2nd hole on Colt's Alternate nine is also very good, as is the picturesque valley 8th, though it lost some of its visual appeal when an enormous bunker cut into the upslope was broken into several smaller traps.

Despite its undeniable beauty, the most notable difference between St George's Hill and other heathland layouts in the area is the grand scale of the undulating terrain and Colt's brilliant use of the elevation changes within his design. Indeed, if Swinley Forest was Colt's 'least bad course,' as the designer himself once noted, then St George's Hill may well be his 'most good' one.

Sunningdale Golf Club

OLD COURSE OPENED 1901
DESIGNERS Willie Park Jr,
Harry S. Colt

NEW COURSE OPENED 1923
DESIGNERS Harry S. Colt,
John Morrison

*'All that one would hope to find
in the ideal golf club is in abundance
at Sunningdale.'*

SIR MICHAEL BONALLACK

OPPOSITE The approach shot
into the penultimate green on the
Sunningdale Old Course.

Home to the earliest outstanding inland course in Britain, the Sunningdale Golf Club is a true pioneer that helped to popularize one of the finest natural golfing regions in the world. The club was the inspiration of Tom Roberts, a homeowner within the sandy Sunningdale farmlands outside of Surrey, who managed to convince St John's College in Cambridge to lease their neighboring grounds to him for golf. He then persuaded a hundred keen golfers to contribute bonds to help establish the club and commision Willie Park Jr to design and construct its course.

When Park's course opened in 1901 it put both Sunningdale and London's Heathland on the golf map, and its success paved the way for other inland sites to be considered for development. One man who benefited from the growth of heathland golf was Sunningdale's first secretary, Harry Shapland Colt, who also had a major influence on the development of the Old Course while at the club. Prior to leaving his post to pursue a blossoming design career, he oversaw the redesign of many of the Park holes when the rubber-cored ball was introduced, and he organized the planting of thousands of trees, which are now such an integral feature of Sunningdale's once barren landscape. Later, with the club looking to meet an increasing demand for golf by expanding its facilities, he returned to design its New Course.

Opening in 1923, the New Course is built right alongside the Old Course but has its own distinctive character. The Old is heavily bunkered, and has a majestic collection of mature pine, oak

and birch lining its fairways, while the New Course has fewer bunkers but is a more exacting test from the tee, with longer carries and tighter fairways lined by a more intimidating cover of heather. Colt's green sites are also less forgiving. The middle section is the strength of both courses, with the New Course boasting an impressive run of solid holes from the 4th to the 14th. The Old Course is less consistent but has six or seven absolute standouts.

Occupying most of the prime land, the shorter Old Course starts with a reachable par five down a slight hill and ends with a long par four back up the slope. In between, it stretches out in a large loop along the western boundary of the property. The clever short par four 3rd and the one-shot 4th, played up into a hill ledge and across an expanse of heather, are its first significant holes. These are followed by an excellent trio of two-shotters. The 5th boasts golf's earliest-known man-made water hazard, and the 7th is played across a wonderful fairway that twists through the pines and rises into a terrific plateau green set on a small crest. Other noteworthy moments include the view from the elevated 10th tee and the crafty short par four 11th, which heads blind over a nasty bank to a fairway sloping away from the green. The 12th, across a series of ditches, is also very good, as is the long par three 15th and the three substantial par fours back along the trees that close the round.

By contrast, the New Course is built across a more open and uniformly undulating landscape

with deep, punishing bunkers and greens that are more demanding on your approach play, many being built up with false fronts and subtle tiers. The central section of Colt's original layout was considered too hilly by the membership and by 1934 had been replaced with five new Tom Simpson holes (6 to 10), which only a few years later were reconfigured on additional land by John Morrison, a partner in Colt's design firm. The opening and closing holes are a touch underwhelming here but the heart of this course is exceptional, starting with the excellent right-bending 4th and then along through a series of attractive short holes and demanding par fours which are set through thick heather and relentless on those inaccurate from the tee. The strategic simplicity of gorgeous holes like the 7th and 12th and the heavier undulations of the 8th and 9th are among the highlights.

Situated on a fabulous property, Sunningdale is a one of the world's premier golf clubs and among the most impressive 36-hole venues anywhere outside the United States. Whether you prefer Old or New, there is no denying that each is outstanding, and a round on both is a pretty special day's golf.

OPPOSITE Colt's brilliant
par three 5th hole, The New Course.

The Royal St George's Golf Club – Sandwich

COURSE OPENED 1887
DESIGNERS Dr Laidlaw Purves,
Frank Pennink,
Donald Steele

'The first nine holes – tremendous fun, not very good golf. Second nine holes – tremendous golf, no fun at all.'

WALTER HAGEN ON SANDWICH IN 1928

Established in 1887, the Royal St George's Golf Club was primarily founded by quality-deprived London golfers looking for somewhere relatively close to enjoy a seaside links. The driving forces behind the club and its search for a suitable home were Scots Dr Laidlaw Purves and Henry Lamb, who scoured the English coastline east from Bournemouth until they finally stumbled upon a vast expanse of tumbling dunes located between the picturesque town of Sandwich and the sea.

A scratch golfer, Dr Purves created the club's first links. The current layout still follows the general direction of his holes and most of his greens and tees are still evident even if no longer in play. The Purves course was originally quite short, and his holes have been lengthened considerably since the early 1900s, when the new rubber-cored ball first made them inadequate. Frank Pennink made significant alterations during the 1970s, removing the blindness of the 4th and 14th fairways and adding new holes at 3, 8 and 11. Prior to the Open championships of 1981 and 2003, Donald Steele was responsible for half a dozen tee extensions, the removal of some further blind aspects and the shifting of the famous 14th green closer to the out-of-bounds fence.

The resultant layout is one of the more demanding, yet interesting, in the British Isles, with eighteen strong holes running to all points of the compass and some of the most intricate green shapes in golf. Totally natural, the greens often feature steep false fronts that make both the aerial and ground routes treacherous but ensure that chipping and pitching options are endless. As much as the modern Sandwich is long and difficult, the primary facet of the challenge it provides is still the crumpling, bouncy fairways, which are notoriously hard to hold and continually surrounded by deep impenetrable rough areas. The key to playing well here is to accept that good drives may bounce off a straight axis into the light rough and work instead on getting your approach shots into par-saving positions and avoiding cardinal mistakes like going left on the 4th, 7th, 9th, 11th or 15th. These greens, along with the fine finishing trio and the gorgeous front nine dunes, are the highlight of a course with at least ten outstanding individual holes.

Although it may sound cliché, Sandwich truly does test all elements of your game. The stances within fairways are rarely flat and even, the wind is a constant factor and the variety of shots demanded of each player, both from the tee and around the greens, ensures that no aspect of your game is left unchallenged. There is no denying that the layout is highly unconventional, but to those who accept that unusual bounces, half-par holes and indirect routes to flags are part of their sport, it is also thoroughly enjoyable.

Whether you base the quality of a course on the individual standard of each hole or the collective strength of all eighteen, Royal St George's is arguably one of the finest links in the world, with a stack of great holes and the most fascinating collection of greens in England.

OPPOSITE The fractured fairway and skyline green of Sandwich's 10th hole.

Swinley Forest Golf Club

COURSE OPENED 1909

DESIGNER Harry S. Colt

Sweeping left and then rising to the right, the 12th at Swinley Forest is one of England's finest par fours.

OPPOSITE The 4th is the first of Swinley's five magnificent short holes.

Located in the heart of the Surrey-Berkshire Heathland, the Swinley Forest Golf Club is one of the purest examples of classic inland golf in all of Europe and perhaps, even more impressively, one of the best few courses by master designer Harry Colt.

A private members-only club, it was formed by Lord Derby, a minister of the crown during the reign of Queen Victoria, who was once late for an appointment with Her Majesty at Windsor Castle after being held up by a slow foursome at Sunningdale. When the Queen enquired as to why a man of such means could not own his own course, Lord Derby responded by forming an exclusive club and handing Colt, who was still serving as secretary at Sunningdale, a piece of land he had purchased within the greater Swinley Forest for the building of his new course.

A heathland setting of rare beauty, privacy and tranquility, Swinley Forest was also blessed with enough interesting ground movement to allow Colt to create exceptional golf holes. He apparently started the design process by first locating green sites for his short holes and then routing the rest of his layout around these areas. With extraordinary vision and variety, he built a world-famous set of par threes, carefully spacing them through both nines and including a long-iron into a natural shelf at the 4th, a ridge green with a steep falloff at the short 8th, a fairway

wood across a deep valley on the long 10th and finally a mid-iron into a beautiful pushed-up knoll at the 17th. That he found five short holes as attractive and diverse is a credit both to his skill as a designer and the suitability of the site for golf. Yet while these moments steal most of the headlines, longer holes such as the 6th, 7th, 9th, 14th and 15th are also fantastic. As is the incomparable 12th hole, one of the greatest two-shot tests in golf, the drive needing to draw and the approach fade to negotiate the heather, pines and rolling fairway in order to reach a severely contoured green set into an elevated bank.

Despite being cut through impressive forests of pine and birch, Swinley enjoys a special feeling of spaciousness as the trees rarely interfere with play and the holes are instead dominated by a hearty cover of heather, which provides definition to the fairways and beautifully frames the green sites. The intricate putting surfaces, positioned in a variety of superb natural areas, are a feature throughout the layout, as are the rippled and bumpy ground contours that create uneven bounces and varying stances to further complicate approach play into these tricky targets.

Steeped in the traditions of early 20th century golf and once described by Colt as his 'least bad course,' Swinley Forest is a layout of rare quality and one that even the most seasoned golfer will feel privileged to have played.

Rye Golf Club

COURSE OPENED 1894
DESIGNERS Harry S. Colt,
Tom Simpson,
Sir Guy Campbell

'I will not say there are not greater links than Rye, but I will say that there are few which combine and gather into one place so many of those qualities which make the game of golf unique.'

PATRIC DICKINSON

OPPOSITE Miss the green at your peril on Rye's terrifying short 7th, as they say the hardest shots here are the second to the par threes.

Prestigious and extremely private, the Rye Golf Club in the south of England is significant not just for its cherished links but also as the birthplace of one of golf's great architectural careers. A qualified lawyer, Harry Colt was appointed a partner in a law firm in nearby Hastings in 1894 but almost immediately turned his back on that profession to help establish the club at Rye and then design its course. He later became the club's secretary before moving to the newly formed Sunningdale Golf Club and then on to 50 years of further design endeavors. Though his work at Rye has been significantly altered over the years, the links remains very true to his design ideals.

Colt's course was built partly on the inland side of a road running through coastal linksland between Rye and Camber, but as the road grew more popular the club moved closer to the beach and into the area's heavier central dunes. The layout was first modified by Tom Simpson in 1932 and then by Sir Guy Campbell in 1938 before final alterations were made during an in-house restoration program undertaken to repair damage caused during the Second World War. Like Colt's original plan, the current links play mostly back and forth along a series of ridges and across the sort of rippling, heaving ground and resultant humps and bumps that would not look out of place on a course like Sandwich. The variety of its daunting green sites, which seem simple but are severe, is matched only by the strength and

diversity of its extreme driving challenges, with the tight fairways routed through shallow valleys, along sandy crests or angled across the steep hills.

Rye opens with its only par five, the hole tormenting those unable to get off to a flying start with the knowledge that there are few more birdie opportunities to follow. The first real standout hole is the 4th, which features one of the toughest tee shots in the world. Following a crested ridge, the fairway falls on both sides to punish those unable to drive dead along its narrow axis. The 6th is another superb driving hole, this time blind and diagonally over a large dune. Next up is the best of Rye's infamous par threes, the 7th, which like the 14th has an elusive elevated target and wicked surrounds including deep bunkers and timber slats cut into its bank to cruelly prevent stray golfers from putting back onto the tiny peak. Elsewhere, Simpson's 9th is a fun short four, while the long and bunkerless 13th is a remarkable hole with the approach crossing a tall dune ridge into a hidden green, a little like the Klondyke at Lahinch, except that here you have to use trigonometry and align two posts on top of the dune to work out your angle into the flag. The closing run is particularly strong and includes the wonderfully crumpled ground of the 15th, 16th and 18th, which form a fittingly unconventional end to a unique experience.

As its main sand structures run parallel to the coastline, the golf here is almost always played

with the winds whipping across you, making the slender fairways and small greens even more difficult to hit. The lies are also a key feature of the course. Varying from uneven to extremely uneven, most shots are played with an irregular stance, to the point where should you fluke a level lie, you almost have to check that you remember how to play such a shot.

While the links has benefited from its move into the hills, changes made on the flatter section of the site have been less successful. Most notable is the pushing of the 10th green away from the road, which subsequently caused adverse alteration to the 11th and the loss of exciting driving lines on the 16th and 18th. More recently an area right of the 11th fairway was excavated as part of the Eurotunnel project, the resultant lake sadly out of place on a links of such class. These points should not dissuade one from attempting to play here, however, for the short holes are very special and shots like the drive on 4 and 6, approach into 13 and fairways at 9, 15, 16 and 18 are truly unforgettable.

ABOVE The bumpy approach into Tom Simpson's short par four 9th.

OPPOSITE Harry Colt's well-preserved par three 5th hole.

St Enodoc Golf Club – Church Course

COURSE OPENED 1907

DESIGNER James Braid

The 6th hole, complete with its enormous Himalaya bunker complex.

OPPOSITE St Enodoc's par five 10th hole, which plays beneath a massive ridge and heads toward the town's ancient stone church.

OVERLEAF Wonderful views of the Cornish coastline from the 16th green.

Golf was first introduced to the charming Cornish sailing town of Rock in 1890, when holidaying Londoners formed the St Enodoc Golf Club on its sandy headland. Situated on the North Shore of the Camel Estuary and enjoying superb views across the Cornwall coastline, the St Enodoc linksland is an unusual landform that was shaped when great Atlantic gales blew vast deposits of sand up onto the bluff. These deposits created the large dune ridges and deep sandy swales that James Braid used so expertly within his 1907 design of the club's Church Course.

Braid incorporated all of the noticeable features of the site into a routing that takes you across bumpy linksland, into heaving dunes and beside some lush farming pastures. Highpoints are dotted throughout the round but are especially prominent early. The first six holes are exceptional, starting with a stunning opening par five that crashes down toward the magnificent coastline and its distant green. The next heads back up into the hill and is followed by two outstanding par fours, the 3rd, a long hole that plays diagonally across an ancient rock wall, and the 4th, a world-class drivable four that rises into a small target with an out-of-bounds fence tight on its right side. Cleverly, the green is angled to best accept shots from this side rather than the lower left plateau. The 5th is then a fine par three added years later by Tom Simpson while the 6th is a sensational par four that twists into a sliver of fairway and is then semi-blind across the enormous Himalaya bunker. Possibly the biggest sand hazard in golf, Himalaya is cut into the face

of an 80-foot dune and is an especially fearsome sight for those with a tendency to catch their irons a little thin.

The rest of the thrills are spread more evenly through the remaining holes, with the blind drive on the 7th, the strategic par four 9th and the approach into the perilous ledge green on the 14th the best of a central section linking the awesome start to the strong finish. This area also includes the Church hole, the 10th, which curves through a natural valley beneath a massive dune ridge toward an ancient stone church. Dating back several hundred years, the building was only restored during the Victorian period after having been buried for decades beneath the sands. The hole itself is attractive but a little too narrow off the tee, while the subsequent loop around the church is strangely mediocre. The best of the back nine follows the par three 15th, which plummets from the higher pastoral ground back onto a closing coastal stretch that includes a terrific tumbling par five, a long one-shot hole back into the heavy hills and a brutal finisher played from an elevated tee down an undulating valley.

A great mix of scenery and strategy, the 69 par here will offer ample birdie opportunities to those on top of their game but is far from a pushover, as trouble lurks constantly and the site is exposed to violent prevailing winds off the Atlantic. With a number of great holes and some of the finest sea views in Britain, St Enodoc is a tremendous day's golf and one of the game's genuine hidden delights.

West Sussex Golf Club – Pulborough

COURSE OPENED 1930
DESIGNERS Cecil Hutchinson,
Sir Guy Campbell,
Colonel S.V. Hotchkin

Located just beyond the small village of Pulborough, the West Sussex Golf Club was the brainchild of Commander George Hilyard, a close friend of King George V, who supposedly conceived of the course while shaving and looking out across neighboring farmland. Recognizing the potential of its softly rolling heather-strewn slopes for golf, Hilyard helped assemble the necessary people to create a club. Remarkably his chosen site proved a geological godsend, as the course is built on some of the brightest white sand in Britain yet surrounded by the harsh clays and marshes of the Sussex downs.

Set within a picturesque forest of pine and birch, the course was designed primarily by Sir Guy Campbell and Cecil Hutchinson, who were in partnership with Colonel S.V. Hotchkin when they started the project but apparently not when they finished it. There is evidence, however, that Hotchkin spent time on site and had a hand in the design, though disagreements, possibly over the now legendary consecutive par threes at 5 and 6, brought the partnership to an end with Hutchinson and Campbell completing the job and being credited by the club for its design.

Blessed with an ideal base for inland golf, the design here is suitably sensitive to the surroundings, with all the undulation utilized, the bunkering both visually and strategically outstanding and the shaping and construction of the course first-class. As was common practice in the 1930s, the round begins with a friendly five that does little more than get play away and into the rich golfing ground that

follows. The next hole is a bunkerless falling four and the start of a long run of glorious golf, as memorable as any stretch of holes in southern England. Standouts include the highly strategic 3rd hole, the rumpled 4th fairway, the strong par four 7th and the short 8th with its gorgeous green site elevated beyond a small gully. Most notorious, however, are the back-to-back par threes at 5 and 6, the first a sublime short-iron into a well-bunkered green and the second a fairway wood played down across a marshy scrub toward a slim target cut into the side of a hillock and sandwiched between bunkers and an out-of-bounds fence.

Both the terrain and the quality of golf is more varied on a back nine that includes a very strong closing set of holes and individual gems like the flat, but spectacularly bunkered, par four 13th and the long 14th, which tumbles across clever sand traps set well back from its tight target. The natural and bunkerless 16th is another great hole and features a drive across a crest to a diagonal shelf of fairway followed by an approach into a green saddled within a heathery knoll.

Though it may be short by modern standards, Pulborough is a real throwback to the Golden Age of golf, when a day's play meant less than three hours toil and both enjoyment and strategic endeavor were essential virtues of course design. While understated and underrated are both apt descriptions of West Sussex, make no mistake about its quality. The course is exceptional, and a round on this small, sandy jewel comes very highly recommended.

OPPOSITE Heather, pines and blinding white sand typify golf at West Sussex. Pictured is the delightful par three 5th.

Woodhall Spa – The Hotchkin Course

COURSE OPENED 1905
DESIGNERS Harry S. Colt,
Colonel S.V. Hotchkin,
Harry Vardon

The 12th is Woodhall Spa's prettiest but most dangerous short hole.

OPPOSITE The par three 5th, guarded by some of Hotchkin's deepest trench-like bunkers.

The charming resort village of Woodhall Spa in the Lincolnshire countryside owes its existence to the discovery of mineral water in the 19th century, a discovery that almost destroyed a golf club which would later put the village on the international golfing map. Though the Woodhall Spa Golf Club was created in 1890, the increasing popularity of the town saw its first two courses swallowed up by urban expansion. Local landowner and prominent member Stafford Vere Hotchkin was the man who saved the club by first leasing it a narrow tract of heathland for a new course and later becoming the driving force behind its success.

Harry Vardon designed the original layout on the Hotchkin property, but his 1905 course was lengthened and altered substantially by Harry Colt between 1911 and 1914. During this period Hotchkin was actively involved in all aspects of club operations, and following the First World War he took back control of the property and became responsible for the maintenance and upkeep of the course. This was a significant period in the development of Woodhall Spa as Hotchkin, an honorary Colonel, then spent the best part of two decades indulging his interest in design by continually tinkering with the layout, leaving Colt's routing but repeatedly changing the tees, greens and, most noticeably, the hazards.

Built primarily on sandy soil, the Hotchkin Course is set among banks of fescue and heather, with its flowing fairways generally lined by mature canopies of pine and birch. Its primary feature is undoubtedly the bunkers, which are huge and mostly the work of the Colonel, who personally dug them deeper each year to create canyon-like traps capable of dealing severe punishment to even the best players. Believing vehemently that bunkers should be hazards, his fairway traps all typically extract a full stroke penalty while finding greenside bunkers will often cost you more, those on the 4th, 5th and 12th among the deepest on earth. Although penal when found, the placement of hazards is quite strategic, with many protruding into the line of play to catch both those being overly aggressive and those too eager to avoid trouble on the opposite side.

What sets Woodhall Spa apart from the other heathland layouts of England is the relentless and sometimes overwhelming nature of its challenge. Apart from the opening hole you never really get comfortable, as disaster lurks constantly throughout the round. The course is dotted with really strong par fours like 2, 3, 4, 7 and 13 and an attractive group of strategic three-shot holes, but its best moments are slightly more subtle and include the short par three 5th with its narrow green ringed by a seemingly bottomless pit of sand. The par four 11th is a brilliant hole, across heather and through gorse from the tee and then into a terrific green placed beyond a messy hollow set deceptively back from the putting surface. Best of all, though, is the short 12th, which requires little more than a mid-iron but is played to a slim plateau green flanked by horrendously deep traps.

Woodhall Spa has a fearsome reputation and is one of the toughest inland courses in Britain. Though Hotchkin later became a course designer of note, this was his passion, his property and ultimately his obsession, and he was adamant that the challenge of Woodhall Spa should stand the test of time; something few who play here would dare deny that he achieved.

The Royal Birkdale Golf Club

COURSE OPENED 1897
DESIGNERS Fred Hawtree,
J.H. Taylor,
George Low,
Fred Hawtree Jr,
Martin Hawtree

First established in 1889, the Royal Birkdale Golf Club moved to the magnificent sandhills of Southport five years later, where its George Low-designed links managed to exist in relative obscurity for more than 30 years. That was until its site was sold in 1931 to the Southport Corporation, which wanted Birkdale to become a championship venue and gave the club a 99-year lease and the encouragement to undertake a grand remodeling of its links. Fred Hawtree and J.H. Taylor were then employed to redesign the course and bring it up to championship standards. The fact that Birkdale has since hosted virtually every major event on the British mainland suggests the pair succeeded spectacularly.

Though the Birkdale site features some of the most impressive dune formations in England, the Hawtree/Taylor design philosophy was to thread the holes through the deep natural valleys running between the sandhills, thus avoiding the need for blind play, bumpy fairways or unfair bounces. Where valleys and flat areas did not exist the club even created them, cutting away part of the sandbank to the side of the first green to allow those bailing right to have a view of the flag and, most controversially, slicing through a ridge in 1967 to open up the 4th fairway. This hole is now a long and featureless par three but, to be fair, the club's plan was only to shave back the top of a dune that extended across the hole and obscured the base of the pin. A misdirected contractor unfortunately removed the whole obstruction.

A number of additional changes were made by Hawtree's son Fred Jr during the 1960s. His most significant work was to add the terrific par three 12th hole, which was part of his father's original plan but not built at the time because of insufficient funds. He also added several hundred yards to the layout by repositioning a couple of greens and tees and advised on the removal of a supposedly great par three at the 17th, incredibly because the club felt a short hole at the end of a tournament was unsuitable. A third-generation Hawtree, Fred Jr's son Martin, later helped the club reshape, resurface and redesign all eighteen greens after the 1991 (British) Open. With targets often cut into clefts against the dunes and shielded from the winds, there are some very attractive green sites here, which thanks to the upgrade are now in superb shape year round.

There are few surprises at Birkdale, with the holes fair and hazards generally located to the sides of the playing areas and laid out in full view from the tee. Major challenges to par are presented by the length of the holes, the ever-present winds, savage roughs and wild willow scrubs. The links has very few weak holes but only a handful that really get the juices flowing, with most of those coming between the deadly short 7th and the long 13th with its green tucked beneath several large dunes. The best of these central holes is the 9th, a tremendous four across the most undulating fairway on the course, and the previously mentioned 12th, which is played into a narrow green nestled into a rugged dune and guarded by pot bunkers. The majority of the

OPPOSITE Birkdale's best! The undulating 9th hole is a terrific par four that is blind from the tee and then turns right toward a plateau green.

remaining holes are best described as solid, with one common complaint of the layout being that by shying away from attacking the hills the course perhaps lacks a few more standouts and the fun and sportiness that make seaside golf in Britain so enjoyable. The quality of the only blind and wild hole on the course, the 9th, suggests that such criticism may well be warranted.

Despite the drawbacks, this is an uncomplicated and logical links that most will enjoy playing because good shots are rewarded and straight balls will always find short grass. Widely admired for its fairness, the major attraction of Birkdale, however, is its wonderful setting, excellent greens and the fun of playing such a renowned championship venue.

OPPOSITE Short but tricky, the 7th hole is played across the roughs to a swollen green ringed by sand.

The Berkshire Golf Club – Red Course

COURSE OPENED 1928

DESIGNER Herbert Fowler

The Calamity-style 10th hole on the Red Course, its tee shot played across a yawning chasm and into a green on top of a ridge.

OPPOSITE Herbert Fowler's rugged bunkering and the Berkshire's beautifully dramatic landscape are evident in this picture of the par three 13th hole on the Blue Course.

The Berkshire Golf Club was born on a beautiful stretch of heathland close to Windsor Castle, its home an ancient forest leased from the British Royal family, who for centuries had used it as hunting ground. During the First World War the land was cleared by the British Defence Force, which performed military maneuvers on the site between a Red and a Blue army. The club's two courses were later named after these brigades with the Red Course occupying the more undulating higher ground.

Both courses were designed by Herbert Fowler, a Golden Ager with a talent for building natural courses, who believed that god created golf land and that 'the less man meddled, the better for all concerned.' At the Berkshire his terrain was ideal for exciting golf, the undulating forest covered in majestic chestnut, birch and pine and full of interesting ground movement. Fowler's routing and the flow of his holes, particularly on the Red Course, is outstanding, with the unusual mix of six par threes, fours and fives making up the layout. A remarkably cohesive journey, each hole falls perfectly across the site and so good was his routing and subsequent design that little revision has been made since its 1928 opening.

The Red's opening holes skirt the perimeter of the property and form a solid introduction to a course which really kicks up a gear from the gorgeous 5th through to back-to-back short par fours at the 11th and 12th. The 7th, 10th and 16th are all great long par threes, while the best of the two-shot holes is the beautiful 8th, played through the pines and turning slightly as it first crosses a ridge and then rises into a narrow green. Though some criticize the three-shot holes for being a little short, the rolling 17th is a very fine challenge and most of the others are right on the balance of par and offer real eagle-to-bogey possibilities.

The variety of the Red Course is not just in its unique mix of par holes but also the use of its physical features, with strategic holes laid naturally across an attractive and diverse landscape. The Blue Course is similarly striking and has some wonderful short holes such as the 4th, 13th and its classic opener, though the longer holes through the flatter portion of the property tend to lack the interest of the Red Course and the heather is slightly less prominent. The bunkering and greens, however, are equally impressive throughout both layouts. The greens are quite subtle but feature clear and clever slopes, while the rugged bunkers are fringed with heather and typically deep enough to extract a genuine penalty when found.

Herbert Fowler was clearly a talented designer and at the Berkshire his use of all the available contour and slope, within the design, as much as the wrinkled and links-like fairways, continue to give his courses their timeless feel. The pick of the golf, the Red Course may be less demanding than some of Fowler's other designs, but is as enjoyable as any he created and the equal of most in this fantastic region.

Royal West Norfolk Golf Club – Brancaster

COURSE OPENED 1892
DESIGNERS Holcombe Ingleby,
Horace Hutchinson

One of Brancaster's unusual sleeper-faced bunkers protects the 4th green.

OPPOSITE The flooding of the entrance to the heavily fortified 9th green creates a daunting approach.

Located on a narrow spit of endangered linksland, the Royal West Norfolk Golf Club was founded in 1892 in the quiet town of Brancaster on the north-west tip of Norfolk. Discovered and designed by Holcombe Ingleby, with assistance from golf writer Horace Hutchinson, the course is squeezed between a large coastal sand ridge and a protected tidal saltmarsh. It only takes one look at the links to understand the precarious nature of its existence, as one side is constantly battered by fierce winds and huge seas while its other side floods during high tide, making the course inaccessible for hours and cutting off those caught playing without checking their tidal charts.

Arranged in a single out-and-back loop along the sea dunes, with the inward nine playing into some of the stiffest prevailing winds in Britain, the layout has never been redesigned but has changed considerably over time, mostly because of the loss of duneland and the narrowing of its playing areas. Several tees along the dunes have been lost through the years, while the 11th hole was completely destroyed during severe storms in 1942. What remains is a quirky kaleidoscope of eccentric golf holes full of deep sleeper-faced bunkers, tiny pots, quick and heavily fortified greens and partially flooded marshlands. These marsh areas actually create some very fine fairway corridors and are used strategically within the design, especially on the heroic par five 8th played twice diagonally across the floodplains and demanding those wanting to get home in two take the aggressive and longer carry on both shots.

The full Brancaster experience begins at the wood-paneled Victorian clubhouse, which enjoys splendid views over the North Sea and an opening hole played along the dunes to a terrific little green tucked into the sand. The next all-star hole is the 3rd, its approach blind over a huge sleepered embankment and into a slim green. Turning straight toward the sea, the 4th is a crosswind par three of considerable challenge, its built-up target set beyond a bank fortified with daunting sleepers. The 5th features a bizarre blind drive through two posts on the top of a ridge, while on the back nine the one-shot 10th is a fine hole that can be brutal as you turn to experience the headwinds for the first time, and both the strong par four 14th and the short 15th have cool sunken and obscured green sites.

Despite its idiosyncrasies, Brancaster is a more substantial test than first appears, with some excellent design elements, well built and well positioned hazards and an interesting variety of green sites. It is not really recommended for general consumption, though, as many will be unimpressed by the fact that the course floods and that there are poor holes, blind greens, unfair bounces and average conditioning. However, for those who enjoy their golf adventurous and a little unconventional, Royal West Norfolk is like stepping back in time and is a real treasure that should be savored before too much more of it is lost.

Alwoodley Golf Club

COURSE OPENED 1907

DESIGNER Dr Alister
MacKenzie

The fairway on the short par four 4th hole comes complete with medieval farming furrows.

OPPOSITE MacKenzie's earliest masterpieces are on display at Alwoodley. Pictured here is the one-shot 14th.

Born on the ancient farming grounds of Wigton Moor outside of Leeds, the Alwoodley Golf Club was formed in 1907 by fourteen businessmen including a local doctor named MacKenzie, a headstrong character who acted as the club's first secretary. During preliminary planning for the course Dr MacKenzie, who had nurtured an ambition to design golf courses ever since serving in the Boer War, sketched out his own design ideas and a routing map that was later shown to the renowned architect Harry Colt when he inspected the site. Colt was apparently pleased with MacKenzie's plan and approved its use, the doctor then staying on to oversee construction and later becoming a partner in Colt's thriving design business.

The site itself was a thin strip of rural farming land, gently rolling and still covered in agricultural furrows that dated back to medieval times and remain evident on several fairways. A fan of St Andrews, MacKenzie used a similar routing, with the course laid out in a single loop that curves at the far end. His holes regularly cut back across the site, however, to break up play and experience the winds whipping across the Yorkshire moors from a range of directions. Aside from an extension to the 10th and a new 11th, both suggested by MacKenzie, the course in play today is remarkably close to his original sketched plan.

A consistent and attractive journey, the layout's better moments include a short downwind par five at the 3rd, a long headwind par four at the 4th, the innocuous-looking but beautifully bunkered 5th and the three-shot 8th, which doglegs across a nasty patch of heather and sand set well back from the target to dictate your strategy for the approach. The uphill par three 11th is another highlight, as are the Redan-like 14th, heavily contoured 15th green and the sunken 17th with its target blind beyond a slight crest. The 10th is also noteworthy for its big left-slinging drive, which is similar to the shape of shot required from the famous 13th tee at MacKenzie's Augusta National. The second half of the hole then drops across a gully where the original hidden green was first built.

Those familiar with MacKenzie's best work in America or Australia will find familiarity in his holes here and in particular the cunning bunker placement and clever greens that are tilted or tiered to provide strategic advantages to certain driving decisions. During the 1990s, with parts of the course looking tired, the club embarked on one of the most successful restoration programs in Britain, altering little of the design and focusing on selectively clearing trees to restore the original open heathland character of the site. This also allowed the club to restore long-suffering heather areas while some much-needed championship tees were added to maintain the relevance of the holes. One suspects the good doctor would approve of this faithful 'back to the future' type approach to restoration.

Though MacKenzie's philosophy was born before Alwoodley was created, his sound design principles and techniques were first tested here, and it was this work that won him the design job at the neighboring Moortown Golf Club and from there on to a career as successful as any in golf.

Royal Liverpool Golf Club – Hoylake

COURSE OPENED 1869

DESIGNERS Robert Chambers,
George Morris,
Harry S. Colt,
Donald Steele

*'Hoylake, blown upon by mighty
winds, breeder of mighty champions.'*

BERNARD DARWIN

Located on a triangle of linksland in the small town of Hoylake, the Royal Liverpool Golf Club owns the second-oldest links in England and started life in 1869 on the racecourse of a local hunt club. Its first course was a nine-hole layout designed by Robert Chambers and George Morris, the brother of Old Tom, which was extended in 1871 to eighteen holes and then reshaped by Harry Colt during the 1920s. Colt's work was substantial and included the building of brilliant new greens at the 8th and 12th, an entirely new 13th hole and making major changes to the 11th, 16th and 17th holes.

Aside from its outstanding links, the club also has a significant tournament history, having hosted the inaugural Amateur Championship and both the first international match between England and Scotland, and the first between Great Britain and the United States for what is now known as the Walker Cup. More recently, Donald Steele lengthened the course in preparation for the 2006 Open Championship, held at Hoylake after an absence of almost 40 years. Aside from stretching the course well beyond 7,000 yards, his changes involved numerous new tees and bunkers and an all-new 18th hole. He also rebuilt several greens, including the once fearsome 17th, which like the 7th formerly had an out-of-bounds area hard up against its putting surface. The modern Hoylake is therefore made up of original hunt club holes, a handful by committees, several Colt greens and numerous new Steele additions, yet it somehow

manages to remain coherent and very true to the spirit of the original design.

The links is mostly built across a flat and fairly bleak sandy plain, its primary defense being the strong winds which blow across from the Dee Estuary and the firm and fast conditions its tight turf provides. Holes are not overly bunkered, but each hazard is extremely punishing and cleverly positioned to catch those who stray, while the greens are arranged in such a manner as to insist that those hoping to score well attempt a variety of approach shots. The round starts into the prevailing winds with one of the most intimidating openers in golf, the fairway bending at right angles around a practice paddock with out-of-bounds down both sides. It is followed by a beautifully bunkered short four that can be played long or short from the tee, depending on your bravery, but has an away-sloping green that is tricky to hold from off the short grass.

Next up is a series of solid holes that lead to Colt's corner, a stretch of golf from the 8th through to the 13th played across the most significant sand formations on the site and enjoying the bulk of Colt's remaining design features. The par three 11th is a great hole that looks out over the barren mudflats of the estuary, while, of the longer holes, difficult fours at 10 and 12 are very good, as is the par five 8th with its terrific raised green protected by a single gathering bunker. Typical of Hoylake, this hole punishes those unable to thread the ball into a seemingly vast chase-in area that is actually

deceptively tight. The bowl green on the 9th, sweeping par four 12th and beautifully bunkered short 13th are further sandhill highlights before play moves onto the flatter plains for a demanding closing run defined by the three tough long holes from the 14th to the 16th. The par five 16th, which again skirts along the out-of-bounds practice ground, is successfully used as the closing hole for major events.

Rather than a string of world-class moments, Hoylake works best as a quality collection of strong holes linked together with impressive base features such as charismatic greens, deep and well-positioned revetted pot bunkers and plenty of directional change. Despite its unmistakably classic feel, the course has evolved considerably to keep pace with the modern game. Although it continually strives to remain a relevant championship test, the club has very sensibly resisted over-bunkering its holes, with the result being a stern links that challenges the great players yet remains both totally playable and utterly enjoyable for mere mortals.

OPPOSITE Another Colt gem, the 12th hole bends sharply left around bunkers and features this brilliantly conceived green, which is elevated and protected by a deep hollow on the right to catch those cowering away from the dunes.

Ganton Golf Club

COURSE OPENED 1891

DESIGNERS Various

Ganton's deep and distinctive bunkering, shown here on the 6th fairway.

OPPOSITE The short par three 5th hole.

Located between York and Scarborough and more than ten miles from the North Yorkshire coastline, Ganton is one of the most demanding courses in Britain and probably the most authentic inland links in the world. Thousands of years ago its site was actually an inlet of the North Sea, which receded to leave behind a pure linkscape complete with a sandy soil base and blessed with the sort of humps and ripples usually reserved for ground much closer to the sea.

Golf was first played here in 1891 on a course laid out through the whins and native grasses by Tom Chisolm and Robert Bird, but in the years subsequent to this has had a seemingly endless list of architectural influences. The foursome of leading professionals Harry Vardon, Ted Ray, James Braid and J.H. Taylor redesigned the layout in 1905, while Harry Colt, Dr Alister MacKenzie, Tom Simpson, C.K. Cotton and Frank Pennink are among the others who have also had a hand in shaping its holes.

Like the classic seaside links, the course continually changes direction to take advantage of the winds that whip through the site. Holes mostly run back and forth across the landscape yet cleverly only once are they consecutively in the same direction. Small trees line the boundary of the property but within the design the terrain is mostly stark, with holes often carved through chunks of gorse introduced to the area, probably by Colt, in the 1930s. Ganton is a great matchplay course, as several of the longer holes sit on the edge of par and most provide a balanced test of

your strategy and shotmaking ability. Driving is your greatest challenge, as danger lurks constantly and sprayed balls typically find the savage roughs or deep and fearsome bunkers, neither of which are places to seek refuge for those hoping to scramble a respectable score. As there are only two short holes on the course, there is little let-up for those struggling with their driving accuracy.

Unlike the better courses around the southern Heathland, Ganton isn't bursting with stupendous features but is instead blessed with a routing full of strong golf holes that will keep you on your toes throughout the journey. Early highlights include the short par four 3rd and Colt's impressive 4th, its fairway dipping across a shallow valley and then into a back-to-front-sloping green. The bumpy par five 9th, with a slim target and clever false front, is another high point, while the 5th and well-bunkered 10th are both fine short holes. The finishing stretch from the 15th is extremely solid, with the 16th demanding a bold carry across one of the biggest bunkers in the world and the 18th, an excellent Cape-style par four around gorse, offering players the chance to end on a high or slide further into the mire.

Critics of Ganton are likely to point to the ferocity of its challenge and the harshness of its landscape as the major drawbacks, but although the course is unlikely to ever win a beauty contest, it is surprisingly attractive to play and does provide all golfers with a thorough examination of their skills.

Notts Golf Club – Hollinwell

COURSE OPENED 1901
DESIGNERS Tom Williamson,
Willie Park Jr

The downhill par three 13th hole.

One of England's most distinguished clubs, the Notts Golf Club was founded in Nottingham in 1887, its early members golfing on common ground they shared with two other clubs. With its council landlord threatening to turn part of the layout into a cemetery, the membership soon decided to seek its own home and in 1899 stumbled upon vast heathlands at Kirkby Forest owned by local ecclesiastical commissioners. Though its undulating sandy soil was deemed ideal for golf, the site was fourteen miles north of the city and members only narrowly voted in favor of the move. Willie Park Jr was then contracted to design an eighteen-hole layout which, until the property was purchased in 1924, the landlords insisted could not be used on Sundays.

Dubbed Hollinwell, after a natural spring or 'holy well' found beside the 8th hole, the Park course opened in 1901 but was altered the following year by J.H. Taylor and club professional Tom Williamson, the pair adding bunkers and also lengthening it considerably in preparation for the new rubber-cored ball. Williamson, who also served as head greenkeeper, later added the opening three holes on land leased west of the club's snaking entrance road, while both Frank Pennink and Donald Steele have advised on minor modifications since the 1960s.

The perimeter of the Hollinwell course is dominated by large bracken- and pine-covered hills, while the internal holes are beautifully cut through paddocks of pink fescues, with heather and a variety of gorse also prominent. From flattish heathland to woodland and then onto the back nine where holes play through valleys and up into some of the site's larger hills and ridges, the rich variety of terrain is impressive.

Notts begins with Williamson's three fine western holes before moving over the driveway and onto the gently rolling moorland of the remaining outward nine. Early standouts include the clever par five 3rd and the strong two-shot 2nd, which bends into a green nestled beneath a pair of pine hills. The quality increases slightly from the partially blind 10th, with both the 11th, played up through a slender valley, and the wild 12th, which heads along a ridge and across two deep depressions, among the back nine highlights. The next, a long par three down through a gorgeous fescue vale, is the prettiest hole on the course, while the most fearsome is the two-shot 15th, its long approach rising into a narrow saddle through the hills to a tiny green with a steep false front. The short par four 16th is also very good, as are the beautifully undulating three-shot 17th and the tough par four finishing hole.

Although the bunkering is not as severe as other northern inland classics like Woodhall Spa and Ganton, the course is well defended by its length and the thick fescues that attractively line its tight fairways. In many ways Notts was ahead of its time. Its charming layout was built long, and more than a century later continues to provide a relevant challenge to good players and still bring pleasurable enjoyment to the average member.

Royal Lytham & St Annes Golf Club

COURSE OPENED 1898

DESIGNERS George Lowe,
Harry S. Colt
with revisions by
Herbert Fowler,
Tom Simpson,
C.K. Cotton and others

A much respected championship venue, the Royal Lytham & St Annes Golf Club was formed in 1886 when a Scottish schoolmaster, who had relocated to golf-deprived North Lancashire, managed to convince the local gentry of St Annes to establish their own course. As interest in the game started increasing so too did the surrounding township, and the club's first links was repossessed for a housing development. An alternative site was found on the inland side of the town's railway line and in 1898 the current course, designed by the club's first professional, George Lowe, was opened for play.

Almost immediately, Royal Lytham focused on establishing its championship credentials and by 1919 the club had called in Harry Colt to strengthen the Lowe layout. Colt repositioned a number of greens and tees to give the course its current configuration. He also lengthened the holes and added numerous bunkers, a practice the club has vigorously continued over the years as it strives to remain a relevant test for leading professionals. Indeed, the overwhelming impression of the modern Lytham is a course which probably exists more successfully now as a championship venue than as an enjoyable members course. The links are among the most challenging in England and certainly the most intimidating from the tee, with narrow fairways cramped by endless revetted bunkers and thick choking roughs.

The course itself is not particularly attractive, as it is laid out across a flat field that does not have sea views, shaggy dunes or tumbling fairways and is surrounded by housing to its north and a railway line along its south-western boundary. A relentless examination of your ability to hit straight shots, the test begins with a long par three opening hole surrounded by sand, then moves on to a series of fine par fours, highlighted by the 3rd with a terrific green that drops away dramatically. Most of the outward holes are helped by the prevailing breeze, your approach to the difficult plateau 8th green a real standout, though made more demanding by its elevation and a wind pushing your ball toward the trouble. The closing stretch from the 14th is a terrifying run of tough par fours, where finding short grass from the tee is quite an achievement but absolutely vital if hoping to post decent numbers. The final two holes, in particular, are unbelievably tight.

Possibly born out of its initial inability to test the world's best players or the lack of any natural physical obstacles, Royal Lytham has continued to toughen its holes from decade to decade to the point where today's links barely resemble the layout Lowe and Colt created. The course is now the sternest and most penal driving test imaginable, the holes so cramped and over-bunkered that unless you are striping the ball down the middle of every fairway, you will strike sand, and when you do the penalty is invariably severe.

The peerless Bernard Darwin once wrote of Royal Lytham, 'hit your ball to the right place and the way to the hole is open to you, but hit your ball to the wrong place and every kind of punishment, whether immediate or ultimate, will ensue.' This description of a strategic links seems no less appropriate today than it was in the 1930s, it's just that the accumulation of more than two hundred bunkers has made the 'right place' even harder to find.

OPPOSITE The entrance to Lytham's reachable par five 7th green.

Woking Golf Club

COURSE OPENED 1893
DESIGNERS Tom Dunn, Stuart Paton, John Low

Tucked away in an idyllic corner of Surrey, the Woking Golf Club was first laid out by Tom Dunn in 1893, though it owes most of its appeal to a brilliant set of greens created by members Stuart Paton and John Low during the early 1900s. Paton and Low transformed Woking from an ordinary layout into a strategic classic, and so impressive were their green site creations that they inspired club member Tom Simpson to pursue a career in golf course architecture.

The pair's first significant collaboration was to add central Principal's Nose-style bunkers and a tilted green to the previously bland short par four 4th, which heads straight along a railway line. Simpson was apparently so taken with the new hole that he once spent an entire day studying it, although others, such as the long valley par three 2nd and the uphill par four 3rd, with its bowl-shaped putting surface, are equally interesting. As are the early back nine holes that head back and forth across crests and valleys and through the thickest cover of heather on the property. The 11th, 12th and 13th are all excellent holes dominated by great greens, the 12th being reminiscent of the famous 14th green at Augusta National, while the 13th is a brilliant target cut by a gully, with three or four distinct sections that are the devil to putt across should you find the wrong area.

There are several other outstanding holes here, but the overriding impression of Woking is its total absence of any commonplace moments. Although some are turned off by the lack of championship length, if you can look at its holes through nostalgic eyes and resist the impulse to propel that new Titleist down each fairway with your heaviest and most high-tech artillery, you will definitely enjoy this test and appreciate the quality of a design that remains as intelligent today as it was when first created.

Wentworth Club – West Course

COURSE OPENED 1926
DESIGNER Harry S. Colt

A famed golfing destination in the heart of Surrey's Heathland, Wentworth was the vision of Walter George Tarrant, who employed Harry Colt to design two courses on his Wentworth estate during the 1920s. Renowned internationally as the venue of the World Match Play Championship, the West Course is Wentworth's star attraction and winds through the heavily wooded estate in a large loop, its tight fairways lined by tournament-ready roughs and a gorgeous mix of pine, oak and birch.

Tough going out, the course is ideal for head-to-head golf as it steps up a gear from the 11th with the finishing holes played across more impressive undulation and the round culminating in consecutive par fives that tend to throw up as many eagles as birdies. Although the short holes are far from Colt's best, both the 2nd, with its signature Spanish oak guarding the green, and the cross-ravine 10th are very good, as is the stretch of golf through the tall pines from the 11th to the 15th.

The club prides itself on presentation and is always in great shape, though its choking rough areas do alter some of the design intent and the loss of much of its heather has left the course lacking the visual character of others on the heathland. The less renowned East Course has an even more attractive mix of woods and heath and, despite being shorter and a little dated in parts, its par of 68 is still quite a challenge.

Wentworth is rightly famous as a superb tournament venue and a fine place to golf. If you think it is all there is in Surrey, however, you desperately need to sample the other charmers featured in this book.

OPPOSITE Guarded by a large Spanish oak, the par three 2nd on the West Course at Wentworth.

Silloth on Solway Golf Club

COURSE OPENED 1892
DESIGNER Willie Park Jr

The Silloth on Solway golf course is located in sandhills just outside the Cumbrian coastal town of Silloth and is blessed with views across the Solway Firth to Scotland. One of the most original to be found anywhere in England, the course is also one of the most attractive, with its medium-to-large dune formations full of a heather, gorse and fescue covering that provides a wonderful contrast to the playing corridors.

Like nearby championship links in Ayrshire and Lancashire, fairways here are full of dangerous pot bunkers and tight bumpy turf, yet Silloth is different for the unusual manner in which the site's natural elements are incorporated into the design. Where the Open venues tend to play along logical lines, Silloth is less conventional and full of hidden greens, blind driving zones, large central hills that obscure targets on par fives and small plateau greens on long, downwind par threes. The opening stretch is terrific, but can seem almost illogical as the layout opens with the first of several blind dell greens and is followed by hidden fairways at the wonderful 3rd and 4th holes. The 4th is truly superb, and from a concealed valley demands a precise approach into a narrow, bunkerless green that falls away almost ten feet on either side. The front nine culminates in an awesome crosswind par three over a ridge and into a tiny shelf green that drops sharply on one side and is heavily bunkered on the other. The remaining short holes are also memorable, while funky par fives at 13 and 14 are other huge highlights.

After experiencing the best holes here it is hard to believe that this charming golf club still manages to exist in relative anonymity. Like North Berwick, Machrihanish and Brora in Scotland, Silloth on Solway is golf at its most raw and the game is poorer for the fact that courses like this are no longer being built.

Hillside Golf Club

COURSE OPENED 1962
DESIGNER Fred Hawtree

The Hillside Golf Club was formed in 1911, though its current course only dates back to the 1960s when Fred Hawtree built nine new holes among giant sandhills acquired adjacent to the Royal Birkdale Golf Club. As at Birkdale, much of the golf follows deep valleys through the attractive duneland, although the routing composition and mix of holes here is slightly less impressive.

The course starts inauspiciously along a railway line, with most of the front nine played over gently rolling ground. The back nine, however, wanders through some of the largest dune formations in Lancashire and wins most of the positive reviews, despite a couple of the big dune holes disappointing. The best areas on the course are in the central hills around the turn, from the par three 7th through to the treacherous fall-away green on the par four 12th. Played uphill into a sandy basin, the short 10th is a wonderful hole but the real star at Hillside is the 11th, a world-class par five that sweeps down through tall dunes, then along a glorious ridge to a green guarded by a deep revetted bunker.

Once proudly described as eighteen mini-tortures, Hillside is a club that wears the difficulty of its course as a badge of honor. Despite the relentlessness of its challenge, this is a links of surprising variety as tough driving holes tend to have simpler approaches, while the more open landing areas generally lead to the more severe greens. Donald Steele has recently reworked several holes here and repositioned a number of bunkers to ensure that the Hillside test remains as fierce as possible.

OPPOSITE The par five 11th at Hillside plays through some of the region's more impressive dune formations.

Ireland

Although Ireland has become one of the most popular modern golf destinations in the world, British golfers were flocking to its famous resort towns during the early 20th century, long before the protracted period of civil strife destroyed a tourism industry that has only recently been resurrected.

The obvious appeal of Irish golf is its spectacular coastline and dramatically bulging duneland, which is much more naturally attractive than the softer, lower, rippled links of Scotland. Ireland remains divided politically, but the golf and hospitality is exceptional on both sides of the border. The island's two biggest links, Ballybunion in the Republic and Royal County Down in the North, were the first to be discovered by the Americans and are outstanding, as are Royal Portrush, Lahinch, Carne, Doonbeg, County Sligo, Waterville and a number of unheralded and unpretentious clubs throughout the land. Many of these were created by the late Eddie Hackett, one of modern golf's most important designers. For 30 years Hackett was Ireland's only real golf architect. An unassuming chap, he worked for modest financial gain and often tried to convince clubs to hire other architects. Famously, both Tralee and Ballybunion (Cashen) followed his advice. A true minimalist, Hackett had a primitive method of routing holes and building courses and was reluctant to shape the land. Where interesting contours did not exist some of his holes are a little dull, but where the land avails itself of good golf he generally extracted maximum enjoyment. A classic example is Carne, the best of his creations and a course he built when well into his eighties.

There are numerous courses in Ireland unlucky to have missed out on being featured in this book, including the half-Hackett Enniscrone links, as well as some of the real charmers near Dublin such as The Island and County Louth's fine links at Baltray. Those featured, however, are the crème de la crème, and an itinerary that includes just half of these courses will take you to some of the most breathtaking corners of this brilliant country and also to some of its most historic sites. The Old Head of Kinsale in the south, for instance, is the only known place where traces of the ancient Eiraenn Celtic tribe, who gave their name to Ireland, have been found, while in the North it was within the dunes at Portrush that Magnus Barefoot, King of Norway, is believed to have perished during an 1103 battle with Irish forces. While not all courses occupy such significant sites, the Irish are great storytellers and you will hear amazing tales told in the 19th hole of every club you visit here.

One quick word of warning. The success and profile of modern resort courses like Mount Juliet, K Club and Druids Glen masks the fact that most inland courses in Ireland are moderate, at best, versions of American-style parkland golf and should only be considered when the exciting and charming links have been exhausted.

The beauty of Ireland is its constant scenery and the ease with which one can travel around the island. You are best advised, however, to do so at a leisurely pace, so you can immerse yourself in both Irish culture and the culture of Irish golf.

OPPOSITE Irish golf is famous for its sea views and large dunes, and the new Doonbeg links in County Clare is well endowed with both. Pictured is the drivable par four 6th.

The Royal County Down Golf Club

COURSE OPENED 1889
DESIGNERS George Coombe,
Harry S. Colt,
Old Tom Morris,
Donald Steele

*'The kind of golf that people play in
their most ecstatic dreams.'*

BERNARD DARWIN ON
ROYAL COUNTY DOWN

OPPOSITE Planted on the advice of
Harry Colt, the gorse at County Down is
particularly prominent on the holes he
inspired. Shown here is Colt's 4th hole,
played toward the Mountains of Mourne
and across an intimidating sea of gorse.

The most exhilarating golfing experience on the planet, the links at Royal County Down is located in the small town of Newcastle, along the sands of Dundrum Bay and in the shadows of the mighty Mountains of Mourne as they famously sweep down to the sea. The club was formed in 1889 and its first eighteen-hole course was designed by Old Tom Morris, who was presented with an ideal piece of golfing ground when he arrived in Newcastle to prepare his plans. The designer spent two days on site and charged the club just £4 for a course which was open for play within a month, proof of how suitable the virgin land here was for golf.

Old Tom's routing had the course set out in a single tangled loop with holes regularly trampling east and west across the site's duneland. This layout changed dramatically over the next two decades, however, and mostly at the hands of George Coombe, the club's autocratic 'Convenor of the Greens' and one of Ireland's first plus markers. Inspired by the potential of its incredible setting, Coombe continually altered the holes and by 1907 had replaced all of the Morris holes and rearranged the course into two north-south loops returning to the clubhouse. In 1926, Harry Colt was employed to help the club overcome its perceived weakness of having too many gathering greens and semi-blind approach shots. Colt's plan included a new 4th hole, several additional bunkers and the merging of two blind holes into the 9th, arguably the greatest par four in the game. He also adjusted several greens and introduced the now infamous gorse to the tumbling dunes. Though the club continued to make minor adjustments, the layout Coombe started and

Colt finished is basically what remains today.

What makes Royal County Down so impressive is the combination of thrilling design and the inspired use of its magnificent dune structures, which are probably the most attractive in golf and certainly the most conducive to exciting play. Lined by purple heather, golden gorse and fearsome bunkers fringed with coarse sea grasses, the fairways are often routed right across the rugged hills. Numerous drives are played blind over the dunes with only a small white rock atop their peaks to indicate your ideal driving line. Such moments brilliantly test both your mental and physical abilities in equal measure, as you must be able to stand on the tee with an element of uncertainty and still strike a meaningful and accurate blow down the fairway. The intimidation of driving blind on holes lined by such formidable rough areas can be overwhelming, although the landing areas are not as narrow as they appear and the hazards are actually set reasonably back from the preferred playing corridor. Stray here and you usually get caught, but County Down can be more forgiving than it first appears and, if you are in control of your golf swing, is a links that, despite its reputation, can be tamed.

The front nine features the most exceptional stretch of golf holes on earth, starting with a great par five played along a jumbled ridge that separates the links from the sea, and then moving on to consecutive world-class par fours, the 2nd a daunting driving challenge across a steep ridge and the 3rd played through fescues and traps and into a magnificent green set beneath a glorious dune. Colt's long one-shot 4th and the semi-blind par fours at 5 and 6 are also great

holes. The approach into the small upturned saucer green at the 6th is particularly tricky and shows off the links' subtle side. As does the gorgeous 7th, which turns back toward the mountains and may be the world's most underrated short par three. The genius of the hole is its putting surface, which appears tiny from the tee as the left side falls away behind a deep frontal bunker and the higher right side is hidden by a small knoll. The 8th is then a terrific two-shotter that rises gently toward a difficult crowned green. Best of all, though, is the awesome 9th hole, with its blind drive plunging across the side of a hill and its wonderful green resting beyond cross-bunkers and in a saddle between two dunes. The view out over the sea and across the town of Newcastle to the mountains from atop this fairway is remarkable, and as golfers we are blessed that such a beautiful setting is available for our recreation.

Despite some problems toward the close, the back nine is also outstanding and the stretch from the 10th to 15th as strong as anything else in Ireland outside the opening holes here. Both the 10th and 14th are excellent par threes that demand shots with different shapes, while the 11th is a nasty four with a daring drive across the steepest hill on the course. The par four 13th is another beautiful hole, its approach crossing a gorse-covered sand ridge into a partially obscured green with just the yawning left-side traps visible and ready to catch those unable to throw the ball into the more open, but hidden, right side. The finishing trio, however, is strangely anticlimactic. The 17th is a very odd hole, while the bunkering on Donald Steele's new 16th is a little out of context with the rest of the layout. The 18th has also been reworked by Steele

but, despite being an improvement, it cannot mask the fact that this course really is a tale of two sides, one excellent and the other extraordinary.

There is no finer links than Royal County Down and despite one's best efforts, it would be nigh on impossible to accurately describe the pleasure of playing here. Suffice it to say that once experienced, it will leave you with an enhanced sense of golfing perfection. If you had just one round of golf left to play, it would be hard to mount an argument against that being at County Down.

ABOVE The rugged beauty of the 3rd hole at County Down.

OPPOSITE The finest nine holes in golf end with a magnificent par four, this the view from the fairway crest on the 9th.

Ballybunion Golf Club – Old Course

COURSE OPENED 1926
DESIGNERS Tom Simpson,
Lionel Hewson and various

'The beauty of the terrain surpasses that of any golf course I know, not excepting Pine Valley in America.'

TOM SIMPSON ON BALLYBUNION

Blessed with the most formidable dune structure in Ireland, golf was introduced to the small Kerry town of Ballybunion in 1893, though its first club folded within five years because of financial difficulties. The present Ballybunion Golf Club was not formed until 1906, when prominent townsfolk commissioned local golf writer Lionel Hewson to design them a new nine-hole course on their spectacular coastal linksland. By 1927 the links had been extended to eighteen holes, and in 1936 the club employed Tom Simpson to make further revisions and help shape a great piece of land into a great golf course.

When Simpson first toured the site he was genuinely impressed with the existing course and delighted by its prospects, even remarking to the club that, 'never for one moment did I imagine, or expect to find, such a really great course or such a glorious piece of golfing ground.' Aside from relocating the current 7th, 9th and 13th greens and adding several bunkers, most notably in the middle of the first fairway, his report to the club was full of only minor alterations or 'finishing touches,' as he called them. The club could not afford to implement all of his changes immediately, but over the next three decades continued to refer to the Simpson report when future amendments were made. That Ballybunion was initially created by somebody else and existed successfully before Simpson's visit does little to dismiss claims that he improved the layout and

is the man most responsible for its elevated international profile.

Stretching from the town road right to the edge of the Irish west coast, the Old Course at Ballybunion twists through a collection of soaring sandhills, the layout ducking in and out of the dunes with great irregularity and spreading the seaside experiences throughout the round. Remarkably, the inland golf and some of the transitional holes into and away from the water are among its most memorable moments. Early examples include the relatively simple opening hole and the par four 2nd, a smashing hole squeezed up through a narrow gap between large dunes. Following a solid par three and a couple of fairly nondescript par fives, the real fun begins at the short 6th, which takes the golfer toward the coastal cliffs for the first time and to perhaps the most evil green site in all of Ireland. With both fairway and green set obliquely along a narrow ridge, the decision from the tee is whether to lay-up high and pitch along the length of the ridge or to play long and try a delicate chip and putt for your birdie. This is one of those classic risk/reward holes where every straight inch gained with your driver makes the approach slightly easier, but every yard strayed makes it more difficult. The next, dramatically played along the very edge of the Atlantic, is the first of Ballybunion's internationally famous par fours, while the short 8th and vastly underrated 9th, both away from the sea, are also outstanding.

OPPOSITE **Approaching the 17th green on the Old Course at Ballybunion.**

Featuring a collection of pin-up holes, the back nine begins with a terrific short par four that heads toward the shore and offers countless options of attack. Further highlights include the four-and-a-half par 13th, par three 15th, steeply uphill 16th, and the fabulous 17th, its skinny fairway falling toward the ocean and then twisting around a massive dune as it follows the beach. Stealing the show, however, is the magnificent 11th, an extraordinary hole that hops along the edge of the cliffs and through deep dunes to a green nestled beyond a shallow sand saddle and set before the crashing seas. While glamorous holes like 7, 10, 11 and 17 attract most of the headlines here, the entire experience is awesome, from a routing that attacks the hills in a variety of ways, to greens whose simple appearance continually mask the intricacy of their clever slopes.

The club also has a fine second course, The Cashen, which opened in 1980 and was built to capitalize on the success and popularity of its venerable classic. Course designer Robert Trent Jones described its virgin site as the 'finest piece of linksland in the world,' and while the layout does boast beautiful natural green sites and dramatic fairway passages through the heaving dunes, it lacks the broader and more playable fairway corridors of the Old Course and has too many small, steep and overly contoured raised greens. The Cashen Course does have its fans, but for first-timers to Ballybunion it should really only be considered when the Old Course timesheet is full.

OPPOSITE One of Ireland's most memorable holes, the 11th on the Old Course is a stunning par four perched on top of seaside cliffs.

Royal Portrush Golf Club – Dunluce Links

COURSE OPENED 1933
DESIGNER Harry S. Colt

Himalayas, Portrush's short
par four 8th hole.

OPPOSITE Skirting the top of a
massive dune ridge, the 14th hole
(Calamity) at Royal Portrush is one of
the most celebrated in the British Isles.

Situated on Northern Ireland's beautiful north coast, the Royal Portrush Golf Club occupies an ancient dune system that runs alongside the Atlantic Ocean and overlooks the Giant's Causeway headland and its towering limestone cliff edges. Founded inland of the sandhills in 1888, the club gradually shifted toward the town's heavy coastal dunes and by 1929 had acquired enough land to build two full courses, Harry Colt employed to design them both. Presented with a rippled landscape covered in undulation, Colt decided to use the higher, more exposed ground, which was full of deep valleys, long ridges and large plateaus, to build his famous Dunluce Links and set the much underrated Valley Course within the site's sunken sand basin.

Enjoying the pick of the linksland, the Dunluce course is a masterpiece of golf architecture. The brilliance of Colt's work is apparent in holes that beautifully follow the curvature of the sand formations and feature some of the most cleverly conceived green complexes in golf, the targets built to accommodate only those playing at the top of their game. Lined by thick roughs and deadly gorse, the fairways mostly nestle in natural valleys between the intimidating dunes, though Colt was also unafraid to occasionally route them across their plunging crests.

For those approaching from Belfast, the Portrush experience starts with a memorable drive into town along the twisting Antrim coast road. This winding drive takes you along the Causeway cliffs and past the ruins of the ancient Dunluce Castle before suddenly opening up to present the town and its magnificent links in all their seaside glory. The round itself begins with a front nine of rare quality; the uphill opening hole does little more than get you away, but is followed by a seven-hole stretch as profound as any you will play. The 4th, for instance, is a cracking hole that requires strong and straight shots squeezed firstly between bunkers and an out-of-bounds fence and then through two small dunes guarding a superb mini-dell green. The 5th then skims bunkerless across small ripples to a marvelous target perched right at the brink of the Portrush cliffs, while the 6th is a fabulous par three that features a large tiered green angled to reject anything not struck precisely.

The next gem is Himalayas, the short par four 8th hole, which bends through a gorgeous dune valley and toward a seriously slender green. Taking in the invigorating scenery from this tee with both the Himalayas and Skerries (13) in full view, the Calamity Corner (14) a few hundred yards away and memories of the opening stretch fresh in your mind, this feels like the greatest links of them all. It is probably a measure of the front nine's greatness, therefore, that in some ways the back nine is a touch disappointing. There remains some wonderful golf, but one or two nondescript shots and the flatness of the finishing holes

keeps it from reaching the dizzying heights of the opening nine. Highlights are generally concentrated on a five-hole series that starts with the strong par four 12th, its green built on a ridge that falls away cruelly on both sides and is difficult to hit unless approached directly from the middle of the fairway. The 13th is then a wild ride from a blind low tee across a large crest that opens up to present golfers with beautiful views of the Skerries Islands just offshore. Next up is Portrush's star attraction, the huge one-shot Calamity, which skirts the top of a massive ridge, its entire right side collapsing violently down into a deep chasm. Of the remaining holes, the falling 15th is adventurous though a tad extreme, while the par four 16th is an excellent test and the 18th, converted from a soft five to a stiff four, is now an appropriate conclusion to such a demanding round.

Despite some disappointment with the finish at Portrush, there are only a handful of courses more enjoyable and very few places that you will long to return to more. It is believed that Colt regarded Dunluce as his finest achievement and it is clearly the best of those layouts credited solely to him. With an inspired setting, ideal golf land, a superb design and wonderful construction, Royal Portrush is close to the perfect example of a quality links and sits comfortably among the best dozen or so golf courses on the planet.

OPPOSITE Great golf and superb coastal views from the Skerries (13th) hole.

Lahinch Golf Club

COURSE OPENED 1892
DESIGNERS Old Tom Morris,
Dr Alister MacKenzie,
George Gibson,
Martin Hawtree

*'Lahinch will make the finest
and most popular course that I,
or I believe anyone else, ever
constructed.'*

DR ALISTER MACKENZIE

A links of unparalleled originality, the Lahinch Golf Club was born in 1892 when Scottish officers of the Black Watch Regiment stationed in Limerick came upon a vast expanse of duneland on the edge of the small seaside resort town of Lahinch and decided to build a golf course. Their original layout only skirted the site's heavy sandhills, but in 1894 it was redesigned by Old Tom Morris. Morris regarded the links as one of the finest natural courses he had seen and pushed more of it into the dunes. Westward Ho! professional George Gibson later added a few more beachside holes but the most significant phase in the development of the course came in 1927 when Dr Alister MacKenzie moved all eighteen into the heavier coastal dunes, added a number of new green sites and stretched and modernized the layout.

The Lahinch that gradually rose to international prominence was a combination of the work of all these designers. Her most famous holes, the Dell and Klondyke, were both by Morris, while the flowing routing, strategic driving lines and wonderfully intricate and unconventional green complexes were a result of MacKenzie's ability to successfully tie together his own ideas with Gibson's and Morris's best moments.

Overlooking the stunning County Clare coastline, the course first plays along the sea toward an estuary that dissects the site before heading back along the main coastal road into town. After a solid opening, the first hint of brilliance comes at the 3rd, an awesome driving hole over a large dune slope that turns seaward and follows a succession of humps and hollows into a clever plateau green. Next are Klondyke and Dell. Unmistakably Lahinch, these two Old Tom originals are among the most famous holes in Irish golf. The Klondyke is played from a coastal ridge into a narrow valley, which then leaves you a completely blind second over the immense Klondyke sandhill to a green resting against the boundary wall. It is followed by perhaps the only hole in golf more distinctive, the famous Dell, Lahinch's signature since 1894 and still as controversial as ever. The tee shot here is little more than a short-iron, but the shallow target is nestled between two steep dunes and totally hidden, with just a white rock on the frontal dune to indicate where the pin is located.

Debate still rages as to whether these are quality or just quirky golf holes, but there is absolutely no denying that the 6th, 7th, 11th, 12th and 14th are all outstanding. As is the reachable par four 13th, which is the most ingenious of MacKenzie's work. Nestled among dangerous sandhills, the green is an awfully tempting target, but the successful drive needs to negotiate a narrow central fracture and flirt with a huge pit in order to reach its angled surface. The Sandwich-style 9th hole is another gem, this time rising up a slanting fairway and then heading into a

slender shelf green cut into an undulating hillside. Although a couple of the closing holes are a little lacklustre, the entire journey is an extremely strong challenge and the course is full of fun and surprise.

Over the decades the club has had problems with coastal erosion and also lost various elements of its design, often during ill-advised remodeling projects. In 1999 it decided to reverse this trend and employed Martin Hawtree to put as much MacKenzie back into Lahinch as he could squeeze into the remaining dune areas. Completed in 2003, the upgrade was substantial and involved work on thirteen holes, including two new par threes and, thankfully, the restoration of several MacKenzie greens that had been softened over the years. The Hawtree program has been a success, and what works best about the modern Lahinch is that despite the differing design influences through the decades the course still manages to provide a coherent test with few, if any, commonplace holes and several that are candidates for inclusion in any greatest golf hole discussion.

Lahinch is to Irish golf what North Berwick is to Scottish golf; not the birthplace of the sport but the absolute embodiment of everything great about the game here and a spiritual base for the passionate links aficionado. It may not be the best course in the world but those unimpressed by the Lahinch layout ought to stop their search for great golf, for the game doesn't really get much better than this.

ABOVE The 11th hole is an excellent par three that was built during the Martin Hawtree restoration.

OPPOSITE One of the best short fours in the world, the 13th is a MacKenzie gem that works because the green is an enticing target, despite the dangers that guard its narrow entrance.

County Sligo Golf Club – Rosses Point

COURSE OPENED 1931
DESIGNER Harry S. Colt
with Charles H. Alison

The 7th hole features Sligo's trickiest approach across this dangerous, diagonal burn.

OPPOSITE The beauty of Rosses Point is evident from the 9th tee, with Benbulben Mountain and Drumcliffe Bay as your backdrop.

Superbly situated at the tip of the Rosses Point Peninsula and less than five miles from the town of Sligo, the largely unheralded County Sligo Golf Club is one of the strongest and most scenic links in Ireland. Founded in 1894 on land owned by an uncle of Nobel Prize winning poet W.B. Yeats, the club originally golfed on a simple nine-hole layout close to the current clubhouse, which was extended to eighteen holes in 1906 and then given to the great Harry Colt to redesign in 1927.

Clearly impressed with the long stretch of windswept coastal land at his disposal, Colt arranged his holes in a single counter-clockwise loop along the Atlantic shoreline, the routing bearing remarkable similarity to his beloved St Andrews. The bunkering was not added until the holes were in the ground and patterns of play had been established. Somewhat controversially, his associate Charles H. Alison was sent to finish the job, and Alison left the club with deep, hungry hazards that were initially unpopular with members but are now a real feature of the layout.

The course itself starts rather inauspiciously by tracking up and then down a steep incline before settling onto low-profile links terrain sandwiched between the beaches of the Atlantic Ocean and the surrounding mountainside. At the northern end of the Peninsula the golf briefly turns inland toward the towering Benbulben Mountain, the inspiration for much of Yeats's literature, before heading back along the Bay of Drumcliffe and making a stunning re-entry onto the main seaside linksland at the beach-carry par three 13th. Built mostly across minor ripples and relatively unexciting undulation, Colt's talent for using the land's existing contours is evident throughout a layout that features simple but stern holes that are often visually deceptive and complemented by superbly contoured greens.

After a somewhat scratchy start, the middle section of the course is particularly strong and includes gems like the 7th hole, its approach played diagonally across a deep burn that also snakes around the side of the green. The elevated 8th green is equally impressive, and followed by a delicious short par three that stares straight at Benbulben and introduces you to a series of fine holes at the far end of Rosses Point. The best golf, however, is saved for the late holes along the shoreline. These include the magnificent par four 14th, which bends twice and is cut by a twisting burn, the seemingly simple one-shot 16th, and Sligo's superstar hole, the 17th, a par four of mighty proportions routed across some of the most dramatic duneland in the country.

Aside from the 14th and 17th, at first glance none of the holes at Rosses Point appear obvious stunners, but Colt's intelligent design and outstanding greens are so effective that you often only realize the genius of a hole after succumbing to what at first seemed its innocuous challenge. Indeed, County Sligo is a links that works best by providing a constant and consistent test for all golfers, its final six holes as thorough an examination of your ball-striking abilities as you will find anywhere in this part of the world.

Carne Golf Links – Belmullet

COURSE OPENED 1993
DESIGNER Eddie Hackett

'I am thrilled with the way the dramatic Belmullet Course has turned out and again reiterate my first opinion that ultimately there will be no better links in the country, or, I doubt, anywhere.'

EDDIE HACKETT

OPPOSITE Wild and rugged, Carne is one of modern golf's most exciting creations. This the highly original 15th hole.

One of golf's true hidden gems, the Carne Golf Links was developed to increase tourism into the Erris region of Ireland's Gaelic North West, and in particular its remote and economically depressed Belmullet Peninsula. About as far west as you can go on the mainland, the course was built on a heaving dunescape of immense proportions and was the last to be designed by Ireland's 'Mr Links,' Eddie Hackett, who designed a large portion of the country's links and had an uncanny knack of finding natural golf holes on natural golf land. Here his fairways, tees and greens are all naturally sited on a property so full of excitement that deciding what to leave out, rather than what to include, would have been one of Hackett's greatest challenges.

His layout features distinctly contrasting nines, with the outward holes set over smaller sand ripples that overlook Blacksod Bay and the homeward side winding through some of Ireland's largest dunes and heading out toward the isolated Atlantic coastline. It is quite possible for the opening holes to be forgotten for the thrill of the back nine, but its less overwhelming landscape tends to mask some very fine golf. The opener, for instance, is an ideal start, with a drive needing to bypass a small knoll that splits the landing zone and separates the aggressive and dangerous driving line from the safer, more conservative play. Also memorable are the unorthodox blind par three 2nd and the corrugated 3rd fairway, although the outward highlight is clearly the brilliant par four 8th, which features an attractive bowl-like target totally surrounded by massive sandhills.

Though the short par four 9th is another fun hole, the entire side is a mere prelude to the adrenalin rush of the mighty back nine, whose sheer size and scale is only apparent once you have traversed the crest of the 10th fairway and stared down at a target framed by a dune ridge that rises more than 100 feet above the green. From this point Carne feels like pure fantasy, the remaining holes set among sand formations so high they seem to stretch into the clouds and dwarf the golf fields beneath them. In truth, Hackett barely designed this part of the course; instead, he let the land dictate play and merely uncovered playing corridors and green sites created by centuries of whipping winds and receding seas. Perfect examples are the back-to-back short par fours at 11 and 12. The second is a mirror image of the first with both holes playing down through a deep valley, then bending at right angles around a gigantic hill before heading steeply up into a perilous green shelf.

Other wild moments include the par four 15th, which features some of the funkiest undulations on the site, and the plunging par three 16th with its tee atop an enormous sandy peak. The beautiful par four 17th is probably the toughest hole on the course, as its fairway turns through a narrow valley enroute to a

small kidney-shaped green that slopes toward a ravine and will only accept the most precise running approach. Another highly original hole is the reachable par five 18th, which collapses into a yawning chasm near the green from where that precious last-gasp birdie is virtually impossible.

Although the golf here never really gets right down along the coast and its views do not rival those of Doonbeg, Ballybunion or Royal County Down, Carne does boast some of the most exciting and natural dune holes in Ireland and is the sort of quality experience that only a designer with enough self-control and experience to know what to use and what to leave alone could have created. Hackett himself once said that as a designer you are, 'only as good as what the Lord gives you in features,' and at Carne he was presented with such a stunning dunescape that it is no surprise this is his most significant creation. He was also convinced that it would one day be regarded as the best links in Ireland, a sentiment that on the surface seems to overlook the strength of its competition, but one that does not seem half as absurd when you finally see this place.

OPPOSITE If big dune golf is your thing, you will definitely enjoy Carne. Pictured here is the awesome scale of the par four 11th.

Doonbeg Golf Club

COURSE OPENED 2002

DESIGNER Greg Norman

'This is a course I want to be identified with, one I will be able to say with pride – I did that one.'

GREG NORMAN

Stretching along a curving beachfront ridge at Doughmore Bay in the tiny town of Doonbeg, the spectacular new Doonbeg Golf Club is surrounded by some of the giants of Irish golf and is destined to become one itself. The links occupies ancient sandhills that tower up to a hundred feet and were first considered for golf by the founders of the nearby Lahinch Golf Club, who ultimately felt the town was too isolated for their club. A century later, and though still remote, the magnificent Doonbeg dunes were finally bequeathed to golfers in 2002 with the opening of Greg Norman's remarkable modern links.

Norman spent a tremendous amount of time on site during the design of Doonbeg, immersing himself totally in the project for several years, aware that this was an opportunity to create something very special. Importantly, his big dune landscape was also blessed with the natural playing corridors and smaller internal ground contours so essential for interesting golf. With such a suitable canvas, the design team built the course with a shovel rather than a bulldozer and merely mowed down the fescues to uncover holes already laid out in the dunescape. Only a handful of fairways and greens were shaped to any degree, while the bunkering was dug by hand, the hazards left rugged and generally either sod revetted or fringed with shaggy tufts of native grass.

The design process was hamstrung, however, when an endangered microscopic snail was discovered in some of the principal dunes, preventing their development and forcing the layout to be rerouted several times. A key design decision for Norman then became whether to sacrifice any further duneland by focusing on a logical and coherent layout, or using all of the available drama through design to create as many spectacular holes as possible and living with a few routing issues. Norman chose the latter and, despite tees that hit over greens and awkward cross-fairway walks, so dramatic and visually compelling are the best holes here that, on balance, it is hard to argue with his decision.

Arranged in a single loop that continually ducks in and out of the towering sandhills, the course begins from a high tee looking out over the site's stunning coastline, the sense of excitement heightened by a wonderful par five that ends with a target tucked into a huge sandy amphitheatre. From here the course shifts onto flatter inland farming ground that skirts the edge of the dunes, re-emerging after some solid but subdued golf into the heavy hills at the par four 5th, its approach heading through a sand saddle and over a gorge toward a green lying before the ocean. The next is played across the 13th green and along wild beachfront dunes. Aside from a diabolical green site on the long 8th, the talking point of the remaining outward holes is the short par three 9th with its sublime target set beside the sea.

The course then again skips along former farmland for three holes, including the

controversial 12th and its donut-shaped green, before moving back into the big dunes at the reachable par five 13th, an audacious hole that is semi-blind across a crest and then into a narrow target resting atop a ridge and beyond a vast expanse of sand. Softening the landing area and shaving part of the driving dune has helped the playability of this hole enormously. Remaining back nine highlights include Norman's favorite hole, the strong par four 15th with its green sitting within a massive sand crater; and the demanding finishing hole played blind along the beach to a well-bunkered fairway and wildly contoured green. The star attraction, however, is the 14th, an evil 100-yard par three played straight at the ocean and a slender shelf of green shaved into the side of a soaring ridge. Despite its youth, this hole has already become a legend in Ireland.

With as many glamour holes as any links in the British Isles, Doonbeg is a terrific experience and, thanks to sensible modification, has improved considerably in the years since opening. Not surprisingly, it has polarized popular opinion, with many highly critical of its seemingly dangerous and illogical routing and others convinced that, by virtue of its many highlights, it is likely to be one of the golfing achievements of the 21st century. While it is unfair to compare Doonbeg with famous neighbors like Lahinch, and its 100 years of maturity, there have been few more impressive virgin courses built in this region during the last half-century.

ABOVE Doonbeg's beautiful beachside par three 9th hole.

OPPOSITE Designer's choice, the par four 15th features a thrilling approach into this memorable green complex.

Waterville Golf Club

COURSE OPENED 1973
DESIGNERS Eddie Hackett,
Tom Fazio

'Everything about Waterville is spectacular, the setting is one of the best I have seen anywhere in golf.'

TOM FAZIO

OPPOSITE Waterville's 11th hole is a par five that meanders through an attractive dune corridor.

As unlikely a combination as extravagant American architect Tom Fazio and a quaint village links may seem, at Waterville, along Ireland's Ring of Kerry, an unexpected transformation has further strengthened the town's historic ties with its frequent American visitors. Golf here can be traced back to 1889, when a nine-hole course was built primarily for workers from a trans-Atlantic cable station built in the village. Abandoned by the 1950s, when the cable station ceased operation, the links lay dormant until an Irish-born American, John Mulcahy, bought the land and employed the prolific Eddie Hackett to design the new Waterville links.

Located along the Atlantic Ocean, on a peninsula of land bordered by an estuary of the Inny River, the Hackett design included a front side built over less exposed terrain away from the coastal dunes and a back nine that occupied rugged sandhills and touched both the mouth of the estuary and the Atlantic shoreline. Opening in 1973, the original Hackett course was the longest in Ireland but oozed old-world charm. It amassed itself quite a devoted and loyal following until sold in 1987 to a small group of Irish Americans who later embarked on what seemed a radical renovation program with architect Tom Fazio.

The Fazio project started in 2002 and involved redesigning a number of the flatter greens, replacing the 6th and 7th holes and remodeling the less dramatic outward nine to provide more dune contours along the lower inland portion of the property. He also moved greens on 2, 15 and 16 and tightened landing areas on the long 18th, making it

a classic closing par five along the ocean that rewards aggressive and well-played shots close to the beach. With the possible exception of an over-shaped 6th hole, the changes have been a big success and, to Fazio's great credit, the new Waterville still feels about a hundred years old.

Though the early holes toward and along the estuary are very solid, the best golf comes later in the round, from the strong par four 9th hole and through most of a superb back nine. Snaking through a rugged dune valley, the three-shot 11th is terrific, as are approaches into the softly rising 10th, 14th and 15th greens. Also memorable is the par three 12th, played across a deep sandy crater where Catholics used to huddle for secret mass during the 18th century, when it was illegal in Ireland to do so and punishable by death. The closing run from the 14th is particularly strong and includes Hackett's wonderful par three 17th and Fazio's finest work, the 16th, where he removed a string of bunkers on the outside of the dogleg and shifted the tee closer to the river and the green closer to the ocean to create a marvelous mid-length four along the sea dunes.

Still one of the longest layouts in Ireland, the one minor criticism of Waterville is that it lacks subtlety. The par threes are all strong, but a clever short one or a genuine drive-and-pitch hole would have done wonders to break up the challenge. Nevertheless, taking a low-key links designed by a true minimalist and handing it over to Tom Fazio to tweak was an enormous gamble by the club's owners, but one that has thankfully paid off in spades.

The European Club

COURSE OPENED 1992
DESIGNER Pat Ruddy

The 10th hole at Pat Ruddy's
European Club.

OPPOSITE Distinctive sleeper-faced
bunkers protect the entrance to the
green on the par five 3rd.

Unlike the majority of modern golf developers who seek immediate headlines and hefty financial returns with their compromised estate master plans, when Irish writer Pat Ruddy decided to build his own golf links it was done with little fanfare and with the long-term foresight of a true golf visionary. A devotee of the classics, Ruddy's vision for the European Club was a private golf-only playground he would build for his own personal enjoyment but then share, when ready, with discerning like-minded golfers.

The designer's first concern was finding an ideal site for his modern links. By helicopter he scoured Ireland's coastline looking for quality linksland, managing to spot a stretch of coastal dunes along the Irish Sea some 40 miles south of Dublin. Convinced of its suitability for great golf, he purchased the property and then, with a 'build it and they will come' mentality, spent several years meticulously planning his course and personally shaping its fairways, greens and bunkers until he felt it ready for play.

Full of interesting elements, the Ruddy routing is made up of two counter-clockwise loops, the first mostly away from the sea and the second touching its shoreline. Most of the golf is set within a series of medium-sized sandhills and, although some holes through the dune corridors designed themselves, the majority were caressed into life by an attentive architect. Focused on variety and careful not to over-design his holes, Ruddy cleverly attacked the sand formations from all directions, leaving the links always at the mercy of the elements and unlikely ever to become tedious.

The opening holes are superb. The rising first fairway introduces you to the site's gorgeous duneland while the 2nd is an excellent short hole and the 3rd a terrific downhill par five that narrows as you approach a forward- and right-sloping hillside green. Both the par three 6th and the long, strong and penal par four 7th are nasty holes, but these are immediately followed by the best stretch on the course, which includes the deep valley 8th, attractive green complexes at the 10th and 11th and a series of holes – 12, 13 and 15 – that are routed right alongside the sea. The pick of these central holes, however, is the par three 14th, which is played across a valley and into a falling ridge green.

About the only minor criticism one could make of the links is the fact that some of the fairway bunkers and tight landing areas are ineffective under certain conditions. The course is also a touch long, especially from the back tees, and does lack a clever short four. The beautifully built green sites are outstanding, however, as are the distinctive sleeper-faced bunkers, which are well placed throughout the course but used sparingly within the fairways.

Pat Ruddy knew that, like all great links, his course would be far from perfect the day it opened and he has spent the years since its 1992 opening tweaking holes to further improve upon what he first created. Despite still being a work in progress, the European Club is a substantial achievement and already one of Ireland's must-play links.

Old Head Golf Links

COURSE OPENED 1997
DESIGNERS Ron Kirby,
Dr Joe Carr,
Eddie Hackett,
Liam Higgins,
Paddy Merrigan and others

The penalty for a miss is obvious on the short 16th.

OPPOSITE Pushed perilously close to the cliffs, the 4th is a dangerous par four that heads toward the Old Head lighthouse.

OVERLEAF Spectacular views across the 7th green and entrance isthmus back down the Irish mainland.

Surrounded by massive cliffs and crashing seas, the extraordinary Old Head Golf Links is built atop an ancient sandstone promontory known as the Old Head of Kinsale, which protrudes out from Ireland's southern coastline. This historic site, whose earliest settlers predate Christ by several centuries, had been used as grazing ground until the late 1980s, when brothers John and Patrick O'Connor purchased the property with a vision to convert it into a golfing field.

Recognizing the potential of its 200-acre diamond-shaped headland for golf, the O'Connor's had to endure a protracted battle with local authorities for permission to build a road onto the site before they could proceed with their course. During this period a number of course architects and possible routings were considered, and the final Old Head layout turned out to be the work of several key figures, including the owners, who insisted upon pushing holes dangerously close to the edges of the cliffs to maximize the golfing drama. Although internal out-of-bounds areas are a regrettable by-product of the clubhouse location and its busy access road, the design itself is quite good, with most of the better holes strategic and the tamer inland holes, which don't work quite as well, saved by their compelling scenery.

The realization that Old Head is something special hits long before you step onto the first tee, the sense of excitement building from the drive toward the rocky headland, which takes you across a narrow isthmus and past ancient stone circles, castle ruins and remnants of a medieval church. Engulfed by remarkable 360-degree ocean views, the course begins with a relatively benign opening hole but soon steps up a gear at the 2nd which, like the 4th, skirts along the edge of the ocean cliffs with anything pulled or hooked plunging 300 feet down into the Atlantic. Sandwiched between these holes is a par three that also dangles perilously on the edge of the abyss. Fortunately from the 5th you can catch your breath, as the next seven holes are inland of the perimeter and, although difficult, they are not life threatening.

Next to make the highlights reel is the impossibly dramatic par five 12th. Routed back along part of the isthmus, its drive is a blind blast from beneath the cliffs to a sliver of fairway located well right of where you imagine. Anything short or left from the tee swims with the fishes, while anything too far right may end there on the second swing as the rest of the hole is downhill along a narrowing tightrope. The cliff-side 15th and 16th holes are also an adrenalin rush, though both are upstaged by the raw drama of the monstrous par five 17th, which is initially blind across a crest but then dives down along the cliff edge. From here you climb nearly a hundred steps to reach an 18th tee box placed beneath the famous Old Head lighthouse and enjoying wonderful views down the incredible Irish coastline.

Despite widespread fame and acclaim, Old Head continues to divide opinion, with some convinced it is God's gift to golf and others believing that 'all it lacks is good golf holes.' The average golfer, however, will struggle to find anything that surpasses the Old Head experience, and though purists can argue the merit of its holes individually, they cannot dispute the fact that it is one of the most spectacular courses on Earth.

Portmarnock Golf Club

COURSE OPENED 1894
DESIGNERS W.C. Pickeman, George Ross

Covered in low-set dunes and small sandy hollows, the 27-hole Portmarnock Golf Club occupies most of a 500-acre peninsula wedged between the Irish Sea and a tidal inlet to the north of Dublin Bay. Originally accessible only by boat, Scottish insurance broker W.C. Pickeman and his friend George Ross discovered the site in 1893 and designed the club's first eighteen holes, which remain its championship layout.

With a greater resemblance to the small-scale links on the Open Rota in Britain than the wild and exciting creations along Ireland's coast, Portmarnock is an ideal championship venue that professional golfers, in particular, tend to enjoy, as it lacks the nasty surprises and hidden hazards found elsewhere in the region. Most holes challenge you to drive straight, and although the narrow dimpled fairways twist through thick fescues and are dotted with deep pot bunkers, the landing areas are generally in full view from the tee and mostly flat. The bounce is also usually predictable and the hazards stern but not impossible to recover from.

Better holes include the par four opener, pressed right beside the sea, excellent par threes at the 7th, 12th and 15th and the string of medium-length par fours through the middle of the round. The downwind 14th, which plays into a small raised tabletop target that is heavily bunkered at the front, is another standout, as are the beautifully bunkered par four finishing holes, where avoiding the sand and thick roughs from the tee is the key.

More a great collection of holes than a collection of great holes, there are very few here that would be considered among Ireland's best but barely any that could be described as weak. Like all true links, Mother Nature was the first architect at Portmarnock, though what makes the course a classic is the hand of man in designing clever and consistent golf holes across her low-set links features.

Tralee Golf Club

COURSE OPENED 1984
DESIGNERS Arnold Palmer, Ed Seay

Although first formed within the town of Tralee in 1896, the Tralee Golf Club now plays on a course built in 1984 and situated along the Kerry coastline at nearby Barrow. Designed by Arnold Palmer and partner Ed Seay, the front nine at Tralee touches an ocean inlet and rocky shore, while the back is carved from an immense dune ridge that tumbles down toward the area's spectacular beach.

Despite this magnificent coastal setting, recommendation does come with some reservations as none of the inland golf will inspire and the early seaside holes, such as the par five 2nd, which bends around the beach where parts of the film *Ryan's Daughter* were shot, are a touch awkward. Similarly, the attractive 8th follows a picturesque inlet but is spoiled by an ill-positioned dune that pinches its fairway too tightly. By contrast, the par three 3rd, played across a rocky cove, is a terrific hole but the remainder of the front side is fairly tame. It is the steep dune holes on the back nine that provide most of the excitement. The best of these is the 12th, a bruising two-shot hole that falls into a narrow landing zone and then crosses an enormous gorge to reach its plateau target. Also memorable is the three-hole beachside corner from the short par four 15th, which includes an all-or-nothing par three and an uncomfortably narrow mid-length par four that are only marginally playable. Most difficult of all, however, is the short 13th, where one must cross a massive crater to find a shallow green sliced halfway up an enormous sand dune.

There is no questioning the attraction of this piece of land, but the lack of internal undulation away from the sea and the sheer size of the back nine dunes suggest the routing options here were limited and perhaps the site was not as ideal for golf as it appears.

OPPOSITE The daunting approach into the 12th green at Tralee.

Portstewart Golf Club – Strand Course

COURSE OPENED 1992
DESIGNERS Willie Park Jr, Des Giffin

Situated along Northern Ireland's magnificent Causeway Coast and only a few miles from Royal Portrush, the Portstewart Strand Course was created in 1992, though it features eleven holes designed by Willie Park Jr back when the club was first formed in 1894. Park's superb opening hole, which follows the beach and plunges down and around a small ridge, remains in play, but during the 1980s the club acquired 60 acres of virgin duneland beyond its green and enlisted a local school teacher, Des Giffen, to build seven holes for its new course.

The Giffen holes, 2 through 8, occupy some of the heaviest sand formations in Northern Ireland and mostly run through deep dune corridors or across broad valleys. Holes that head up into dunes, such as the 5th and 7th, are outstanding, as is the 8th, which hugs a hill as it boomerangs around to the left. The wild 9th is also terrific and reintroduces golfers to Park's original holes. Unfortunately, the rest of the course is routed away from the heavy dunes and feels totally different, as the ground is much flatter and less interesting. Aside from a tremendous shelf green site at the mid-length par four 11th, the back nine is best remembered for a series of tough par fours that make up the closing stretch.

Giffen did an admirable job in the sandhills but in some ways the variance in terrain hurts the Strand Course, as does the hundred-year gap in design philosophy, the Park holes somehow more adventurous despite the less dramatic land. This disparity should not put you off a visit, however, as the terrain here is ideal for golf and the course is a terrific back-up option for visiting golfers who have exhausted their playing privileges at Royal Portrush.

The K Club – Palmer Course

COURSE OPENED 1991
DESIGNERS Arnold Palmer, Ed Seay

The Staffran Estate in County Kildare had a history dating back almost 1,500 years prior to paper and packaging magnate Dr Michael Smurfit purchasing it in 1988 with a view to creating a luxury golf and hotel destination. Located less than 20 miles from the center of Dublin, the Kildare Hotel and Country Club, or 'the K Club', was opened in 1991 and is now home to a superb five-star hotel and two contrasting, but distinctly American-style, resort courses built on either side of the Liffey River.

Routed through established park grounds, the original Palmer Course is the pick of the golf and, despite water coming into play on fourteen holes, is less tricked-up than the over-the-top Smurfit Course. While sculptured water hazards are the central feature of the layout, the better holes are those close to the river and include the fine three-shot 7th, requiring a bold drive and a precise lay-up into the narrowing fairway to set up a pitch across the Liffey to a tight target. The short par four 8th and riverside par three 17th are both noteworthy, while away from the river the dangerous par four 15th and all-water 16th, with its island fairway and island green, are also very good.

The Palmer Course is an especially effective matchplay venue, as it oozes drama and has countless places for matches to swing. Aggressive, risk-taking golfers will almost certainly love its many gambling opportunities, the mix of small, built-up greens and tempting tee shots surrounded by water likely to leave you dipping regularly into the bag for new balls if your game is not 'on.' Though well below the class of Ireland's best links, the K Club is nevertheless great fun to play socially and clearly the best of Ireland's inland resort courses.

OPPOSITE The pitch across the Liffey and onto the green at the par five 7th, with the K Club's luxurious hotel in the background.

Wales

S ituated between England and the Irish Sea, Wales is one of the oldest nations in the world and famous for its coastline, castles, mountains and male choirs. Less recognized as a tourist destination than elsewhere in the British Isles, Wales is also the least frequented golfing country of the region, which is a major part of the attraction as its best courses remain largely undiscovered.

In many ways overshadowed by the great success of golf tourism in Ireland and Scotland, Wales is now trying to take advantage of the overcrowding and overpricing that this success has brought by promoting itself as a low-cost, high-quality alternative to more traditional golf destinations. There is a genuine charm and attraction to playing in Wales. The scenery is usually spectacular and the leading private clubs are unpretentious and welcoming to visitors. The golf itself is unhurried and highly original, and often so quirky that even the daft holes and features seem cool. Despite being full of raw, exciting links and the sort of moderate green fees Ireland was famous for before the tourists invaded, in truth the general quality of golf here is a long way below that available across the sea.

As in Ireland, the game was first exported to Wales during the 1880s, to the town of Tenby in the south-west. Most of the subsequent layouts were then scattered along its attractive coastline. The country's two leading championship courses are the celebrated Royal Porthcawl links west of Cardiff and Royal St David's, set in the shadow of the World Heritage-listed Harlech Castle. While Porthcawl is an outstanding course, Royal St David's, which is surrounded by monstrous dunes but routed across much flatter ground, is fairly tame compared to the better links available elsewhere in Britain. More noteworthy are places like the remarkable Nefyn & District Golf Club or Pennard and Southerndown, which are both set atop high plateaus that were sprayed with sand centuries ago and now feature the crumpled fairways and humps and hollows of traditional beachside links. The oldest Welsh golf club, Tenby, is a terrific links experience, as are Aberdovery, Ashburnham and three holes on the back nine at Pyle & Kenfig.

High-end American resorts and country clubs are largely foreign to Wales, but there are a handful of worthwhile parkland courses such as the Rolls of Monmouth, laid out on the estate of the founder of Rolls-Royce, Marriott St Pierre and the Vale Resort courses in Glamorgan. While the 2010 Ryder Cup at Celtic Manor will no doubt increase the profile of Welsh golf, those visiting and not playing Royal Porthcawl, Tenby, Pennard and Nefyn & District will not only miss the best golf in Wales but the very essence of what the game in this part of the world is all about. Indeed, a trip to these four featured tracks plus Southerndown, Ashburnham, Aberdovey and Royal St David's is an inexpensive way to educate yourself in the charms of genuine links golf, and a perfect prelude to the sterner and more fertile links grounds of Scotland, Ireland and England.

Royal Porthcawl Golf Club

COURSE OPENED 1913

DESIGNERS Harry S. Colt,
Fred Hawtree,
J.H. Taylor,
Tom Simpson

The undulations and deep pot bunkers
guarding the short par four 9th hole.

OPPOSITE Porthcawl's magnificent
finishing par four, reachable but sloping
toward the sea and surrounded by trouble.

Superbly located on the Glamorgan Coast between Cardiff and Swansea, the Royal Porthcawl Golf Club was formed in 1891 by a group of Cardiff businessmen on common land in the seaside town of Porthcawl. In 1895 the club found a permanent home on an adjacent seaside site, its original layout modified in 1913 by Harry Colt and again in 1925 by the firm of Hawtree and Taylor. Tom Simpson made further alterations in 1933, with all three contributing to the quality of what is unquestionably Wales' most significant golf course.

The course itself is situated on softly contoured linksland that overlooks the Bristol Channel and leans gently down toward its shore, ensuring the water is in full view from virtually all parts of the property. Though it lacks the marked undulation and heaving sandhills that typify golf in south-west Britain, like all great links Porthcawl does enjoy tight, bouncy playing surfaces, thick fescue roughs and is totally exposed to the elements coming in off the coast. Cleverly routed with the frequent high winds in mind, the layout takes full advantage of the shoreline early on, then heads into the gorse-covered inland areas with holes later looping back on each other and playing to all points of the compass as they again near the shore.

The round opens with three holes adjacent to the beach, the 2nd almost in the sea with its fairway creeping down and toward a green pressed hard against the coastal fence. The 3rd also follows the fence and is a quality links hole full of natural ripples and deep traps. From here Porthcawl wanders up to higher ground where both the 5th, played into a green perched on a spur and set between an out-of-bounds rock wall and thick gorse, and the short 7th are fine holes. The golf then zigzags down the hill, past the narrowing and dangerously bunkered 10th green, before reaching a strong closing stretch that includes a series of tough, long holes and a fabulous short par four finisher. Playing back across the first fairway, the 18th is probably the links' most memorable hole as it ends with a delicious away-sloping green set right in front of the sea.

Although its total yardage may seem a little light, Porthcawl is not an easy course to master, with finding fairways and avoiding the hay and hazards the key to good scoring. While the narrow fairways are bunkered sparingly, the greens are generally well protected by revetted hazards that are typically deep and small but feature large collection areas that make them easier to find and usually more difficult to escape from. The turf throughout is as keen and bouncy as any you will play from and the large greens are mostly quite flat, with some tiers and swales but nothing like the extravagance of a Pennard or Royal St George's.

An extremely consistent layout from start to finish, there is not really a weak moment at Royal Porthcawl, although the par fives are probably not its strong point, as the three heading away from the sea are generally played downwind and fail to test three-shot strategies for the skilled player. The course also lacks the truly great holes that make similar low-set championship links such as Carnoustie and St Andrews so outstanding. Despite these minor shortcomings, this is still a terrific examination and clearly remains Wales' most suitable championship venue.

Nefyn & District Golf Club – Old Course

COURSE OPENED 1907
DESIGNERS James Braid,
J.H. Taylor

Nefyn's wonderful par four 13th hole.

OPPOSITE The par three 16th crosses a bottomless pit and enjoys superb views of the Nefyn headland.

Situated on the isolated Lleyn Peninsula and reminiscent in scale and scenery of the Old Head of Kinsale, Nefyn & District is an unconventional golf club that was first founded as a village nine-holer in 1907. The course was then extended to eighteen in 1912 before J.H. Taylor and James Braid were asked to revise the layout in the 1930s and add an additional nine holes. Strangely, only 26 exist today: ten outward holes, apparently by Taylor and Braid, and two inward sets of eight.

With two distinct landforms, the early part of the Old Course is set along a vast coastal headland while its final holes occupy a tiny promontory that protrudes out from the peninsula and rises several hundred feet into the Irish Sea. The round begins with a downhill par four played toward the coast, which is followed by a four-hole stretch that dramatically hug its cliffs. The most noteworthy of the holes along the headland is the almost world-class 2nd, which features a thrilling drive over the corner of the cliffs and a green perched high and close to its edge. With a more formidable greenside bunker and an angled green, this hole would be terrific and provide a real advantage for those driving nearer the sea. The solid 3rd, 4th and 5th holes also run alongside the ocean, but from the 6th the course turns away from the water and returns to the central clubhouse with the remainder of the front ten fairly pedestrian.

Part of the original short course and located on their own spectacular spit of land, the final eight holes, by contrast, are far from mundane and feature a mix of mad and magnificent golf moments. The 11th, for instance, is a short par four where the only play is to hit a middle-iron into the base of a steep hill followed by a wedge up into a blind bowl. Even more unusual is the par five 12th, its blind drive seeming to plunge straight into the sea, the fairway beneath not apparent unless you walk down the hole to confirm its existence. A busy beach road and huge bottomless pit then lurk down the left side of a heavily left-sloping fairway, with smashing the ball up near the green in two about the only way to keep it in play. More conventional is the brilliant clifftop 13th, which is played obliquely along a narrowing ridge, your drive needing to flirt with the ocean and a massive ravine in order to set up a decent shot into a small target squeezed into the Peninsula's rocky tip. From here the course turns back for home with the par five 17th, which overlooks the earlier headlands, the most memorable of the closing holes.

In many ways Nefyn is the archetypal Welsh golf course, a fun layout in a stunning location let down by some ordinary design. The golf does get breathtaking in places, but a number of potentially great holes are spoilt by rudimentary greens and bunkers, many being flat, uninteresting and offering straightforward recoveries. Regardless of whether this general lack of polish, or the odd mediocre hole, affects your enjoyment of the round, the attractions of Nefyn are nevertheless apparent to all who play here.

Tenby Golf Club

COURSE OPENED 1888
DESIGNER James Braid

The oldest golf club in Wales, Tenby Golf Club formed in 1888, although its current links was mostly designed by James Braid during the early part of the 20th century. Situated in the south-west corner of the country, the course is routed across superbly undulating linksland, with wonderful views over the Tenby beach and out to the monastery island of Caldey.

Featuring a number of naturally sunken green sites, blind drives over expansive dunes and thick fescue roughs, the links provides a genuine test of all aspects of your game, especially the ability to control ball flight, as it is exposed to strong gusty winds and the firm fairways and tight targets are narrow and notoriously hard to hit. Tenby's four-hole opening stretch is among the toughest in golf. It starts with a lengthy par four played blind across heavy dunes and includes the extraordinarily difficult 3rd hole, with a slender fairway and skinny tabletop green that falls steeply on both sides. Despite only being a short-iron approach, many players actually choose to pitch short of this brilliant green in order to prevent the embarrassment of missing the target and then chopping back and forth from side to side. Other standout features include the deep ravine guarding the par three 12th, the drivable 13th and a beautiful approach into the final green. Unfortunately, the three holes located on the inland side of the town's railway are a little disappointing by comparison to the compactly grouped holes on the main paddock.

A challenging layout for all levels of player and especially fun along the main dunes, Tenby has never been in better shape and, despite its modest yardage and par of 68, remains one of the sternest examinations in Britain.

Pennard Golf Club

COURSE OPENED 1896
DESIGNERS James Braid, C.K. Cotton

Located on the Gower Peninsula in South Wales, the Pennard Golf Club is one of the most interesting golf courses in the British Isles. Despite occupying classically undulating linksland full of bumps, humps, swales and tumbling dunes, it is actually situated some 200 feet above the sea on a spectacular sandy promontory. The site also houses the remnants of a 13th century castle, which some locals believe was cursed by vengeful Gypsies when nasty castle owners turned them away during severe storms. Wild winds and sand squalls ensued, covering the heads in sand, condemning the castle and bestowing to golfers this unusual, elevated linkscape.

Golf was first played on the site in 1896, though today's modest layout is mostly the work of James Braid and C.K. Cotton several decades later. While many will be put off by scratchy conditioning, basic green and bunker shapes and a number of blind shots, the course is a real adventure and awfully difficult for first timers, especially on holes like 3, 4, 6, 8, 9 and 14, where ideal landing areas are not always apparent. Pennard's most remarkable hole is the outrageous 7th, which heads toward the sea between the ruins of the castle and an ancient church, its small green then cruelly sitting on a ledge and sloping away from play. Other genuine highlights include a number of attractive dell greens, the drive down the tumbling 10th, the heaving 14th fairway and the three cool closing holes.

Pennard is definitely not a layout for those looking for lush lies, as course conditions here are generally quite poor. For purists and links addicts, however, the tight, bouncy turf is perfectly acceptable and there is much to admire about this raw and rugged golf experience.

OPPOSITE Pennard's brilliant 7th hole, heading through castle and church ruins.

Australasia

OPPOSITE Australia and New Zealand are golf
destinations of considerable merit, from the established
classics of the MacKenzie era to modern masterpieces such
as Barnbougle Dunes (pictured, the 110-meter 7th hole).

Australia

OPPOSITE The distinctive bunkering style of the Melbourne Sandbelt on display at the short 9th hole at the Commonwealth Golf Club.

A vast island continent, Australia is a sports-mad, golf-rich nation that has produced a number of the game's great players and houses some of the finest courses anywhere on the planet. With relatively inexpensive green fees, endless sunshine and one of the highest golf courses per capita ratios in the world, there is no end to the golfing options available to those traveling to these golden shores.

Like its population, the majority of Australia's best golf is concentrated in the south-east corner, where the mild climate is ideal for outdoor activity and the soil and terrain more naturally endowed for the game than anywhere outside the British Isles. The most internationally significant area is the Melbourne Sandbelt, which was uncovered when Royal Melbourne shifted into the city's southern sandhills around 1901. Blessed with a fertile, sandy soil that presents perfect year-round turf conditions, the Sandbelt's best classics are world-class and were mostly influenced by the brief 1926 visit of Dr Alister MacKenzie. MacKenzie arrived in Australia to design Royal Melbourne West, but he also helped plan bunkering systems for Kingston Heath, Metropolitan and Victoria, and trained Alex Russell to continue his design philosophies after he departed. The famed architect also initially routed the brilliant New South Wales golf course in Sydney and then left plans and ideas that the charming Royal Adelaide would later enact.

Although a long period of inactivity followed MacKenzie's visit, his work significantly lifted the standard of course design throughout Australia. The modern growth in new course development, which was triggered by substantial Asian investment, started in the 1980s with the introduction of resort and residential golf, primarily to subtropical holiday spots along the Queensland coast. Though most of the early resorts were built on reclaimed swamps, thankfully there has since been a shift back to traditional golf land, with some spectacular modern seaside sites uncovered here over the past two decades. On either side of the Sandbelt, the stunning Mornington and Bellarine Peninsulas have slowly developed into outstanding regions in their own right, while sun-soaked Perth has become a quality golf alternative and the discovery of Barnbougle Dunes has single-handedly turned the island of Tasmania into a genuine golf destination.

Beyond the courses featured in the following pages, if you are looking for first-class golf then consider both Kooyonga and The Grange while in Adelaide, the beautiful Royal Canberra layout in the nation's capital, Royal Sydney, The Lakes and Terrey Hills in Sydney and Yarra Yarra, The Capital, Spring Valley, Huntingdale and Southern as Sandbelt backups. If modern resort golf is your thing then the largest, and warmest, states of Queensland and Western Australia feature a number of worthwhile and very distinctive options such as Brookwater, Laguna Whitsundays, Club Pelican, Hope Island, The Glades, Joondalup, The Vines and The Cut, a new estate course located among coastal dunes at Port Bouvard near Perth. Magenta Shores, south of Newcastle, and the 36-hole Moonah Links development on the Mornington Peninsula are other exciting modern creations.

The Australian classics from the MacKenzie era, with the benefit of more than 70 years to grow and mature, remain the country's most celebrated layouts, but the modern golfing renaissance here has been prolific and the quality of its finest creations has reconfirmed the oft-held belief that Australia is one of the great destinations in world golf

The Royal Melbourne Golf Club – West Course

COURSE OPENED 1931
DESIGNER Dr Alister MacKenzie

'It burns me up that with the billions of dollars spent on course construction in the past 50 years, all the architects together haven't been able to build another Royal Melbourne.'

GENE SARAZEN

OPPOSITE The reachable par five 2nd on the West Course, with the club's trademark bunkers dictating the strategy of approach.

Australia's foremost golf club, Royal Melbourne's origins date back to 1891 when a group of prominent Melburnians formally introduced the Royal and Ancient game to Victoria by establishing the Melbourne Golf Club on leased land near an inner-city railway station. As urban encroachment threatened the existence of their course, the search for a more permanent home brought the club's council to a racetrack built among the heathland scrub of Sandringham in the city's south. What they uncovered within the undulating sand dunes was the ideal location for their new links, a discovery that inadvertently led to the birth of the Melbourne Sandbelt.

The course opened for play in 1901, but by the early 1920s housing had engulfed the western corner of the property. The club decided to sell this part of the site and move slightly east to its main paddock in Black Rock, where an additional 68 acres of land was available. Although only six of the original holes were lost in the relocation, it was decided that the entire course should be upgraded and redesigned. Dr Alister MacKenzie was recommended to the club and accepted its invitation to advise on the new course, starting out in 1926 on his groundbreaking Australasian adventure.

MacKenzie's stay in Black Rock was brief, and while on-site to survey the land he was accompanied by Australian Open champion Alex Russell and head greenkeeper Mick Morcom, who was well read on the subject of golf architecture. MacKenzie was clearly satisfied that both men were capable of interpreting his ideas and philosophies, and when he departed he left the construction of his West Course under their supervision. He later described Morcom as the best greenkeeper he had ever come across and appointed Russell as his Australian design partner.

Much has been written on the qualities of the West Course but, put simply, it is the combination of great land, great design and great construction that makes it so special. The timeless strategy of the MacKenzie design is as profound as it is simple and is based on wide fairways that are playable to the average golfer yet demand that those more skilled drive the ball into dangerous corners to get close to the flags. Full of dramatic sandhills and bold contours, the site remains one of the finest in golf, its fertile soil and naturally rugged appearance truly a gift from the golfing gods. Morcom's bunkering is spectacular, as are his greens, which for decades have consistently provided the purest putting surfaces in the world. Large and beautifully contoured, they are built to accommodate approaches from a number of angles, with each progressively more demanding the farther the tee shot strays from the perfect line.

Picking out West Course highlights is as difficult as mounting a compelling argument against its long-held position atop Australian golf ranking lists. Individually there are at least ten outstanding holes, including six that are world-class, such as the all-carry par three 5th, with its

awesome bunkering and slippery raised green pressed against a magnificent scrub-covered dune. The 6th is also remarkable and has become a textbook MacKenzie par four, its grand sweeping fairway, tantalizing corner bunkers and superb green setting as manageable for the first-timer as they are challenging to the professional.

There are plenty of other standouts, including the brilliant three-shot 4th hole, the drivable par four 10th with its teasing target perched beyond the largest and deepest sand hazard in the country, and the breathtaking greenside bunkering at the 17th. The final hole is also noteworthy, with a thrilling tee shot played across a steep sandy ridge to a blind, dipping fairway. Both tee and green on the 18th have been shifted since MacKenzie departed but, like the majority of alterations made through the years, the changes have been minor. The obvious exception is the 7th hole, built by Ivo Whitton in the late 1930s to allow extra room for the first tee on the East Course. The green on the 12th was also shifted significantly to the left and slightly back to create a wonderful kink at the end of its fairway.

Perhaps the most interesting change, however, was made to the 15th hole long after MacKenzie had discovered the penal artificial mounding of the existing fairway and declared, 'we'll leave it as is, to show future generations how silly golf course architecture used to be.' The fact that he left this deliberate blemish to underline the inadequacies of penal design shows he was probably a man who did not believe in the notion of the perfect golf course. Although his point was well made, years later the club improved the hole by removing the central section of these mounds.

It seems a great shame that MacKenzie never saw the finished product at Royal Melbourne because, despite leaving Australian shores to create countless classics across the globe, there is little doubt the West Course retains the truest interpretation of his design philosophies. Indeed, it is hard to imagine that the game of golf gets any better than Royal Melbourne. To all, from purist to weekend hacker and professional, it remains the absolute embodiment of golfing perfection – if indeed such a thing exists.

ABOVE The short 5th is the only hole at Royal Melbourne that Mick Morcom constructed under Dr MacKenzie's direct supervision.

OPPOSITE View from the corner bunkers on the par four 17th.

OVERLEAF MacKenzie's strategic masterpiece: the grand, sweeping par four 6th hole.

The Royal Melbourne Golf Club – East Course

COURSE OPENED 1932
DESIGNER Alex Russell

The opening green on the East
Course, protected by classic
Sandbelt bunker shapes.

OPPOSITE Russell's flat but exciting
par three 16th hole, his East Course
design complemented by Mick
Morcom's exquisite shaping.

The concept for Royal Melbourne's East Course was born shortly after Alister MacKenzie had left Australia and while his famous West Course was still under construction. The club's plan to build a new clubhouse on the current 7th West was well advanced when two parcels of land east of the main Black Rock site became available in 1929. The prospect of 36 holes appealed greatly to the membership, who decided to proceed with the second course and shelve plans to relocate its clubhouse. With MacKenzie back in the United States his new partner Alex Russell was put in charge of the design, with Mick Morcom again responsible for course shaping.

Given the very nature and distribution of the available land, the East Course differs considerably from the West Course. Holes are played in a single loop away from the clubhouse, across several roads and covering three separate allotments. Despite the obstacles and inferior terrain of the eastern property, Russell's routing works surprisingly well, with balanced nines, a great variety of holes and the same beautifully constructed bunker and green sites as the West. Sensibly, the long holes tackle the wind from each direction, while the only minor criticism of his arrangement is that all four wonderful par threes play to the north.

The course starts and finishes on the main site, alongside its more famous sibling, with these seven 'home paddock' holes incorporating the most dramatic undulation on the course.

The closing stretch is exceptional, while the short-four, long-four, mid-four start presents clear risk/reward options from the tee and birdie-to-double bogey possibilities. Aside from the excellent and heavily bunkered par three 16th, these are the holes that combine with the best from the West to form Royal Melbourne's world-renowned Composite Course. First conceived in 1959, the traditional Composite Course routing is astonishing, with Russell's six all-star holes standing comfortably alongside MacKenzie's and blending into one outstanding layout.

Royal Melbourne's East Course is often unfairly rated because of the esteemed company it keeps, yet any track with holes the quality of the first and final four is very special. There are many other highlights as well, including the cross-bunkering on the 10th and the approach through the saddle of sand at the difficult 12th. Although variations in terrain and the disparity between its best and worst holes prevent East from outranking West, there are only a handful of Australian courses that boast anywhere near its number of world-class moments.

After the good doctor departed Australia Alex Russell was a man in demand, kept busy overseeing the MacKenzie projects and completing work of his own. Despite a flurry of design activity, the East Course remains his masterpiece, fittingly standing alongside the greatest accomplishment of his illustrious mentor.

New South Wales Golf Club – La Perouse

COURSE OPENED 1928
DESIGNERS Dr Alister
MacKenzie,
Eric Apperly

'At Sydney, I made an entirely new course for the New South Wales Golf Club at a place called La Perouse. This is a sand-duned peninsula which overlooks Botany Bay and presents, I think, more spectacular views than any other place I know, with the possible exception of the new Cypress Point golf course I am doing on the Del Monte peninsula in California.'

DR ALISTER MACKENZIE

OPPOSITE New South Wales' famous cross-ocean 6th hole.

Situated on the rugged cliffs of Sydney's La Perouse headland, the spectacular New South Wales Golf Club overlooks Botany Bay, where Captain James Cook first sailed into Australia aboard the *Endeavour* in 1770. For golfers, however, it was the visit of another intrepid British pioneer that gives this site its special historical significance.

During his 1926 stay in Australia, legendary designer Dr Alister MacKenzie visited the La Perouse site to design a course for the newly formed club. Enthused by its potential, MacKenzie produced the initial routing map for the course, though its subsequent success cannot be solely credited to his design genius, as the work of Eric Apperly in completing the architect's plans after he departed was also pivotal. MacKenzie left New South Wales bunkerless, with Apperly entrusted to position the hazards once patterns of play had been established. The resultant bunkering, though not as stylish as some of MacKenzie's more famous features, does complement the design and is well suited to the landscape.

Apperly also made a number of changes to the layout during the subsequent years, the most significant being the shifting of the 5th tee and the building of the world-renowned 6th hole in the 1930s. The tee on 5 was originally positioned on an elevated sand dune left of its current location, with the rocky Cape Banks shoreline visible from the tee. After the army reclaimed some coastal land during World War II, the tee was moved inland, making the hole straighter and the drive blind across a ravine and over an enormous rise. From the summit of the fairway the hole plunges almost 100 feet down toward a tiny green and the mighty Pacific Ocean. This view of falling fairway and crashing waves is one of the most magnificent in Australian golf. Equally memorable is the fabulous par three 6th, played from a rocky outcrop behind the 5th green over the sea to a small, sloping target back on the mainland.

Completing a stunning stretch along the coast, the uphill 7th, heading away from the sea, is another superb hole that, although straightened, remains largely as MacKenzie intended. A second coastal loop on the back nine, 13 through 16, is also world-class, with a series of difficult par fours played along and away from the cliffs. The best of these is the 14th, an extreme short four that is blind across a wild fairway ridge into a hidden valley; followed by one of the game's great pitch shots up into its exposed skyline green. Offering no respite, the 15th is then the hardest hole on the course and demands a strong, straight tee shot through a narrow chute of dunes and tea-tree to reach a saddle at the fairway's crest. Missing the drive usually means reloading, while a good tee shot here sets up an uninterrupted view of a beautiful green site shifted almost 100 meters to its present position by Apperly.

Wonderfully rugged and exposed, the entire course offers tremendous views and a series of

dramatic holes built around, over and through the hills and valleys that lead toward the coastline. The routing, as much as the setting, makes La Perouse special, and despite more than 70 years of tinkering and evolution, twelve holes and the majority of the standout moments remain either MacKenzie originals or variations on a theme he first suggested. Of those altered, the most notable are the four Apperly par threes, which form the best set of short holes in Sydney, and the par five 8th, which is a combination of two MacKenzie holes.

In the decades since Apperly's passing, a number of Australian designers have been involved in reshaping problem areas here, including the firms of Peter Thomson, Jack Newton, and Greg Norman, who, along with Bob Harrison, strengthened the soft opening hole and also reshaped the troublesome skyline green on the 3rd. The most significant improvements, however, were made during a recent in-house restoration program which involved rebuilding the more exposed traps with a traditional revetted face.

While there are still some weaknesses in its extremities, and the architecture and construction may be more sophisticated elsewhere in Australia, few courses of any era, or from any country, are as exciting to play as the timeless New South Wales Golf Club.

ABOVE The view from the 14th tee with the drive crossing a thick ravine and the pitch played into a small clifftop green.

OPPOSITE A distracting setting and falling fairway complicate your approach on the legendary par five 5th.

Kingston Heath Golf Club

COURSE OPENED 1925
DESIGNERS Dan Soutar,
Dr Alister MacKenzie

'Never yet have I advised upon a course where, owing to the excellence of design and construction work, the problems have been so simple.'

DR ALISTER MACKENZIE

Shortly after World War I, prominent Melbourne solicitor Stanley Dutton Green led a committee of disgruntled city golfers on a search to acquire sufficient land within the growing Melbourne Sandbelt to construct their own championship golf course. Their search for the ideal site brought them south to Cheltenham and a small, gently undulating parcel of land that was soon purchased to become the home of the Kingston Heath Golf Club.

Fascinated by British design, Green corresponded with Open champions J.H. Taylor and Harry Vardon, who convinced him that with the advent of the rubber-cored ball, the new course should be built of a length to 'stand the test of time.' The committee agreed, and called in Sydney professional Dan Soutar to design the layout. Soutar walked the property twice without comment before coming to rest amid dense scrub near the center of the site and declaring, 'Here is where we start, an ideal ready made short hole for the 10th.' He later changed the direction of the 10th hole but continued to plan the entire course from this point, and when finished had met the club's brief and created what was officially the longest course in Australia.

Measuring a little over 6,200 meters when first opened, the fairways, tees and greens were built by Royal Melbourne superintendent Mick Morcom in 1925, while the bunkering was deferred on news of the imminent arrival of famed architect Dr Alister MacKenzie to design

Royal Melbourne West. MacKenzie provided a detailed report on the bunkering of each hole at Kingston Heath and also felt compelled to suggest one important change to the overall course design, converting the blind par four 15th hole into an ingenious uphill par three. MacKenzie clearly thought highly of Soutar's routing and the fact that he could find just one design fault was in itself a glowing endorsement of his layout. It is interesting to note that the designer was paid £25 for his tireless work, while the club reluctantly paid MacKenzie ten times that amount for bunkering plans that he finished in a matter of days. Although seemingly inequitable, the club was left with one of the country's great par threes and possibly the best bunkering system in the world.

Kingston Heath's entire collection of short holes is outstanding. The signature 15th is the star attraction but the beautifully bunkered 5th and the treacherous 10th are also impressive. Of the remaining holes, strong par fours like the 1st, 6th, 8th, 9th, 11th and 16th stand out, as do each of the par fives and a number of fascinating semi-blind shots. Perhaps the best hole of all, however, is the drivable but dangerous 3rd, which features a shallow green that is angled to accept only the most precise pitch shots. Although most of the Soutar/Morcom course remains in play, long-standing superintendent Graeme Grant did make some alterations during his tenure. These included the rebuilding of several greens, the

addition of a deep depression protecting the front of the par five 7th and the controversial, and less successful, central bunker on the wonderful 11th hole. The putting surfaces, especially those Grant reshaped, are superb and it would be hard to argue that the greens on any classic course, other than perhaps Royal Melbourne, are better than the Heath's.

With the exception of dense tea-tree and heavy undergrowth that was badly burnt out following a major wildfire in 1944, the natural process of the course's evolution has gone relatively smoothly. Some overplanting problems have been corrected and the vast areas of low-growing heath grasses, which give the course its unique character, are now thriving after a recent restoration. Aside from brilliant bunkering, wonderful greens and incredible construction, the Heath's charm lies in the use of these native grasses and the manner in which the holes and hazards seamlessly integrate into the surrounding vegetation.

A special privilege to play and one of the finest examples of golf course architecture from any era, Kingston Heath's greatest defense from low scoring continues to be a strategic layout that is playable to all yet demands absolute precision from the professional wanting to score birdies. Though it no longer plays like the monster it once was, the combination of an ageless design and stupendous bunkering has helped the course remain a supreme test of one's golfing smarts.

OPPOSITE The Heath's classic bunkering style and use of native grasses are prominent as you approach the 9th green.

The National Golf Club – Moonah Course

COURSE OPENED 2000
DESIGNERS Greg Norman,
Bob Harrison

'Moonah was our first experience in true linksland and we had to adapt our style to the ground and wind. There were natural golf holes everywhere and it was our responsibility to try to find the best of them. It took months before we were ready to start construction.'

BOB HARRISON

OPPOSITE The first of Moonah's marvelous par fives, the 2nd highlights the suitability of the club's duneland for golf.

Founded in 1987, The National Golf Club was born as an eighteen-hole course in the Cape Schanck hills overlooking Bass Strait but grew into Australia's largest private golf facility in 2000 with the opening of two spectacular seaside links situated on the Mornington Peninsula's rolling farming pastures. Built on heaving coastal duneland of Irish proportions, the Greg Norman and Bob Harrison designed Moonah Course is the pick of the club's three tracks and one of the world's most exciting modern creations.

Boasting stunning rural and ocean panoramas and occupying an attractive series of jumbled dunes and ridges, Moonah's virgin land presented Norman and Harrison with a number of natural golf holes and the team spent hundreds of hours on site developing alternate layouts and considering various combinations to squeeze as many great holes as possible into their course. The pivotal hole in this process was the 11th. Tucked away in the north-west corner of the property, it lies on land the designers were so keen to include that they had to trade off routing difficulties to get to it. The hole itself falls beautifully across the undulations, with the tee shot played into an elevated saddle surrounded by sand and the approach over a hollow toward a punchbowl green framed by the distant Bass Strait dunes. To balance the use of this extraordinary land, however, the closing stretch is made up of a series of long holes that head back to the clubhouse and usually into the teeth of the stiff Peninsula winds. To score well at Moonah, therefore, you need to get through the first eleven holes without too many scars, as the battle to hold onto your score coming home is one of the toughest in the country.

Aside from the number of impressive golf holes, the key to Moonah's success as a big dune links are its outstanding bunkers and greens. To remain playable and accommodate the running approach shot, most of the greens were built with open fronts and shaped to follow the general contour of the landscape. Many also come complete with backstops or pronounced side-slopes to allow skilled golfers to work the ball back toward more inaccessible pin positions. The bunkering is Moonah's most distinguishing feature. The small traps were first excavated quite roughly before the edges, and parts of the faces, were seeded with fescues to provide a wild, jagged and ungroomed appearance, not dissimilar to the fearsome hazards at Royal County Down.

Also distinctive is the fairway shaping. While the landing areas are fairly generous, the aggressive player is often able to attack ridges and distant valleys in order to set up shorter and easier approaches. The opening hole sets the tone for the round to follow. Chances are you will not miss its expansive landing area with your first tee shot, but hit too far down the left side and your best chance of par is from one of the greenside bunkers. The next is a

superb par five along and then into an imposing sand ridge, while the 3rd is a brilliant driving hole with a diagonal fracture cutting across its wide fairway and kicking accurate balls toward the target but pushing weaker drives away and leaving a longer and more difficult approach. The tee shot on the 4th is another beauty, this time played from atop a plateau out over sweeping undulations, with the second shot climbing to a green cut into a hillside. Other standout holes include the par four 10th, with its windmill and wild green, the chasing one-shot 17th and the splendid set of par fives, particularly the 7th, which drops and then rises through a tumbling valley into a lovely long depression. The four-and-a-half par 16th hole is another excellent adventure, though a little demanding for most of the membership.

There are not many modern courses as dramatic as Moonah, and although it will appeal to the masses, for low markers who like their golf raw this is a special treat. The other two National courses are also worth exploring. The adjacent Ocean Course, by Peter Thomson, Mike Wolveridge and Ross Perrett, occupies an even more suitable slice of duneland, while the Old Course is a typically extravagant Robert Trent Jones Jr design that features amazing coastal views and one breathtaking work of art, the short 7th, worth traveling from wherever you read this review to experience.

OPPOSITE Moonah's central hole, the par four 11th, with its green set down in a natural hollow.

OVERLEAF The 7th hole on the Old Course at The National Golf Club.

Barnbougle Dunes Golf Links

COURSE OPENED 2004
DESIGNER Tom Doak
with Michael Clayton

'One of the most spectacular properties made available for golf in the past 50 years.'

TOM DOAK ON BARNBOUGLE DUNES

Though the small island of Tasmania has long been a popular tourist destination, for more than 160 years its only real interest to golfers was the rudimentary Ratho golf course, which was the first in Australia and dates back to 1842, making it the oldest course anywhere outside of Britain. It was not until the 2004 opening of the outstanding links at Barnbougle Dunes, in the sleepy seaside village of Bridport, that the entire golfing landscape in this most southerly corner of Australia changed forever.

Occupying a two mile stretch of giant sand dunes along Bass Strait, the course was the vision of a persistent young links fanatic who pestered, harassed and finally managed to convince a gruff potato farmer, and staunch non-golfer, to convert part of his 14,000-acre Barnbougle farmland into a golf course. American Tom Doak was the chosen architect and although the first business model for the development failed, Doak was so eager to build the course that he offered a long-term payment plan for his services, a gesture that managed to convince the landowner to proceed with the development himself.

Working with local partner Michael Clayton, Doak set about shaping the curving beachside sandhills into a quality links. Crucial to the design was a decision to opt for a central clubhouse, which meant holes could be laid out in a loop on either side. This prevented a long continuous stretch into the strong winds and allowed for the closing holes to play right along the beach. Routed mostly through dense valleys, the outward half occupies the heavier dunes, although it opens with a couple of holes on the flatter farming land. The short par four 3rd, its drive partially obscured across a diagonal ridge, is the first hole that dives into the sand. The next is a drivable par four and the first real jaw-dropper, the hole dominated by a massive bunker embedded into a steep hillside, which must be carried in order to get near a green resting within a deep dune bowl. Remaining front nine highlights include a side-slope approach into the 9th and the evil short 7th, which swings back into the prevailing winds to a tiny crowned green that is protected by a deep trap left and steep banks both long and right.

Setting out in an eastern loop, the inward nine is built across broader, more expansive undulations and heads toward a tidal inlet before turning west and returning to the clubhouse alongside Barnbougle beach. Both of the par four finishing holes are strong, while the excessively humped skyline green at the 10th and the reachable 12th, with its enticing target sitting on a ledge, are also noteworthy. The best of the back nine, however, is the 15th, a world-class mid-length par four played along the inlet and its adjacent dune ridge. Those able to find a sliver of fairway on the right here are given the best angle into a narrow green that falls sharply to the left and is especially tough to hit for timid golfers straying left of the central fairway bunker.

OPPOSITE The view of beach and dunes from the 6th tee at Barnbougle Dunes.

Beyond the impressive dunes and beautiful beachside setting, the standout features at Barnbougle are the bunkers and Doak's quirky greens, which are often built with smaller quadrants within the greater green shapes to allow balls to be bounced off wide slopes and fed back toward certain hole locations. Although effective, some of the internal contours, especially on the par threes, do seem a little overdone. With the stiff sea winds that whip through the site responsible for the magnificent sand structures but also some of the most testing links conditions in the southern hemisphere, the designers sensibly left most targets open to ensure the course was manageable for all players under all conditions. The rugged bunkering is particularly striking and importantly not overused, with hollows and clever chipping zones often the preferred method of testing the inaccurate approach.

Despite its basic two-loop routing, the direction of play changes quite regularly, and once the fescue surfaces mature to present the firm conditions synonymous with golf in Britain, this will become a thorough links examination. Thanks to the vision of a young links addict, and the ability of Doak, Clayton and their teams to fashion the raw sand dunes into an exciting experience, Barnbougle Dunes is one of modern golf's great discoveries and the sort of pure, uncompromised golf project the world needs more of.

ABOVE Rugged bunkering and a steep falloff protect the green on the outstanding par four 15th hole.

OPPOSITE View from the 15th tee, the hole playing alongside an inlet and favoring those who drive down the narrow right side.

The Royal Adelaide Golf Club

COURSE OPENED 1905
DESIGNERS H.L. Rymill,
C.L. Gardiner,
Dr Alister MacKenzie

'No seaside courses that I have seen possess such magnificent sand craters as those at Royal Adelaide.'

DR ALISTER MACKENZIE

Founded at Glenelg in 1892, the Royal Adelaide Golf Club moved to the sandy craters and dunes of Seaton along the city's western railway in 1904, to a site that also housed a municipal train station providing members with easy access to their links. The first Seaton course was a modest design by committee members C.L. Gardiner and H.L. Rymill and opened for play in 1905. Rymill then upgraded the layout three years later, adding a thousand yards and incorporating the sandhills into the routing as well as several railway crossings. A subsequent beautification program introduced magnificent pine trees to the site and transformed the raw coastal sandscape into a grand-scale 'British-style' golfing experience.

Like many of Australia's best classics, the course received its most notable overhaul when Dr Alister MacKenzie made a flying visit to Adelaide in 1926 after designing Royal Melbourne West. Because MacKenzie was only in town for a few days he worked fast, preparing a report that converted many of the penal fairway bunkers into undulating ground and reconfigured the eighteen holes to eliminate dangerous rail crossings. He also insisted on making full use of the site's natural features by designing holes over and around the enormous dunes.

Tremendously impressed with the terrain and particularly excited by the abundance of sand, MacKenzie departed the club by boasting that, 'If the suggestions put forward for the reconstruction of the Royal Adelaide course are acted upon, it will be superior to most, if not all, English championship courses.' Despite a persuasive character and lofty reputation, his proposal was not universally accepted and immediately following his departure heavy debate within the club led to a number of his recommendations being renounced. The club did build his inspired short par four 3rd hole, which has not changed, and the awesome sand crater drive at the dogleg 4th, which remains a MacKenzie moment despite the hole being stretched almost 100 meters beyond what he had intended. Eleven greens were also rebuilt, the rail crossings eliminated and over time the 6th, 9th, 13th and 14th all altered to resemble MacKenzie's plan.

Aside from helping members realize the potential of their site, MacKenzie's gift to the club was to leave behind the extraordinary 3rd hole, which with a frontal pin may be the best short par four anywhere in the world. Although a visionary, he had no way of foreseeing the technological advances in our modern game, yet managed to build a drivable blind par four along a heavy dune ridge that remains as mesmerizing when played with titanium as it would have been with hickory. The genius of his design is in the positioning of the green beneath the dune, and the scruffy knoll and small ridge that guard its narrow front. From the tee the critical decision is which club to take and whether to play safely to the top of

OPPOSITE The approach across a sandy crater into Royal Adelaide's 11th green.

the crest or head over the hill toward the green. Like all great tempters, the penalties are harsher the more aggressive you get and the approach more difficult the safer you play. An accurate tee shot with the driver equals a probable birdie and the straight lay-up a comfortable par, but stray with either shot and you are left fighting for a five.

The other obvious standout at Royal Adelaide is the 11th, the infamous 'Crater hole,' its approach played from the peak of a rising fairway over a huge hollow to a green framed by an imposing pine-covered sandhill. Pushing the green site right back into the dune was actually MacKenzie's idea, although his plan for a dogleg from near the present 10th tee was rejected. Holes like the 3rd and 11th became legends in Australia long ago and are duly preserved, while the continued tweaking of others like 4, 8, 13, 14 and 18 has seen them also elevated to a similar status.

Royal Adelaide is an offbeat, one-of-a-kind course that has changed substantially over the years, yet retained its fundamental character and charm. It may not be Australasia's best golf course, but with a core of outstanding holes and an unmistakably adventurous streak, to many it is one of the most enjoyable.

OPPOSITE Blind and pinched between a large dune and a grassy knoll, the green on MacKenzie's incredible 3rd hole is what makes this tempting par four such a classic.

Ellerston Golf Course

COURSE OPENED 2001
DESIGNERS Greg Norman,
Bob Harrison

'At Ellerston we were able to create a course that a golfer of my calibre would love to play every day for the rest of his life.'

GREG NORMAN

Locked away in the secluded high country of the New South Wales Upper Hunter Valley lies the beautiful Ellerston estate, a veritable Shangri-la preserved for the exclusive enjoyment of Australia's wealthiest family. For lovers of equine pursuits, this remarkable property has long been a landmark, for within its natural valleys and tumbling hills are pristine polo fields acknowledged as the finest in the world. The decision to add golf to the property came during 1999, when the late Kerry Packer propositioned Greg Norman Golf Design and instructed them to build him Australia's toughest and most spectacular golf course.

With budget unlikely to be a problem, the critical issue for designers Greg Norman and Bob Harrison became selecting the best site. The team was given carte blanche to use any part of Packer's 70,000-acre sanctuary for their course. Following several days scouring the vast area, the fast-flowing Pages Creek was discovered and instantly recognized as the perfect location around which to build the dramatic course that Mr Packer desired.

The creek is the central feature of the layout and is incorporated into no less than nine holes, with most of the remaining holes built in the higher country leading away from the hazard. Fanatical about the difficulty level, the client's determination to provide the ultimate challenge to the world's best players enabled the designers to take more risks than usual. They created shots and sequences that simply would not be possible on a more accessible course and built a number of severe green sites pressed hard against the edge of the creek. One such site, the 6th, was actually washed away by heavy rains shortly after the course opened. This had not been entirely unexpected, given the area's propensity to flood, so in order to alleviate the worry and expense of continually rebuilding the green an elevated alternative was suggested. Without hesitation, however, Packer ordered the green be rebuilt exactly where it was and instructed his design team to do so each time that it washed away.

Aside from experiencing its exclusivity, the highlights of Ellerston are the demanding longer holes, which are a relentless driving examination, each requiring a long bomb positioned in the premium part of the fairway to ensure an unimpeded line into the green. Eight of the par fours measure between 395 and 415 metres, yet as a set they are remarkably diverse, thanks to the use of contrasting hazards and the constant elevation change. The 7th and 8th are wonderful illustrations, with the downhill 7th measuring 50 metres longer than the 8th but often playing a club shorter, its intimidating tee built into the side of a hill and the drive played along the creek toward a fairway some 200 metres away. The 8th then tracks back up the hill, with its approach crossing a nasty gorge and heading toward a green perched out on a perilous ledge. Equally impressive are the back-to-back par fives at 9 and 10, the 9th featuring a risk/reward drive across a series of diagonal

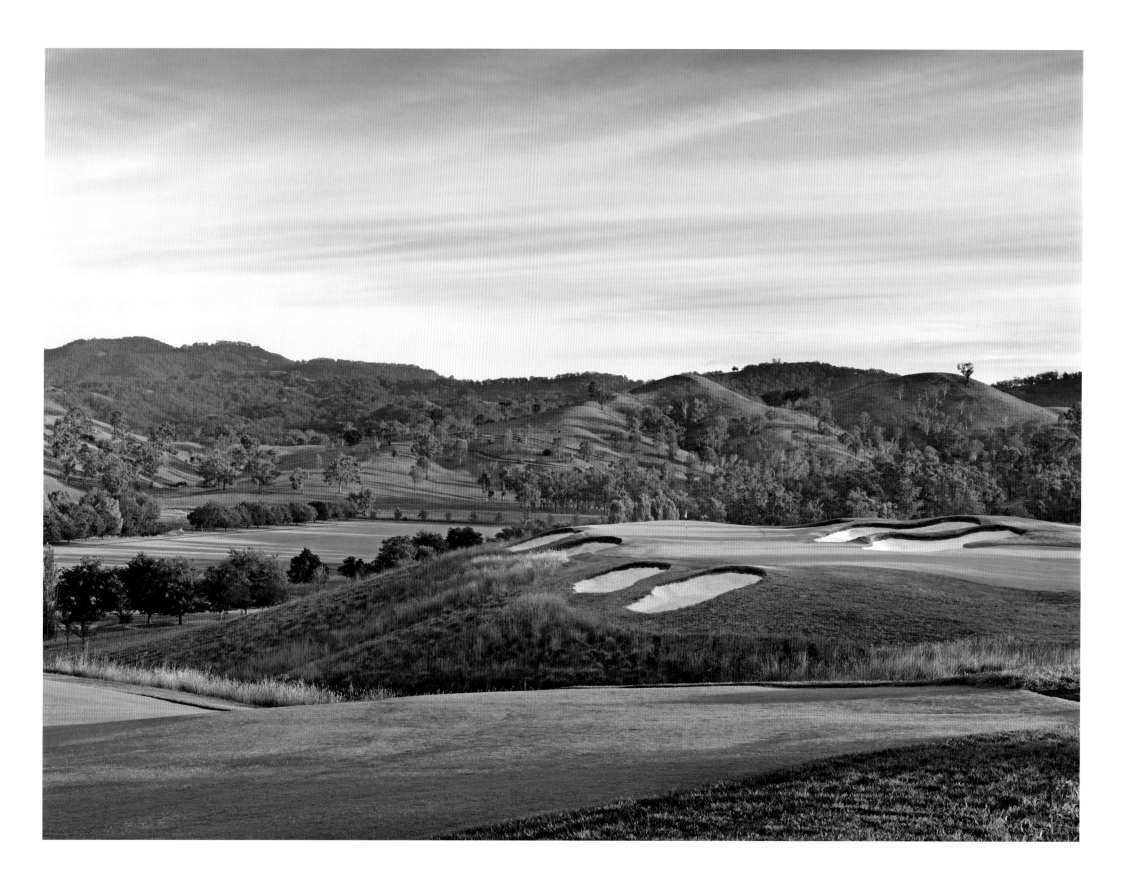

bunkers followed by a steep downhill plunge through a narrow forest, and the 10th meandering along a gully to a gorgeous green pitched beyond the stream. Most memorable of all, though, is the 16th, an audacious right-angle dogleg with its approach an all-or-nothing carry up the length of the creek toward a superb target framed by a sheer cliff face and encircled by the creek's running water.

Throughout the round, the variety and beauty of the green settings, whether dramatically pushed up against the hazard or set in natural gullies or atop small ridges, is quite striking. Most are framed visually by the impressive Norman/Harrison bunker shapes, although bunkerless targets like the 5th, 10th and 16th are among Ellerston's most attractive. The actual Pennlinks bentgrass putting surfaces, which were designed for great speeds, are immense and without blemish. Likewise, the fairway presentation is impossible to fault, the buffalo short roughs providing a contrasting color and texture to the pure couch playing corridors. This buffalo grass does not wear particularly well and is unsuitable for courses with even moderate traffic levels; it is fortunate, therefore, that Ellerston averages less than ten rounds per week!

Much more than just great grass however, Ellerston has some wonderful holes and is one of the most fascinating golf courses built since the Great Depression. A passionate golfer and tournament-broadcasting pioneer, Mr Packer left an indelible mark on the Australian sporting

landscape during his reign as head of its most powerful media empire. Ellerston is an appropriately striking tribute to his imposing presence and, despite its privacy and inaccessibility to the golfing public, cataloguing the planet's premier layouts without its inclusion would leave the directory incomplete.

ABOVE The attractive green on the short, creekside 6th hole.

OPPOSITE Ellerston's impeccable conditioning and the impressive Greg Norman/Bob Harrison bunker shapes are pictured here at the 13th fairway.

The Victoria Golf Club

COURSE OPENED 1927
DESIGNERS William Meader,
Oscar Damman,
Dr Alister MacKenzie

An abundance of sand protects the par three 4th green.

OPPOSITE Another of Victoria's excellent par threes, the longer 7th hole.

Melbourne businessman William Meader is considered the forefather of Victorian golf, having helped establish the state's golf association in 1902 and founding the Victoria Golf Club the following year. Meader was later the driving force behind the club's move into the southern Sandbelt and in 1923, with club captain Oscar Damman, designed the current layout. Course construction was hampered by bad weather and problems with site access, but the delay proved a blessing, as it allowed traveling architect Dr Alister MacKenzie to advise on the bunkering of the unfinished course in 1926.

Clearly impressed with the property, MacKenzie told the club that, 'Little more is required to make this a magnificent golf course' and then proceeded to add finishing touches to the existing routing by mapping bunkers and suggesting a few green changes. Although some downplay MacKenzie's influence at Victoria, it is impossible to deny that, as at Kingston Heath, his input was significant and his superb bunkers define the character of the course.

Perfectly located little more than a wedge from Royal Melbourne, the layout these three men created is outstanding, with a collection of fine holes falling beautifully across a naturally rolling landscape that is somewhat reminiscent of its famous neighbor, albeit on a slightly smaller scale. The central and southern sections of the site are the highlight, particularly holes 9 through 13, which take the golfer on an absorbing journey through the most interesting undulation on the course. The long 9th is a classic Sandbelt par five running across tumbling ridges, while the wonderful short 10th, described by MacKenzie in 1926 as 'a fine drive and pitch adventure,' features a dipping, sweeping fairway and sublime elevated green site. Falling away toward the southwest corner of the property, the charming 12th is followed by a difficult par four that heads blind over a rise, then into an elevated green from a down-sloping fairway.

Many believe Victoria's weakness is the configuration of holes, as each nine closes with back-to-back par fives. Despite being an unusual arrangement, both the 9th and 17th are excellent holes and the short 18th provides a stirring finish, with many matches decided on its enormous front-to-back-sloping green. The only real black spot is the opening hole, a drivable par four with a horrible green that was raised during the 1980s. Until recently the bunkering was also a problem, as years of slow deterioration had changed some of the original shapes and left the club's famous hazards looking dated and tired. Using an aerial shot of the course taken shortly after its 1927 opening, MacKenzie's original concepts were faithfully restored by local architect Michael Clayton, who also lengthened holes like 5, 9, 17 and 18, and tightened some of the landing areas. These changes were relatively minor but have enhanced the layout and again made it a relevant test for the good players.

Long regarded as one of Australia's elite courses, Victoria exists today as a tribute to the hardworking pioneers who laid the club's foundations and the divine contribution of Dr MacKenzie, who helped shape a very good course into a truly great one.

Commonwealth Golf Club

COURSE OPENED 1921
DESIGNERS Sam Bennett,
Charles Lane,
Sloan Morpeth

Bending left around a pond and then heavily bunkered to the right of the green, the 16th is Commonwealth's signature hole.

OPPOSITE The uphill approach into the heavily treed 11th.

Like a number of Melbourne's famous clubs, the Commonwealth Golf Club was founded by frustrated members of a clay-based city course who, in the 1920s, decided to move to the prospering southern Sandbelt. Inaugural professional Sam Bennett designed the first twelve holes before club captain Charles Lane completed the rest and touched up the greens and bunkers. Unusually for its vintage, the layout then evolved primarily without the aid of high-profile, high-priced golf course architects, but instead thanks to a long history of sound internal club management.

What club pioneers created was terrific and based around the strict adherence to the simplest values of strategic design. Beautifully bunkered and exquisitely built, the tilted greens were designed to favor players who can approach from the best angles, with the fairways then shaped to create clear choices from the tee according to one's ability and ambition. This design philosophy is best highlighted on the superb par fours. The famous 16th, for instance, bends left around a fairway lake and features a slippery green that is guarded by a fearsome right-side bunker and angled to reward only the brave golfer who can drive close to the water.

Another standout, the mid-length par four 11th is played around corner bunkers before heading uphill toward a large, tiered green that has a steep slope and is flanked by deep sand traps. The closing stretch is also outstanding. Following the brilliant 16th comes a tremendous short par four, which rises gently to a sharply contoured green that is devilishly difficult to pitch into from the wrong angle. The 18th is then a strong par four, its modern length and classic bunkering making it an ideal finish to the round.

For many decades the members acted as custodians of their course, successfully able to maintain the integrity of its timeless design in-house. The greatest period of reform came during the 1960s, when additional land allowed long-time club secretary Sloan Morpeth to redesign the 10th and 11th holes as well as a number of green sites. Strangely, in the 1990s the club abandoned its internal management policy and embarked on a program to 'modernize' the layout. First came the loss of the beloved drivable opening hole, which was fondly remembered, but underweight, according to a committee that added length and created a dogleg. Architect Kevin Hartley then built a new par three to replace the popular short 7th hole and added a further 200 meters to the length of the course. An existing tree-planting program was also continued, which has yielded a beautiful collection of native flora but caused some problems with intruding limbs interfering with the line of play on several holes.

Commonwealth's continued success can be directly attributed to the design philosophies implemented by its early members. Although modern changes have done little to improve the experience, the contemporary course still has a number of wonderful holes as well as original greens and bunkers that are as attractive and strategic as any on the Sandbelt.

St Andrews Beach Golf Club – Gunnamatta Course

COURSE OPENED 2005
DESIGNER Tom Doak

'There are some great localities for golf around the world and the Cups region is one of them.'

TOM DOAK

Situated in the heart of Mornington Peninsula's Cups country, the Gunnamatta Course at the 36-hole St Andrews Beach Golf Club is the third Australasian layout in the increasing international portfolio of American architect Tom Doak. Occupying some of the most suitable duneland in Victoria for golf, the course was built with minimal earthmoving and great natural features like deep fairway valleys, large basin target areas and natural sandy blowouts, incorporated into the design.

Routed across a vast rolling pasture, the layout is dominated by a series of high hills and ridges that run through the site and divide the golf into smaller pockets. These ridges proved a popular place to locate greens and tees, the targets often tucked into one section, with the subsequent back tee built high on the opposite side to provide golfers with outlooks across the attractive golfscape.

Gunnamatta starts from the top of one of the site's more prominent hills, the outlook and drive from the opening tee as impressive as its obscured green site. The 2nd, a reachable par four that runs alongside an exposed sand dune, is probably the pick of the holes, with its fairway sloping left toward the sandy wasteland and a tempting target situated in a shallow clearing. The approach into the 3rd is another standout; the tee shot is a rather dull affair around a hill, but those driving bravely are advantaged with a better angle across a bunkered dune into the undulating amphitheatre green. Best of the rest

include the short 6th hole, the cruelly domed 9th green, and the strong par four 12th. The last half of the left-bending par five 17th is also excellent, while the 18th is one of the finest modern finishers in the game, a series of central bunkers splitting its fairway and creating a safer lower platform and a tighter aggressive line that leaves a shorter shot into the large, layered green.

The most pleasing aspect of Gunnamatta is its variety and the manner in which the designers created a challenging test that still throws up birdie opportunities to the average player. While the best holes are outstanding, a few, such as the 15th and the heavily dropping par three 16th, are less effective, as are some of the more isolated fairway bunker shapes that don't work as well visually as the rugged traps that blend into their surroundings. The greens themselves are very good and according to Doak are the best set he has ever created, primarily because the existing contours were so simple to shape. Complementing his natural targets are wonderful collection areas that throw up some fantastic short-game situations.

Owing to the suitability of the virgin terrain, this was the easiest course Doak and his team has constructed and, as the designer himself noted, it allowed him 'the highest expression of his minimalist philosophy.' Although less dramatic than both Barnbougle Dunes and Cape Kidnappers, St Andrews Beach is a substantial achievement and an essential inclusion on your increasingly packed Peninsula schedule.

The Peninsula Country Golf Club – North Course

COURSE OPENED 1969
DESIGNERS Sloan Morpeth,
Michael Clayton

'Peninsula North was a wonderful piece of land for golf but it was hampered by some very poor holes that were fortunately very easily reorganized into a significantly better course that took advantage of the potential of the site. The course is not long, nor particularly difficult but it's full of holes that are really fun to play.'

MICHAEL CLAYTON

OPPOSITE Michael Clayton's revised 13th hole, complete with its minuscule target area.

Located in the bayside city of Frankston, the Peninsula Country Golf Club has two excellent courses positioned geographically within the Melbourne Sandbelt, yet only minutes from the thriving Mornington Peninsula. The club was originally founded in 1924 but only became a significant member of the Victorian Sandbelt in the 1960s, when it moved to an adjacent property and local golf identity Sloan Morpeth built its North and South courses.

While Morpeth incorporated twelve holes from the original layout into the South Course, the North Course, which was built on the undulating sandy high ground, was totally new. For more than 30 years the South Course, with its championship length and difficulty, was considered the club's premier layout. The shorter and quirky North Course was built on the more dramatic land but was less regarded because of its unconventional design. At the turn of the 20th century the club employed local golf designer Michael Clayton to oversee major revisions to all 36 holes. The result of work done to the North Course in 2002 was nothing short of remarkable and transformed the little course with infinite potential into the new darling of the Melbourne Sandbelt.

Although the routing was not significantly altered, Clayton's changes were considerable and included a number of superb 'new' golf holes built along existing lines. He also incorporated classic Sandbelt-style bunkering and added areas of native vegetation to create a number of spectacular vistas, especially on the short 2nd and 14th holes, which received the most substantial facelifts. The wild and unkempt appearance of the heathland grasses that line fairways and greens stir memories of its more famous cousins. Indeed, there is now as much of Royal Melbourne and Kingston Heath in this layout as original Peninsula North.

Testing players with strategy and subtlety rather than length, the variety of shotmaking challenges is the course's greatest asset, the par threes running to all points of the compass and the short- to medium-length par fours bending both ways and sloping up, down and across the tumbling hills. The front nine is full of solid holes, but the best stretch of golf starts with the 12th, an uphill par four with a hog's-back fairway lined by a sandy hazard that runs the length of the hole. The next is a short four with a nasty hourglass green that is tiny, tiered and almost impossible to hold, while the once drab par three 14th now plays into a wide, sloping green built into a sizeable sand dune and framed by sublime bunkers.

Aside from Royal Melbourne and parts of Victoria, Peninsula's North Course is as good a golf site as any in Melbourne. Morpeth's original design had always used the natural movement to great effect, but thanks to Clayton the course feels born again, with his commonsense tweaking a welcome relief for golfers constantly battered by older courses striving to be longer and tougher. For so long tarred with a 'potentially good' epithet, the modern Peninsula North is tremendous fun and now a true Sandbelt highlight.

Woodlands Golf Club

COURSE OPENED 1913
DESIGNERS R.S. Banks, S. Bennett, Mick Morcom

Largely unheralded outside Australia, the Woodlands Golf Club is yet another exceptional example of classic golf course architecture within Melbourne's glorious Sandbelt. Although it is now one of the best-bunkered courses in Australia, when formed back in 1913 the club's landlord prohibited any earthworks on the estate and its early members were forced to use portable wire netting as hazards in place of actual bunkers. This policy was altered in the 1920s when the course evolved into its present form and Royal Melbourne greenkeeper Mick Morcom added the famous bunkering.

Short by modern standards, Woodlands is actually quite a difficult test, with tight tree-lined fairways and small elevated greens that get notoriously firm and fast in the summer months and are protected by strategically positioned bunkers and dangerous humps and hollows. Despite its varied mix of intelligent long holes and attractive par threes, the strengths of the course are the outstanding short par fours, like the 3rd, 13th and the easily reachable 4th, its wicked target narrow and all but impossible to hold unless approached straight on. The 7th is another fabulous four, with a tight drive followed by a pitch into one of the finest greens in Melbourne. Other course highlights include the bunkering on the 5th and 15th, strong back-to-back par fours at the 9th and 10th, and the frightfully tight 17th, which has one of the toughest greens to hit of any par three on the Sandbelt.

Woodlands came of age during Australian golf's Golden Era, yet despite retaining the characteristics that make Sandbelt golf so distinctive, the lack of the Dr MacKenzie signature has seen this wonderful course perennially underrated.

The Metropolitan Golf Club

COURSE OPENED 1908
DESIGNERS J.B. Mackenzie, Dr Alister MacKenzie, Dick Wilson, Michael Clayton

The Metropolitan Golf Club was founded by a group of Royal Melbourne members who rejected the club's 1901 move into Melbourne's southern sandhills and opted instead to remain at their inner-city home. After a few years, however, the Metropolitan golfers were forced to relocate, and they shifted to an estate in Oakleigh with less natural undulation than the new Royal Melbourne site but with the same fertile sandy base found throughout the Sandbelt region.

Engineer member J.B. Mackenzie created the first course, his routing taking advantage of the unusual shape of the estate by including several fine doglegs and fairways that ran in a number of directions. The other MacKenzie, Dr Alister, also had a major hand in the design of Metropolitan, advising on bunkering and some minor routing improvements during his 1926 visit to Melbourne. Sadly, with the exception of the final two holes and the tee shot on the 10th, none of the back nine is arranged as either Mackenzie had intended, American Dick Wilson rebuilding this part of the course in 1960 after the club had been forced to sell its beloved southern holes for a school development. Michael Clayton later made alterations to some of the Wilson holes and, despite some decent design work and an excellent long par four at 15, the best golf is concentrated in the much stronger outward side, where holes such as 1, 2 and 5 are the standouts.

With magnificent plantings and some of the purest couch fairways and bentgrass greens on the planet, a round at Metro is an exceptional experience, although the aesthetic contrast between holes, as well as the lack of interesting ground movement on the back nine, ultimately keeps it from Australian golf's top shelf.

OPPOSITE Metropolitan's heavily bunkered short par four 16th hole.

The Dunes Golf Links

COURSE OPENED 1997
DESIGNER Tony Cashmore

Located amid the glorious sandhills of Victoria's Mornington Peninsula, the Dunes was created in 1997 by local architect Tony Cashmore, who completely reshaped a primitive and partially built layout into one of Australia's most cherished public golf courses.

The existing holes had played mostly through deep valleys with little shaping, few bunkers and modest greens. Aside from views and the challenge of Man versus Mother Nature, they did little to attract serious golfers. Cashmore refined the targets and hazards, and transformed the land into a classy dune course by modifying existing shapes and devising new ones to blend holes into a seamless golfscape. With generous fairways set in valleys between the dunes or routed across ridges, and a number of greens built in attractive hollows or on gentle plateaus, the site appears naturally suited for golf, although major earthworks were required on several holes to ensure visual continuity.

The strength of the Dunes is the sum of its parts, with seventeen strong holes and only one, the crazy downhill par three 6th with its hidden pond, likely to make you cringe. It is hard to nominate a hole that does not have great visual interest because, as Cashmore explains, 'The land either yielded natural golf vistas, or was deliberately fashioned to excite the golfers eye from the moment he arrives at the tee.' Beautiful par threes at the 13th and 17th do stand out, however, as does the stretch of left-bending holes from the 8th through the 10th and the attractive valley drive down the 18th fairway.

Fully public and modestly priced, the Dunes is a significant golf course in Australia. Its quality helped popularize the now burgeoning Peninsula region, and its critical success has encouraged other developers to seek naturally suitable golf land in this well-endowed country.

OPPOSITE The short 17th at the Dunes was once described by Tom Watson as an 'exquisite golf hole.'

The Grand Golf Club

COURSE OPENED 1997
DESIGNERS Greg Norman, Bob Harrison

Queensland's private Grand Golf Club was the first designed by Greg Norman and his Australian partner, Bob Harrison, who actually had the layout routed and ready for play in 1990 when their client abandoned the $30 million investment before a single divot could be taken. The course was then left dormant and overgrown for six years, until a consortium of frustrated local golfers bought the land, looking to establish an exclusive members-only retreat free from the Gold Coast resort crowds. They chose an ideal site, as the Grand's greatest appeal is the peace and isolation of its secluded hinterland setting.

With the undergrowth cleared, several landing areas reshaped and all of the greens and bunkers remodeled, the golf holes were rediscovered and the 'new' course ready for play within eighteen months. Although not overly long, the Grand is certainly no pushover, with its short par fours and reachable par fives among the trickiest holes on the course and the clever greenside contouring providing a complete examination of approach play and your powers of recovery. After a couple of relatively soft opening holes the 3rd, which plays across a pond for those driving too safely, is the first stern challenge, and from here the test gets progressively more difficult the farther you travel. The best section on the course starts with the par three 6th, includes a number of slippery back-to-front tilted greens and runs through to the 12th and 13th holes which, along with the 17th, are notorious for the large gum trees that stand in the middle of each fairway and particularly irk the professionals.

A controversial tournament venue, the Grand is a superb members' club that offers keen students of design the most challenging and well-presented test in Queensland.

Newcastle Golf Club – Stockton

COURSE OPENED 1937
DESIGNER Eric Apperly

Originally founded within the industrial city of Newcastle, north of Sydney, the Newcastle Golf Club moved permanently into the remote dunes of nearby Stockton during the 1930s, to the site of a secondary nine-hole course they had built in 1915. Eric Apperly was employed to extend their short course, his full eighteen-hole layout opening in 1937 and remaining virtually untouched ever since.

Located a short-iron from the Hunter River and a few hundred meters from the Pacific Ocean, the Stockton course is built on rolling sandhills, with Apperly carving his holes out of rugged Australian bushland and designing them up, over and around the site's heavy slopes. Although its sandpit-style bunkering lacks the sophistication of the Sandbelt courses, the appeal of the design is its wonderful use of the diverse terrain as holes bend with, rather than against, the wild fairway movement.

After a very fine start, the best stretch of golf begins with the par four 5th, a brilliant driving hole surrounded by dense dunes, with a fairway set diagonally to the tee and narrowing as it plunges down and to the left. Bending around tea-tree and rising steeply into a large elevated green, the 6th is another gem and is followed by a wonderful short par three. The next two are also excellent, as is the par five 10th, a classic roller coaster routed across three deep dips, with each shot blind or semi-blind depending on whether you attack the ridges or lay back in the valleys. The mid-length 11th and short 12th are also strong, and although the remainder of the back nine is less memorable than the font nine, there is hardly a mediocre moment anywhere on this uniquely Australian layout.

OPPOSITE **Bushland surrounds**
Newcastle's famed par three 7th.

Portsea Golf Club

COURSE OPENED 1965
DESIGNERS Jock Young, Sloan Morpeth,
Michael Clayton

The Portsea Golf Club was founded in 1924 among the tea-tree-covered sand dunes that border Victoria's Point Nepean National Park. The first nine-hole course was designed by Scottish professional Jock Young and opened for play in 1926, after fifteen men had taken almost twelve months to clear the site of its dense scrub. Twelve holes were in play by 1932, though it was not until the 1960s that the course was finally extended to eighteen holes by Sloan Morpeth and head greenkeeper Jack Howard, who created eighteen originals but did retain some of Young's existing green sites and fairways. In more recent years, increased competition on the booming Mornington Peninsula has forced the club, through local designer Michael Clayton, to make substantial improvements to its much-celebrated layout. Clayton removed encroaching undergrowth on several holes and strengthened the previously weaker back nine by lengthening 15 and 17, and building a terrific new par three at 16.

Quite literally carved out of the coastal tea-tree, the course falls beautifully across the small site, with fairways set amid the rolling dunes and the more exposed holes offering great views out to Port Philip Bay. A beautifully dipping first fairway is a strong start to the round and followed by superb driving holes like the 5th and 6th, built across wild, sloping ridges, and the wonderful 8th, 11th, 15th and 17th, which also come complete with fabulous fairway undulation.

Measuring less than 6,000 meters, Portsea is a fun course that manages to test every club in your bag. Although the reachable par fives and short par fours ensure plenty of birdie opportunities, the vagaries of the Peninsula winds and the small greens will keep you on your toes throughout the round.

Thirteenth Beach Golf Links – Beach Course

COURSE OPENED 2001
DESIGNER Tony Cashmore

One of the most naturally endowed golf estates in Australia, Thirteenth Beach is a 36-hole development that stretches for two miles along Barwon Heads' famous surf beach. Designed by Tony Cashmore, the older Beach Course is the pick of the golf and starts by taking golfers in a loop away from the shore and through low-lying farming pastures, before turning seaward at the 5th and heading deep into the rugged sandhills for the majority of the remaining holes.

Although Cashmore did a good job shaping the flatter housing precinct land into a convincing golf experience, repeat business here is driven by the dunes, and an excellent series of holes within the natural dells, valleys and thick vegetation of the precious coastal duneland. Particularly striking are the three gorgeous short holes, each framed by messy sand formations and testing a different aspect of your iron play. Despite measuring little more than 100 meters, the 16th is the hardest of these as it is totally at the mercy of the wind and plays to a tiny thumbnail green set on a spur and semi-concealed by a sandy waste foreground. The long 7th and mid-length 12th, with its green squeezed into a natural hollow, are also impressive, while of the longer holes the three-shot 11th along a ridge, the short par four 13th and dogleg 17th are also very strong.

Complementing the raw glamour of the natural landscape and the severity of the coastal winds with generous fairways, large sensible putting surfaces and rugged bunkering, Cashmore has managed to create a fine layout that rises above the disparity in terrain to sit beautifully within its surrounds.

OPPOSITE **100 meters of hell: the wicked little 16th hole at Thirteenth Beach.**

The Golf Club Kennedy Bay

COURSE OPENED 1999
DESIGNERS Michael Coate, Roger Mackay,
Ian Baker-Finch

Located among the windswept sandhills of Port Kennedy, south of Perth, the unheralded links of Kennedy Bay was shaped by principal designer Michael Coate with help from PGA professionals Ian Baker-Finch and Roger Mackay, and is one of the Southern Hemisphere's most authentic links creations.

From a central clubhouse the course is arranged in two loops, each running along a series of small dune ridges and shallow natural valleys. The fast-running fairways and large, undulating greens are lined by thick coastal scrub and protected by more than one hundred revetted pot bunkers. Though a solid test from start to finish, the highlight holes tend to come later on, the heroic par four 15th and short 'Wee Tap' 16th, which plays into a shallow ledge sandwiched between traps, particularly worthy of mention. There is also a fine set of short fours, from the drivable 7th with an enormous raised target contoured to catch those who get 'too cute' with their pitch, to the 'Split Decision' 11th with its fairway strategically divided and green then appropriately angled to favor those taking the tighter, bunkered side.

Like any true links, the region's coastal breeze, known as the Fremantle Doctor, is the course's greatest defense as it swings around and strengthens in the afternoons, totally altering the nature of the holes. Although Kennedy Bay lacks really dirty weather, its design, dunes, tight surfaces and constant battering from the Doctor give it an authentic Scottish feel, with only the temperate climate to remind you this is, in fact, Western Australia.

Barwon Heads Golf Club

COURSE OPENED 1921
DESIGNER Victor East

Founded in 1907, the Barwon Heads Golf Club moved to its present home alongside the coastal dunes of the Bellarine Peninsula in 1920, to a links designed by Royal Melbourne professional Victor East and built using horses to plow the hand-planted fairways, tees and greens.

Encompassing two distinct landscapes, the final twelve holes at Barwon Heads are routed among tight coastal tea-tree, while the opening six head out across a classic piece of exposed linksland. Built within earshot of the ocean and adjacent to the seaside sandhills, these early holes are the standouts, particularly the right-bending 3rd, with its fairway set across the tee and played over an enormous sandy waste area. Generally heading into the prevailing south-westerly winds, the temptation is to carry as much of this waste as possible to shorten the approach into an elevated green. The next two tees offer great views down the Barwon Coast, while the 6th heads back toward the clubhouse and a typically British green guarded by rough-covered hillocks. The remaining holes are a little more demanding from the tee, as the bouncy fairways feature the same natural contours but with tighter, and more severe, rough areas. The highlight of the back nine is the famous par three 13th, its tiny green bunkerless but surrounded by wicked undulation and totally exposed to the elements.

Barwon Heads is a prime example of the sort of classic course technology is supposedly rendering obsolete. Tackled with the latest equipment and without the usually stiff coastal breezes, the track seems short, wide and straightforward. Such conditions are rare for these parts, however, and pitting your skills against this natural golf course and scavenging for pars on seemingly defenseless holes is surprisingly invigorating.

OPPOSITE Bending left through dense tea-tree, the 9th is the start of a stern run of holes at Barwon Heads.

New Zealand

Blessed with one of the world's most beautiful landscapes, there are endless attractions to New Zealand, including its coastline, canyons, alpine mountain ranges, lush forests, friendly locals and unhurried pace of life. There is also golf, with the nation said to have more courses per capita than any other country on earth.

While the first golf balls were struck on the South Island at Dunedin in 1869, the game soon headed onto the greener golfing pastures of the North Island, where all of the country's meritorious layouts were subsequently built. There are now golf courses in every corner of New Zealand, but although there is a real understated charm to the game here, unfortunately – unlike a country such as Ireland – this rarely translates into exciting golf. Indeed, this is one of the very rare established golf markets where the quality of design has actually improved in modern times, with most of the worthwhile layouts built since the 1990s. The obvious exception is the wonderful Paraparaumu Beach near the southern tip of the North Island, which has been unchallenged as the nation's standout course for more than half a century. In the suburbs of its biggest city, Auckland, both the Titirangi and Auckland Golf Clubs are the next-best classics and also well worth a look.

The modern golf boom began here in the 1970s when Wairakei International, near Taupo in the center of the North Island, was opened. Built with federal funds, this highly rated resort evoked pride among Kiwi golfers who felt a sense of ownership with the project. Sadly, Wairakei's lofty profile does not match its badly dated design, the course only marginally more impressive than decent country clubs like the nearby Taupo Centennial, New Plymouth, Hastings or the very funky Rangitikei course near Bulls. It was also during the 1970s that American tycoon Julian Robertson first fell in love with New Zealand. His continuing belief that the country is the world's next major tourist destination has led him to build two stunning new courses, Cape Kidnappers and Kauri Cliffs, which are apparently the first in a string of high-end golf properties he is planning across the country. Elsewhere, Robert Trent Jones Jr designed the prominent Gulf Harbour layout in 1998, which is built on a very pretty peninsula property but spoilt by encroaching housing that occupies some of its best golf land.

Despite some disappointing course developments, these are exciting times for golf in New Zealand, with the world on alert and now watching to see what Mr Robertson will come up with next. There is no doubt that it will be spectacular, as he does not seem to be a man interested in the mundane. Whether he can reproduce something as striking as Cape Kidnappers or Kauri Cliffs remains to be seen but any quality golf project is a welcome addition to the attractions of this wonderful country.

Already one of the best holiday destinations in the southern hemisphere, New Zealand has a million things to occupy the active traveler. If keen on your golf, then the three very distinct courses featured on the following pages are not to be missed.

OPPOSITE With some spectacular modern creations, New Zealand is boosting its reputation as a golf destination of note. Pictured is the dramatic 17th hole at Kauri Cliffs as it heads along a ridge toward the Bay of Islands.

Paraparaumu Beach Golf Club

COURSE OPENED 1949

DESIGNER Alex Russell

The tricky green site on the mid-length par four 15th.

OPPOSITE The Kiwi Postage Stamp, Paraparaumu's short 16th hole.

A short drive from the nation's capital, windy Wellington, New Zealand's most famous piece of golfing ground was first used for the game back in 1929 when a group of local residents created a nine-hole course on leased sandhills within the seaside village of Paraparaumu Beach. The group had plans to expand, but during the Depression its landlord was forced to sell the course and the neighboring land between the links and the beach. A syndicate of Wellington businessmen purchased the property, subdividing the beach area for residential sites and then extending the course to a full eighteen holes in 1937.

A golf club was later formed in 1948 and, with ambitions to improve their layout, the members called in Alex Russell to offer some design suggestions. A one-time partner of Dr Alister MacKenzie, Russell was delighted by the prospects of this rare piece of authentic linksland and set about redesigning the course by keeping some green sites and sticking mostly to the existing routing but reversing nines and altering all eighteen holes considerably. The Australian proved an astute choice of architect, and when he returned to the site in 1952 Russell was pleased at how his plans had been implemented, commenting that it was, 'with the greatest of pleasure that I found my ideas and suggestions translated exactly as I conceived them.' With some minor exceptions the designer's original plans have survived virtually unchanged.

Full of messy dunes and bumpy fescue fairways, Paraparaumu Beach is a subtle masterpiece, with Russell's undulating holes and small greens guarded by fierce traps and testing all elements of your game. The layout plays little more than 6,000 meters from the tips but is far from a pushover, as the target areas are frightfully difficult to find under the naturally breezy coastal conditions. A solid short game is important but driving straight is absolutely vital here, as thick hay borders the fairways and taking your approach from the wrong side on most of the longer holes is a recipe for disaster.

Routed predominantly to the north and south, holes are laid out in a big square rather than a loop so that play changes direction continually, which is important on such an exposed site. After a terrific tumbling opening hole, the 2nd features an obscured green complex and is the first of four very fine short holes. The 5th is also an excellent par three and feels much tighter than it really is, thanks to a semi-natural gully surrounding the target. This gully was actually partly dug by an autocratic club president under the cover of darkness, after his proposal to do so had been rejected by fellow board members. The 16th is another fabulous one-shotter and a virtual copy of the Postage Stamp at Royal Troon, though marginally less terrifying.

The course also has a strong and varied collection of unique par fours, including three

that are truly outstanding. The 8th is a short four across a rippled fairway that bends right into a dune with a tiny green flanked by deep traps that make cutting the corner particularly treacherous. Even better, the brilliant 13th is the best hole in New Zealand and a massive bunkerless par four played downhill across wild rolling terrain, through dunes and then up into a small ridgetop green. The final classic is the intimidating 17th, which narrows from the tee into an ideal left-side plateau and then straightens across a series of undulations into a flattish target guarded by punishing traps.

Perhaps the only worrying aspects of these links are the greens and surrounds, which are much softer than is ideal on such a bumpy site. Russell had warned the club about such a problem back in 1952, as his pitching and chipping areas were designed to be kept tight and firm to present golfers with a range of interesting short-game options. Despite modest length and some concerns with conditioning, Paraparaumu Beach remains a Kiwi classic and, as well as having more knockout holes than any other course in New Zealand, is also the most fun to play.

OPPOSITE A touch of Dornoch, Paraparaumu's 13th hole is played across some wild undulation, its great driving challenge matched by a thrilling approach into a narrow green perched atop a steep ridge.

Cape Kidnappers Golf Course

COURSE OPENED 2004

DESIGNER Tom Doak

'The flattish fingers of land along part of the clifftops were ready-made fairways grazed by sheep. I played 15 of the 18 holes with my crew one day before we had built anything.'

TOM DOAK

OPPOSITE Played across a deep gully with the ocean to your left, the 6th hole is no place for the fainthearted.

Situated on the East Coast of New Zealand's North Island, Cape Kidnappers is a remarkable prestige golf facility designed by American architect Tom Doak. The course occupies part of an isolated 5,000-acre sheep station and incorporates stunning sandstone cliff fingers that plummet 500 feet down into the waters of Hawke's Bay. With a number of holes running toward and away from these cliff edges, and even routed along the bluffs, this is one of the most compelling modern layouts in golf, with some unforgettable coastal views.

The Cape Kidnappers area is as significant as it is spectacular, the bay beneath having strong links to Maori folklore and the cape itself being named by Captain James Cook in 1769, after locals had attempted to kidnap his ship's young Tahitian guide. The golf course site slants gently toward the cliffs, which then collapse dramatically down to the ocean, allowing the golf, in places, to dangle right out onto the edge of the landforms. Given the glamorous nature of such holes, Doak found himself having to work harder to ensure that the golf away from the coast did not suffer by comparison. To his great credit, the success of Kidnappers is the quality of these inland holes, many of which are dominated by pronounced ridges and feature demanding carries from the tees across vast ravines.

Greens throughout the course are excellent. A couple, like 8 and 14, are a touch extreme but the majority are subtly tilted, often elevated and with clever internal contouring that rewards precise approaches kept under the hole. Due to the severity of winds that typically whip across the heads here, the fairways are very generous with Doak giving players plenty of width and using bunkers only sparingly. Unusually, given his strategic design philosophy, there are a number of 'hit anywhere' holes, slashing away wildly on fairways like the 2nd, 4th, 12th and 15th unlikely to cause too many out-of-position problems.

The layout starts away from the magnificent sea views, with the early holes routed across a broad, sweeping landscape that gives little indication of the excitement to follow. With its left side collapsing hundreds of feet down into a cove and a split fairway offering two distinct paths into a plateau green site, the 5th is a superb hole and a wonderful introduction to Cape Kidnappers' infamous cliff-side area. The next is a smashing seaside par three across a deep gully, while other standouts on the front nine include the strategic opening hole and the plunging par four 7th. On the homeward nine the real quality starts with the par three 11th and the long, falling 12th, which features a gorgeous bay backdrop and follows an expansive shelf that narrows as it feeds into a yawning ravine. Perched atop a ridge, the 13th is then a beautiful short hole that falls sharply left into the ocean, its horizon green contoured through the center to feel much smaller from the tee than it actually is. Also worthy of note is

the bizarre punchbowl green on the 18th and the brutal par four 17th, which plays along a gully before crossing a tightly bunkered shelf.

Most interesting of all, however, is the 15th. Named Pirate's Plank, this is a long, wide and flat par five that follows a massive cliff finger as it gently heads down toward the edge of the earth. Bunkerless and strangely bland given its incredible surroundings, the hole basically demands two long and strong woods followed by an approach that is not overhit. On a property so visually dramatic, the only question mark some may have with Doak's work at Kidnappers is whether an extravagant designer, such as Tom Fazio or Jack Nicklaus, could have extracted more from such a site. Certainly a hole like 15 would have looked very different done by another architect but there is, in fairness, a substance to Doak designs which the others sometimes lack, and there is no denying that his Cape Kidnappers creation is an impressive addition to the world's golfing menu.

ABOVE The beautiful 13th is the shortest of Cape Kidnappers' four par threes.

OPPOSITE From a tee pushed right against the edge of the cliffs, the 16th is a shortish par five that flirts with one of Kidnappers' deep inland gullies.

Kauri Cliffs Golf Course

COURSE OPENED 2000
DESIGNER David Harman

Looking out across the 17th green and down along the spectacular Bay of Islands.

OPPOSITE The long, all-carry par three 7th hole at Kauri Cliffs.

The north-eastern section of the North Island was the birthplace of the New Zealand nation and is a region of rare unspoilt natural beauty, with a striking subtropical coastline dotted with gorgeous islands and secluded coves and bays. It was here in Matauri Bay during the 1990s that Wall Street financier Julian Robertson bought a 4,000-acre cattle ranch, with panoramic views over the headland and out to the wild Cavalli Islands, and looked to create his own luxury golf destination. With the odd cluster of the region's giant Kauri trees and a site touching enormous cliffs that crash hundreds of feet down into the sea, Kauri Cliffs was born.

Set mostly on heaving pastureland, this thrilling course was designed by American David Harman and enjoys mesmerizing views of the outer reaches of the Bay of Islands. Though only a handful of holes hug the bluffs above the Pacific Ocean, the land generally leans toward the sea, meaning it is visible from the majority of holes. Away from the cliffs the rolling fairways tend to follow the curvature of the land, Harman making full use of the dramatic site by routing holes along broad crests, across ravines, through deep valleys and by using inland promontories throughout his bold design. Given the wind strength and extreme penalty for missing fairways, the landing areas are fairly generous from the tee, although tighter driving lines are often rewarded with easier approach shots. This is

very much a second shot golf course, however, as the key to scoring well is finding greens that are heavily contoured and presented to play firm and fast.

Starting from a central clubhouse, the course winds its way gradually toward the sea, with a series of solid holes played through shimmering fescue grasses. Standout moments early include the short par four 3rd, which is featureless from the tee but has a pushed up green that is tough to hit from the left half of the fairway. The 4th is a heroic par five for the big hitters who can carry right-side bunkers and then blast over a corner hazard and into a large green perched at the end of a sheer drop-off. Unfortunately, there are few options here for the average player who cannot make either shot. Both the 5th and 7th are long all-carry par threes with the sea out to your right, while sandwiched between is a brutal par four that demands a strong drive across a ravine followed by a blind, rising approach.

The back nine begins with some decent strategic golf within a deep valley, the ocean out of sight for a couple of holes but right back in your face at the long one-shot 14th, which is set hundreds of feet above the water and stares straight down to the Cavalli Islands. The next three holes along the coast are the most dramatic, as the golf gets closest to the cliff edges and the outlooks are totally uninterrupted. Though exciting to play, the horseshoe finish at the reachable par five 15th

is a tad severe and probably makes the safe play too attractive for those looking to make a birdie. The sometimes drivable 16th, heading toward the distant sea, also sadly favors the conservative play. It is followed, however, by the best and most spectacular hole on the course, the elevated tee shot on the 17th played across a gorge to an oblique shelf fairway that follows a ridge as it falls toward a well-bunkered green and an unbelievable backdrop.

With a four-corners wind that swings around on a day-to-day basis, there are set-ups and conditions here that are more trying than others, but the course remains playable for the average golfer thanks to a wide variety of teeing options. Despite its very obvious attractions, ultimately what hurts Kauri Cliffs is the lack of genuine world-class golf holes to match its astonishing setting. With barely a blade of grass out of place, however, as well as superb scenery and some heroic design, Kauri Cliffs is a visual feast that is sure to impress the vast majority of those who golf here.

OPPOSITE The last third of Kauri's heroic par five 4th hole, with its distant coastal views.

Europe

France

For all its historic and cultural significance, famous monuments and culinary delights, France has become the most popular tourist destination in the world, but it is also one of the very best places to play golf, with a varied collection of fine courses found throughout its rich landscape. In almost all of the popular holiday regions there are great golf courses. From the dune gems near Boulogne in the north to the stunning Simpson classics around Paris and the antique courses of Biarritz, the quest for high-quality golf takes you to some of the most enchanting parts of this amazing country.

France has played a pivotal role in the development of golf; in fact, some believe it actually evolved from the medieval Flemish game of 'chole' played by French soldiers during the Battle of Bauge of 1421, where the Scots fought alongside the French against the British army. The first golf course on continental Europe was formed within the Basque region of southern France, the Pau Golf Club (1856), followed by the nearby Le Phare course (1888) built by Willie Dunn for wealthy British holidaymakers in the luxury sea resort of Biarritz. The original Biarritz course was most famous as the home of golf's first cross-ocean par three, a hole admired by C.B. Macdonald and copied countless times throughout the world. Sadly, the club's cliff holes were lost to housing after the Second World War, and though today's course is short and landlocked, it still has a number of outstanding originals such as the terrifying short 14th.

Since the 1980s, golf has experienced tremendous growth here, comparable to the golden period between the two world wars when Harry Colt and Tom Simpson were prolific. Simpson was responsible for what remain France's best five classic courses; Morfontaine, Chantilly and the highly original Fontainebleau course near Paris, the unmistakably British Chiberta course in the dunes near Biarritz, and Hardelot Les Pins, which plays through pine-covered sandhills and features a superb set of naturally sited and contoured greens. Colt's best at Le Touquet and St Germaine are also interesting, particularly the bunkering on dull land at St Germaine, though each is a long way behind his best elsewhere. Like the rest of mainland Europe, much of the modern golf development is unfortunately over-hyped, overly difficult and lacks imagination, Trent Jones' Le Prince de Provence, Moliets, Les Bordes and the Châteaux course at Golf du Médoc among the exceptions.

Despite an indifference to almost anything British, there is no doubt that the French have now fully embraced golf, and indeed, if you look beyond traditional golfing hotspots such as the British Isles, North America and Australia, this is probably the strongest golf country in the world. With so many other reasons to visit France, it is unlikely to ever become principally a golf destination, yet an itinerary that was able to take in Morfontaine, Chantilly, Fontainebleau, Hardelot, Sperone, Chiberta, Biarritz, Le Prince, Médoc and Les Bordes and the associated antiquities of locales like Paris, Chantilly, Provence, the Loire Valley, Bordeaux and the incredible Bonifacio would probably make the ultimate golf and sightseeing combination.

OPPOSITE One of the most underrated golf countries on the planet, France is full of fine golf clubs like Golf de Chantilly, outside of Paris. Pictured is the 18th hole on its Longères Course.

Golf de Morfontaine

COURSE OPENED 1927
DESIGNER Tom Simpson

The 11th is just one of a number of outstanding short holes at Morfontaine.

OPPOSITE The brilliant nine-hole Valliere Course ends with this uphill par three across the heather.

The Morfontaine story began in 1910 when a French duke decided to create his own nine-hole golf course on gorgeous woodlands tucked away in a quiet pine forest outside Paris. Tom Simpson was commissioned to design his layout, which was finished in 1912 and followed in 1927 by an adjacent full eighteen-hole course built for the duke's friends who had formed the Morfontaine Golf Club. The original nine, known as Valliere, was later donated to the club and remains its brilliant short alternate course, with some of the most amazing green complexes in world golf.

An extremely prestigious club that guards its treasured golf holes as much as its privacy, Morfontaine is a rare beauty and remarkably similar to the best in London's Heathland, with shades of Swinley Forest, Sunningdale and St George's Hill but set on possibly even more attractive grounds. While any invitation to play here should be greeted with delight, the way to enjoy Morfontaine, if possible, is to first play the avant-garde short course, which is an ideal warm-up for the longer, and slightly less eccentric, main event. As a stand-alone nine-holer, the Valliere Course would probably rank with Royal Worlington and Newmarket in England as the world's finest, and it is certainly the most fun to play. All seven of its surviving Simpson greens are a work of art, while the 2nd, 4th and 9th holes are awesome par threes and the 5th is a very special short par five, with its fairway bending left toward a partially obscured green sitting in a basin between the dunes.

Like the Valliere, the par threes on the course proper are a highlight, as are some of the longer bending par fours, which demand precision from both the tee and the fairway. The entire layout is highly strategic, however, with a stunning array of short-game challenges presented by the creatively contoured greens and bunkers. Aside from its spellbinding beauty and rolling fairways, which are mostly lined by tall pines and heather-covered hills, Morfontaine is noted for an exceptional stretch of holes through the middle of the round. This section includes strong fours such as the 7th and 8th, fantastic short par four greens at the 9th and 10th and beautiful par threes at the 11th and 13th. The doglegging 8th is a magnificent driving hole across rocks to a crested fairway that bends into a superb green complex, which is progressively more difficult to approach the safer one drives from the tee. Both the 9th and 10th feature severe fall-away greens where Simpson gives you a glimpse at the target but then rejects anything not perfectly struck, the 9th falling sharply away to sand on the right and the 10th with a wicked false front. The finish is also strong, and includes a wonderful long par four at the 16th followed by a short hole played into a shelf green that slopes sharply to the front.

Right until his death, Simpson continually tweaked the holes at Morfontaine, regularly sending sketches and drawings of green and

bunker changes to the club. Some have suggested his continual desire to make alterations was financially motivated, but he clearly cared a great deal about this golf course and one cannot argue with the quality of the end result. Until 2005, when Kyle Phillips completed some minor redesign work, the entire layout had remained virtually unchanged since his final design. Phillips only extended tees on the 3rd and 10th, but he changed the par five 12th substantially by shifting both the tee and green back and creating a pronounced dogleg. A more challenging hole now for the better players, one can only hope that the club will resist further change and continue to preserve Simpson's artistic genius for the golfing world to enjoy.

There are few more attractive places to play the game than Morfontaine, and while the raw glamour of Ballybunion has made it the best known of Simpson's courses, this is his architectural masterpiece and ranks among the best inland golf available anywhere.

ABOVE The unique shaping of Valliere's 3rd green typifies the creativity of Simpson's work at Morfontaine.

OPPOSITE Tightly treed and terrific, the 13th is yet another fabulous par three.

Le Prince de Provence

COURSE BUILT 1991
COURSE OPENED 1999
DESIGNER Robert Trent Jones
with Robert Trent Jones Jr

*'The Prince is one of the premier
golf course designs of my life.'*
ROBERT TRENT JONES

Possibly the world's most exclusive golf club, Le Prince de Provence was actually conceived as part of multi-course residential development by Robert Trent Jones during the 1970s. Scouring the Mediterranean coastline for an ideal site to build the 'Pinehurst of Europe,' Trent Jones found and acquired a 2,500-acre property in the hills high above the French Riviera. He then obtained the largest planning consent ever granted by the French Ministry, which included three championship golf courses, hotels, houses and apartments to be included on his vast estate. Sadly for Trent Jones, this preliminary approval was later rescinded during the detailed planning process, when conservationists pressured authorities
to reject his plans despite the first course having been completed and the development's proposed density being reduced to a third of the original concept.

For six years an impeccably maintained golf course sat dormant without a single round being played. Due to a permit technicality, golf on the site was decreed illegal and this proved the final straw for Trent Jones and his partners, who lost their substantial investment in the property when it reverted to a lending bank. The white elephant was eventually sold to a syndicate of Norwegian businessmen, who scrapped housing and expansion plans and instead decided to create a private single course golf club for a fortunate few friends. With significant financial might, the new owners challenged court orders preventing play on the course, and in 1999 were able to get an injunction on the ruling and begin golfing.

Occupying one of the region's largest private properties, the course is totally secluded and surrounded by the untouched Provence hills. The holes weave through red rocky outcroppings replete with distinctive umbrella pines that are native to this small region of Provence and an integral part of the design on many holes. While the rolling valleys and uniquely shaped pines dominate the landscape, the designer was unafraid to add to what nature had left and was able to build believable undulation into holes such as the 2nd, 7th, 10th, 15th and 17th with great effect. The green contouring is also outstanding, most of the clever slopes presenting a range of short-game options, which is not always the case on other Trent Jones courses.

Consistent throughout with the designer's mantra of easy bogey, hard par golf, Le Prince opens with a series of well-bunkered holes, the most notable early moment being the superb right-bending 2nd, which is played through sand and red rock and into a delicious green site. Shaped and bunkered to resemble Trent Jones' famous 16th at Augusta National, the 4th is the first of a fine group of one-shotters, and although the par fives are slightly less impressive, the reachable 8th is a nice hole and both the 3rd and 12th feature interesting pitch shots. Further highlights include the attractive

away-angled green on the downhill 10th and the bunkers and slopes that artistically frame the 15th and 17th holes. The crested drive and cross-pond approach into the dramatic 7th hole are also terrific, while the 18th is a wonderful closing hole that turns into a small rise with turn-point bunkers and a lone pine guarding the corner. This tree was actually retained by Robert Trent Jones Jr against his father's wishes, and although a tree blocking a bunker is never ideal, this one does work because the temptation to flirt with the right side, despite its dangers, is still quite strong.

Although Le Prince was the brainchild of Trent Jones senior, his son was heavily involved closer to completion due to his father's poor health. It was one of their few joint ventures and clearly impressed Robert Jr, who was delighted that his father found the property and describes his design as 'a true masterpiece.' Indeed, Le Prince de Provence is the embodiment of a life's work from a designer who poured his heart and soul into the property for more than 20 years. It was one of the rare golf course projects that Trent Jones personally invested in and with a conglomerate of his finest holes, plus first-class shaping and construction, is an appropriate tribute to his famous design style.

Golf de Chantilly – Vineuil Course

COURSE OPENED 1909
DESIGNERS Tom Simpson,
Donald Steele

Set in the roiling countryside of Picardie and surrounded by the enchanting Chantilly forest, the prestigious Golf de Chantilly is one of France's great golf clubs. Founded a short walk from the center of the historic town, its members initially golfed on a rudimentary layout that was redesigned in the 1920s by Tom Simpson, who transformed Chantilly into an aristocratic club of real quality. Simpson, who also designed the nearby classic at Morfontaine, originally built 36 holes for the club but its land was owned by the French forestry and over the years nine were lost to roads and parking.

During the late 1980s Golf de Chantilly decided to re-establish the second course and commissioned Donald Steele to build nine new holes on additional land. Curiously, they then opted to exchange three of his holes with the final three from Simpson's Vineuil Course to allow the new layout to return twice to the clubhouse. This was seen as preferable to an out-and-back routing but seems a strange decision, as the flat Steele holes are a poor substitute to the superb Simpson originals, which occupy beautifully undulating ground and formed part of an exceptional six-hole finishing stretch.

Aside from losing these three closing holes, the Vineuil Course has retained its original character and, when used as a tournament venue, it is returned to its former configuration and remains one of Europe's best championship layouts. Holes are generally set well back from the surrounding forest and routed across a gently undulating pasture with attractive fairways lined by waving fescues. The greens here are quite large and the slopes softer than on other Simpson courses, except for highly contoured gems such as 2, 8, 13 and 16. The bunkering is excellent and the shapes remain mostly as rugged and punishing as first conceived. Many of the longer holes feature classical cross-bunkers that are among the most formidable Simpson ever built; thankfully, the recent shifting of a number of back tees has brought most of these traps back into play for the strong golfers.

The course starts with a succession of fine holes over softly moving ground and gradually builds through an open middle section to a thrilling climax played through a deep valley and across a hungry ravine. Highlights include the attractive par threes, cavernous fairway bunkering at the 7th, 8th, 12th and 13th and a trio of tremendous holes from the 16th, which were originally a prelude to the closing holes but now form a fabulous finishing stretch in their own right.

The town of Chantilly is best known for its historic racecourse and famous Château de Chantilly, which featured in the Bond movie *A View to a Kill* and houses the second-largest art collection in France. In golfing terms the Vineuil Course, which is less than five minutes away, is not quite as significant but in its original format is still a golfing treasure. While a game here remains a special treat, missing the three holes to your left as you drive off the first tee is a real tragedy, especially when one considers how ordinary their replacements are. Though hesitant to encourage inappropriate behavior on any golf course, sneaking across and playing these terrific holes after your round on the Vineuil is well worth the risk.

OPPOSITE Vineuil's classic opening
par four, through the fescues and into
the undulating woodland.

Les Bordes Golf Course

COURSE OPENED 1986
DESIGNER Robert von Hagge
with Rick Baril

'Les Bordes was one of my most gratifying personal and professional experiences.'

ROBERT VON HAGGE

OPPOSITE As on several other holes, anything short on the par three 8th is certain to get wet.

One of Europe's highest-profile golf resorts, Les Bordes is a luxury retreat built on a secluded hunting estate deep in the Loire Valley's ancient Sologne forest. It was originally conceived by Baron Marcel Bich, the Bic pen pioneer, and Yoshiaki Sakurai, as a private international golf club for friends and colleagues that was to house France's best-kept and most challenging layout.

After considering a number of prominent course architects, the baron selected American Robert von Hagge as his designer and invited him to Paris to discuss the project. Von Hagge traveled to France unaware of his client's background or the scope of his ambitious plans, and upon arrival was shown a rudimentary layout and master plan for the vast property. The designer then readied his Parker pen to make some alternate suggestions to the plans before him, and it was only after being politely asked by the Baron to use Bic pens when working on the project, that he realized who his client actually was.

For von Hagge and his partner Rick Baril, Les Bordes was quite an undertaking, as the property was flat and featureless, except for small stands of hardwood, and covered mostly in cornfields and marshes. It was originally conceived as a 36-hole project and construction started on holes that required no tree clearing, as the necessary permits had not yet been secured. As the estate was former swampland with heavy clay soils, the playing areas had to be raised, so a number of lakes were built on

land already cleared of trees and the fill used to build up the fairways. The greatest compliment one can pay the design team is how natural the entire golf course feels, and in particular the wetland areas, which come into play on at least a dozen holes, blend beautifully with the forest and its accompanying undergrowth and look to be part of the original landscape. Indeed Baron Bich was so enamored with the total tranquility of the first eighteen when it opened that he immediately shelved plans for the second course. Following his death in 1994, Mr Sakurai became sole owner of Les Bordes and today runs the estate as an idyllic resort for a high-end golf market that demands and appreciates quality.

Similar in both concept and style to a club like Loch Lomond, Les Bordes is a typically extravagant resort-style experience complete with immaculate playing surfaces, punishing penal design, isolated target areas, heroic carries and severely contoured putting greens. While some of the design decisions are questionable, such as building a par five around wetlands but cutting off its fairway to force a lay-up from the tee, the holes are nonetheless attractive, well constructed and very enjoyable to play.

The early holes give you a pretty clear indication of what lies ahead here. An opening island green ringed by a massive sandy waste bunker is followed by two narrow long holes and the first of the eye-catching par threes,

with its small target pressed up against a pond. More meritorious are subsequent moments like the approach into the 9th and the par four 6th, which is played along a deep bunker that contains a cross commemorating a fallen knight. The back nine has more water than the front and probably shades it a little in terms of excitement and good golf, with better holes including the par three 13th and the two-shot 17th, which bends through the birch forest. Also noteworthy, the typically bruising closing hole features a long all-carry approach across water and into a shallow green with a steep step.

Les Bordes is not to everyone's taste but is the best and most significant European course out of the prolific office of golf course architect Robert von Hagge. Though the shaping in places is a little overdone, the course is well-built and the site so pretty that it is easy to see the attraction of Les Bordes and hard not to fall for its charms.

OPPOSITE Tight from the tee and even tighter into the green, the 11th is one of Les Bordes' hardest par fours.

Golf du Médoc – Les Châteaux

COURSE OPENED 1989
DESIGNER Bill Coore with Rod Whitman

Located a little north of Bordeaux, and surrounded by some of the region's famous vineyards, is the 36-hole Golf du Médoc facility and its outstanding Les Châteaux Course designed by Bill Coore and built by his friend Rod Whitman. Routed over fairly unremarkable terrain, the course is a superbly constructed and classically strategic layout, with wide fairways bordered by gorse and thick indigenous grasses leading to clever green sites that are bunkered and contoured to substantially reward those able to drive closer to the hazards.

The strategic appeal of the course is apparent from the very first tee, with the opening fairway split by central bunkers positioned to offer a much easier approach from the riskier right side. The back nine is particularly strong and includes a string of fine holes that climax with the tremendously original 18th. Divided by a diagonal creek and angled to reward bold lines, the 11th is followed by the best par three on the course, a perfectly bunkered flat par four and a beautiful short par five that sweeps around a nasty ditch.

In terms of both the approach and the appearance, the bunkering throughout the course is reminiscent of Dr Alister MacKenzie and some of his work at Royal Melbourne. Coore is clearly an accomplished designer and the best holes here, such as the 4th and 13th, are as good as golf design on dull ground ever gets.

Médoc is probably Europe's most understated quality golf destination, and is a layout that is sure to please all design connoisseurs.

Golf de Sperone

COURSE OPENED 1991
DESIGNERS Robert Trent Jones, Cabell B. Robinson

Famous as the birthplace of Napoléon Bonaparte, the French island of Corsica is a playground for wealthy holidaymakers but home to just one golf course, Sperone, which is built on rocky headlands and overlooks the pristine coves and azure waters of the Mediterranean. The course was designed by Robert Trent Jones and Cabell B. Robinson, who save most of the excitement for a six-hole seaside stretch late in the round, which is among the most scenic anywhere.

The solid front nine winds mostly through rugged Corsican undergrowth with only the odd glimpse of the distant waters and a number of small raised greens to complicate play. The back nine, on the other hand, packs quite a punch and includes a superb run of holes from the 11th, which plays down toward the ocean and a slender ledge green sandwiched between large boulders. The next is a brutal one-shotter across a rocky canyon to an elevated clifftop, while the 13th is a short bumpy par four played along the edge of the sea to a tiny target framed by the sandy Sperone beach. Both the 15th and 16th would be all-world holes with a little tree clearing, the 16th in particular hurt by growth along the cliff edge which separates the fairway from a tee that rests on a rocky peninsula jutting into the sea. The hole then bends left around the cliffs, and were the trees removed it would become one of the most exhilarating driving holes on earth.

Situated at the southernmost tip of the island, Sperone is only minutes from the medieval clifftop town of Bonifacio, which towers above the Lavezzi Islands and the Strait of Bonifacio. This fortified town is a particularly striking sight for those coming by ferry from the nearby Italian island of Sardinia and is itself a must-see European destination, with or without your golf clubs.

OPPOSITE The magnificent Mediterranean outlook from the approach to the 13th green at Sperone.

Spain & Portugal

Valderrama

Praia D'El Rey

El Saler

Troia

Sotogrande

With sun-soaked climates and captivating coastal landscapes, Spain and Portugal have long been popular destinations for northern European holidaymakers looking to escape the cold. Golfers are also heading south to the Iberian Peninsula in ever-increasing numbers, with Spain's Costa del Sol and Portugal's Algarve Coast, in particular, now dotted with golf clubs and plush modern resorts. Though both are gorgeous places to visit, the golf tends to lack the intelligent design found in more traditional golf regions and may disappoint those looking for more than green grass, golf carts and GPS.

Golf was first introduced to the Peninsula during the 1890s with Portugal's oldest golf club, Oporto, the third oldest on mainland Europe. The first Spanish club was not formalized until a few years later, but the game has developed much more quickly here than in its tiny neighbor, thanks in part to the success of champion professionals like Seve Ballesteros, José Maria Olazabal and Sergio Garcia. Spain has also played a significant part in the game's modern boom throughout Europe, with its players driving the Ryder Cup renaissance and the prolific Robert Trent Jones setting up his first European office here in the 1960s after being commissioned to design Sotogrande and the giant of the Iberian Peninsula, Valderrama.

The region's most significant local designer was the unconventional Spaniard Javier Araña, who operated prior to an American architectural invasion and designed the excellent El Saler course near Valencia as well as a string of admirable efforts elsewhere, such as Madrid's Club de Campo course, Aloha near Marbella and Neguri in Bilbao. Sadly, his highly rated El Prat course in Barcelona no longer exists, its land recently acquired as part of an airport expansion. Elsewhere in Spain the charming Harry Colt designed Real Golf Club de Pedreña, where a young Ballesteros learned his craft, is an enjoyable layout, as are the von Hagge courses at Empordà, Las Brisas by Trent Jones and the new La Reserva at Sotogrande by Cabell Robinson. Unfortunately, most of the other high-profile modern courses are not of an international standard.

Portugal has fewer golf courses than Spain but some real quality among its more interesting modern designs. The year-round sunshine of the Algarve makes it the nation's most popular holiday spot, yet aside from Henry Cotton's famous 16th hole at Vale do Lobo (Royal), the golf here is fairly average. San Lorenzo and Vilamoura 'Old' and 'Victoria' do have their fans but are ordinary by comparison to what is available farther north at Troia, Oitavos, Penha Longa and Praia D'El Rey, each within an easy drive of the enchanting capital Lisbon. The highlight of those not reviewed in the following pages is the Arthur Hills designed Oitavos course at Quinta da Marinha. Set among reforested duneland, the layout boasts several holes, such as the brilliant short 14th played across a sandy depression into a saddle green, that are among the best in the country.

The golf industry on the Iberian Peninsula is currently experiencing a period of tremendous growth, a trend unlikely to reverse anytime soon given the amount of new development still taking place here. It is not difficult to see the attraction of the region – there are a number of beautiful holiday spots along both coastlines and good weather is almost assured. For serious golfers, however, the best advice is to select your golf courses carefully to avoid disappointment.

OPPOSITE With pleasant climates and bountiful coastlines, the golfing potential of Spain and Portugal is enormous. Pictured is the 15th hole at Praia D'El Rey, a surprising seaside find north of the Portuguese city of Lisbon.

Valderrama Golf Club

COURSE OPENED 1975
DESIGNER Robert Trent Jones

'I was guided in my design of Valderrama by the ideal of hard par; easy bogey.'

ROBERT TRENT JONES

OPPOSITE The pitch into Valderrama's notorious 17th hole is a special treat for those who have watched leading professionals succumb to the water here. Despite initial input from Seve Ballesteros and others, this par five is now as Robert Trent Jones had intended.

Although Valderrama is a recent phenomenon, its genesis can be traced back to 1975 when the Sotogrande Estate opened a second Robert Trent Jones layout to accompany its famous Old Course. The New Course, as it was first known, had major shortcomings and was sold in 1985 to a business consortium headed by Jaime Ortiz-Patiño, a Bolivian mining magnate who was a homeowner on the Sotogrande Estate and frustrated by the increasing traffic on his beloved Old Course. His group also acquired land surrounding the New Course that was earmarked for residential dwellings but essential to improve and extend the layout. The property was renamed Valderrama and, following a clash with his consortium, Ortiz-Patiño bought them out to become club president and the driving force behind its success.

Trent Jones always believed this course had enormous potential, and when contacted to repair the problems of the under-funded original was naturally delighted to be given a second bite at the design, and even more so to have extra acreage and a client who instructed him to work toward an 'ideal world with money a secondary consideration.' Determined to create a stern test for the world's best players, their first decision was to reverse the two nines, primarily to ensure the course had more of a sting in its tail but also because of plans to add a pond in front of the 17th green to create a dramatic penultimate championship hole. Trent Jones then spent several years personally working hole-by-hole through the layout, altering and reshaping each fairway and creating a terrific set of new greens, most being small, quick and full of breaks that are difficult to decipher. Many are built up and also guarded by punishing bunkers positioned to catch anything wayward and deep enough to extract the maximum penalty.

As a result of a preoccupation with providing professionals with a thorough challenge, for mere mortals Valderrama is a gruelling test that many find narrow and overly penal. The difficulty of the course is tee to green, as holes are cut through an established forest with a number of large, sprawling cork oaks likely to either catch your shot or block your approach if you are not driving the ball precisely. Tough to carry and at times impossible to bend around, some individual trees, like the one in the middle of the 2nd fairway or the beast blocking the right side of the 5th green, do seem a little too intrusive, while the short par four 8th and left-bending 18th are two of the enclosed holes that are horrendously cramped from the tee.

Although the difficulty of Valderrama is relentless, strong two-shot holes like the 2nd, 5th and 10th and approach play into the attractive built-up targets are among the many high points of the layout. As a set, the par threes are very solid, while controversial par fives like the 4th, with its cascading greenside pond, and the infamous 17th are both good

driving holes and great third-shot holes, the only negative being that neither is a realistic chance in two for the average golfer because of the severity of the targets. The 17th is much maligned by professionals because its green slopes steeply toward the pond and many have spun the ball back into water from the fairway. The front of the green plays like the 15th at Augusta and a swale between the green and its back bunkers is similar to Augusta's 13th, which makes missing long and chipping downhill toward the water a particularly nasty option. Played sensibly, though, the pitch across the pond is within most golfers' capabilities and a really fun shot to hit, especially given the hole's history.

Attractive and surprisingly undulating, Valderrama is close to ideal terrain for this sort of design, with none of the gradients too steep for sensible golf. Importantly, given the property's elevation and proximity to the sea, the direction of play changes constantly, making full use of the area's two distinct trade winds. President Ortiz-Patiño, a certified greenkeeper, is famously hands-on here and the club's success is as much due to his vision and drive as Trent Jones's solid design, especially in recent years when Valderrama has come to represent turf excellence. Unquestionably the most demanding course in Europe, and its finest from the last half-century, Valderrama has a huge reputation and is one high-profile course well worth its billing.

ABOVE Featuring a narrow target guarded by a pond, the pitch into the par five 4th hole can be quite a dangerous assignment.

OPPOSITE Tight through the trees and attractively bunkered, the 10th is an excellent undulating par four.

Praia D'El Rey Golf & Beach Resort

COURSE OPENED 1997
DESIGNER Cabell B. Robinson

'This is the kind of landscape we architects try to create, but at Praia D'El Rey it's all here naturally.'

CABELL B. ROBINSON

OPPOSITE Praia D'El Rey's par three 14th hole, complete with its stunning Atlantic backdrop.

An hour north of Lisbon lies Portugal's Silver Coast, an area of outstanding natural beauty blessed with rugged cliffs, pristine beaches, historic towns and the Praia D'El Rey golf course, itself an astonishing sensory experience. Designed by American architect Cabell B. Robinson, who spent 20 years working for Robert Trent Jones, Praia D'El Rey is part of a greater residential development and features a prominent section of spectacular holes that overlook the crashing surf of the Atlantic Ocean.

Opening in 1997, the development was first proposed during the late 1970s, and fortunately prior zoning permissions obtained by the original developer enabled Robinson to utilize the beachfront topography and route three holes right along the cliffs, something no longer possible in this part of the world. Away from the Atlantic, the rest of the course is either set within a fragrant and undulating pine forest or cast from pure white sand dunes covered in a thick indigenous ice plant.

Arranged in two clockwise loops, Praia D'El Rey starts in the thinned-out forest but quickly brings golfers within sight of the ocean at the 2nd and 3rd holes before heading back away from the water until midway through the back nine. The well-bunkered par four 12th doglegs toward the coast and is the hole that reintroduces players to the sea. It is then followed by a stunning three-hole stretch along the shoreline, which includes a beautiful short

hole sandwiched between dramatic par fours that are played through the coastal dunes. These are the holes that will linger longest in the memory, although they are by no means Praia's only attractions. Better offshore moments include the last part of the tumbling par five 2nd, the brilliant 4th and the plateau green on the 6th. The closing sequence is also strong. The 16th is a fine hole with an obscured drive and the 17th is a huge par five through a menacing sandbank that would be a great challenge were it not for the extreme target area.

Given the dramatic nature of the site and the fact that in many areas houses separate fairways and actually occupy some of the prime golf land, there is a major disparity between the best and worst of Praia D'El Rey, but Robinson did an admirable job routing his holes through as much duneland as he was given and with the restrictions involved in building a residential layout such as this. The highlights of his course are fantastic and quite strategic. The reachable par four 4th, for instance, features a massive sandy blow-out that gets progressively more in play the farther one drives from the tee, yet the clever green is tight and tricky to hold from any sort of distance. Similarly, the cliff-side 13th is another tempting gem, which is played across small ripples to a tiny green that is well protected but an enticing target despite the obvious perils.

Although none of the site could be described as dull, the best golf land here is quite extraordinary and a close look at the surrounding property reveals further potential classics were lost to bricks and mortar, which seems a golfing tragedy. There are also a couple of ponds on nice natural dune holes that are not ideal. This is a great place to visit, however, with the views, the weather and the opportunity to experience holes like 4, 13, 14, 15 and 16 something special. Indeed, with this offering less than an hour from Lisbon and close to the fortified medieval town of Óbidos, an historic National Heritage site that was traditionally given as a wedding gift by the King of Portugal to his new Queen, it is hard to understand why the Algarve is more popular with traveling golfers.

While it will break the hearts of some purists to read that the course featured in these photographs is part of an integrated housing development, the seaside terrain here is incredible and there are certainly more than enough quality golf holes within the layout for Praia D'El Rey to be recommended.

OPPOSITE Praia's 4th hole is one of the finest short par fours in the modern game, with the large sandy waste area a greater hazard the more aggressive one gets from the tee.

Campo de Golf El Saler

COURSE OPENED 1968

DESIGNER Javier Araña

Running alongside the Mediterranean's scenic coastal dunes, the 8th is a terrific short par four.

OPPOSITE Heading away from the dunes and into the trees, the 6th hole at El Saler features a green protected by large bunkers and one of Javier Araña's deceptive false fronts.

Designed by Javier Araña, Spain's most accomplished golf course architect, the El Saler Golf Club is located within a nature reserve outside the city of Valencia. Adjacent to the Mediterranean coastline and with a mix of virgin dunes and rolling woodland, the course is Araña's finest and has garnered considerable international acclaim since it opened back in 1968.

While part of this unique course occupies a prime stretch of sandhills, the majority of holes are laid out across pine-laden slopes and surrounded by thick woodland. Most are very good, but the stretch from the 2nd through to the 8th is outstanding and likely to leave golfers with their lasting impression of the round. The rolling 2nd, with its wicked green, and the par five 3rd, which is an excellent driving hole and famous for its enormous greenside bunker, are the best of the forested holes, while both the 6th and 7th, running from dune to pine and back again, are also very strong. The pick of the front nine, however, is the short par four 8th, which borders the sea and features a large sandy waste area between the fairway and the beach and a heavily sloped green that rewards those who can hug the more dangerous left side from the tee.

The golf on the back nine tends to be solid but fairly unspectacular until you reach the long par three 17th and its dune basin target area. Also excellent is the finishing par four that looks down the coastline from high atop a sandhill and tumbles across the undulations as it heads into a superb green site.

With a profusion of pine-covered dunes and a beautiful sea aspect, there are distinct similarities here with a track like Formby in Lancashire, although Araña's design is on a more adventurous scale. Throughout the course he employs artistic, and often penal, bunkering to accompany his bold green shapes, which are full of false fronts and severe contours that are quite tricky to read. Depending on conditions, and the state of your golf game, the false fronts on the greens will either be an added challenge or an overused nuisance. The strong par four 6th, for instance, running away from the sea and across a valley to a well-bunkered green, has a particularly nasty front, which makes stopping the ball downwind almost impossible. The 2nd and 8th, however, work much better because they are shorter and across the wind, and the greens are more in context with the type of shot required from back in the fairway.

It can be warm and humid here and as a result the grass is generally more lush than at the equivalent seaside courses in Britain, which will worry some but may be good news for those hoping to hold the cruel greens with their longer irons. You should also expect kikuyu roughs instead of fescues, a warm Mediterranean wind rather than the arctic chill of a stiff sea breeze and some extreme greens and enormous bunkers, but otherwise El Saler is a fairly authentic links-like experience and well worth a look.

Troia Golf Course

COURSE OPENED 1980
DESIGNERS Robert Trent Jones, Cabell B. Robinson

Designed by Robert Trent Jones and Cabell B. Robinson, Portugal's Troia golf course is an extremely demanding and exposed layout built over spotless sand dunes on the narrow Troia Peninsula, less than an hour south of Lisbon. Within sight of the sea and sandwiched between the peninsula's main arterial road and the ocean, the rolling fairways here are cut through pine trees and guarded by some of the smallest greens in golf.

The short holes are especially memorable. The 4th, like the 11th, is a gorgeous shot into a minuscule target that will only accept a perfectly struck approach, while the 17th is a stunning hole with a tiny green set obliquely beyond a sandy waste and ringed by traps that frame and highlight its curves. Other standout areas include the tight twisting 3rd hole, an evil tiered and raised sliver of green at the long par four 6th and the stretch of quality golf from the attractive 12th through to the 15th. Most of the fairways are narrow, while further complicating play is the large-scale bunkering, which occasionally blocks all access to the putting surfaces, demanding that golfers take the more dangerous aerial route into the greens.

Given the general standard of seaside golf in Europe, Troia is a rare find and much better than the ordinary layouts along the Algarve. Unfortunately, grooming and maintenance can be scrappy and the course is too tricked up to be genuine top shelf, but its diminutive targets framed by sprawling traps are an interesting take on the traditional links concept and there is enough fun throughout the round to please most visiting golfers.

Real Club de Golf Sotogrande – Old Course

COURSE OPENED 1964
DESIGNER Robert Trent Jones

The Old Course at Real Club de Golf Sotogrande, which opened more than a decade prior to Valderrama, was the first Robert Trent Jones course in Europe and one of the few on the continent that he personally designed. Although the standard of shaping and course grooming is a tier below its now famous sibling and the site is a little less consistently dramatic, there are similarities here, notably its established cork, pine and oak forest setting.

First impressions of Sotogrande are not great, as your round starts and finishes on fairly dull ground, but things improve from the 4th, which is the start of a nice stretch through to the 11th, where Trent Jones used elevation changes and built-up greens to create a number of exciting golf holes. Long valley par threes at the 4th and 8th are particularly effective, as are approach shots into plateau greens such as the 10th and 11th, the ledge green on the 5th, and the narrow 7th wedged between a pond and a mound. From the 12th, the course moves onto some strangely bland water holes and although the 15th is very good, it is not enough to save a pretty disappointing finish.

In its heart there are solid golf holes here, but the course is inconsistent and its extremities lack interesting undulation and inspired design. This is a significant club in Spain, however, as it popularized the now heavily developed Costa del Sol region. While Sotogrande is now a rung below the coast's best, it is still a step above the rest.

OPPOSITE Approaching the elevated 5th green on the Old Course at Sotogrande.

The Netherlands

Kennemer

Royal Hague

De Pan

Noordwijkse

There are numerous challenges to the long-held belief that Scotland was the birthplace of golf, the Romans, French, Germans and even the Chinese believing its origins can be traced back to ancient ball and stick games they had invented. The most plausible, however, seems to come from the Netherlands, a country that had strong trading links with the Scottish East Coast during the early part of the second millennium, and had played a game known as 'Colf' or 'Kolf' for more than a century prior to the birth of the Royal and Ancient game. Like golf, this medieval game was played on open country with the player having to drive a stationary ball toward a distant target using a stick that had a curved bottom.

Whether you accept golf's Dutch ancestry or not, there is much more to the Netherlands than clogs, bikes, tulips and windmills. In fact, considering its flat landscape, much of which lies below sea level, the quality of golf courses is surprisingly good. There are little more than a hundred courses in total here but the best are among Europe's finest, thanks largely to the influence of Harry Colt, who was prolific in Holland prior to the Second World War. Also important is an impressive fortified sand ridge along the country's coast that protects its lowland areas from the North Sea and provides an ideal home for three Dutch dune masterpieces – Kennemer, Noordwijkse and the very sporty Royal Hague.

Like most of the established golf countries on mainland Europe, the Netherlands has recently experienced considerable growth in golf course development, with some fairly disappointing results. For the best examples of design, therefore, you generally need to search out courses that pre-date World War II, despite the fact that the entire nation suffered terribly during the war years. Both the Colt gem at Kennemer and the first course at the Royal Hague Golf Club were totally destroyed by the Germans, though Kennemer has since been restored to something like its pre-war glory. While the big coastal dune layouts provide the standout golf experiences, the utterly charming De Pan course, also built by Colt and set within an attractive sandy forest near Utrecht, is the best of the inland golf. There are also fine heathland-style courses at Hilverschume and Eindhoven, which are both quite flat but do boast some interesting holes.

There is no denying that the Scots formalized the game of golf, but the Dutch almost certainly played a part in its genesis. The golfing landscape in Holland may seem worlds away from the links of Scotland, but its best golf actually occupies superbly undulating ground that is anything but dull. Unfortunately, in order to protect its precarious ecosystem there are strict environmental restrictions on golf courses here, including a ban on chemical use. Turf conditions as a result can be a little scratchy, but this policy is essential to protect low-lying farmlands and should not put you off a trip to one of Europe's premier golf destinations.

Kennemer Golf & Country Club – B & C Course

COURSE OPENED 1927

DESIGNER Harry S. Colt

The tantalizing short par four 10th hole
on the Colt layout.

OPPOSITE The 15th at Kennemer
is a mighty par three played to a severe
target perched atop a steep hill. Buried
beneath the green is part of a concrete
wall built during World War II.

A short drive from Amsterdam, the 27-hole
Kennemer Golf and Country Club is situated on
Holland's West Coast and is home to the oldest
seaside golf course in the country. The original
eighteen-hole layout was designed by Harry Colt
during the 1920s, but was virtually destroyed
during World War II when the occupying Nazi
forces built a massive concrete anti-tank barricade
across the links. Parts of the wall have since been
removed but a large section was simply covered
with sand during the restoration project and
remains within the site.

While Colt's original holes did not survive the
war years, there is no doubt that today's layout
would please him immensely, as the course has
been faithfully returned to near his initial concept.
This is largely due to the remarkable collection of
detailed correspondence between Colt and the
club, which somehow survived the conflict. Aside
from the tank wall, which scarred the landscape
forever, the only divergence from his plan was the
lengthening of the 3rd, a hole that Colt never
liked anyway.

Almost a mile from the ocean, the property
enjoys a seaside feeling thanks to an appealing mix
of large rolling duneland and smaller internal
contours that are covered in coastal underbrush
and exposed to the ever-present south-west sea
winds. Just as he did successfully at Muirfield, here
Colt arranged his course in two loops with the back
nine looped around the inner holes and boasting
more of the significant fairway movement. The
front nine is far from bland, however, and opens
with a very fine hole played across a series of

ripples and small ridges to an attractive green site.
The next is a neat par three played over flatlands
and into a heavily contoured plateau green atop a
dune saddle. After a string of solid holes, including
the improved 3rd, the course kicks up a gear at the
brilliant 9th, a strong par four heading along an
angled fairway that gently rises into an excellent
basin green.

The fun continues on the back nine, starting
with the terrific short par four 10th, which is semi-
blind from the tee to a wild fairway that narrows
significantly through dense rough as you approach
its small target. The impressive 15th, played across
a valley to the top of a steep dune, was Colt's
favorite hole and is the standout in a strong set of
par threes. It is also the start of a superb run home
that includes a reachable par five, a short par three
across a thorny gully and a charming finishing four
set in the shadows of the thatched-roof clubhouse.

While the playability of the layout would
improve with tighter fescue grasses in the fairway,
this is a terrific journey from start to finish with
barely an indifferent hole on the entire course.
There is also a third nine at Kennemer, which
opened in 1985. It is a long way behind the quality
of the Colt holes but significant because it was the
last work of architect Frank Pennink, who died
shortly after its completion.

Having emerged from a turbulent history with
one of the continent's most cherished golf courses,
Kennemer could do with a restoration of some of
its tired and neglected bunkering but otherwise
remains a charming links sure to satisfy even the
most discerning golfer.

Koninklijke (Royal) Haagsche Golf & Country Club

COURSE OPENED 1938
DESIGNER Harry S. Colt
with Charles H. Alison, John Morrison

The Koninklijke Haagsche Golf & Country Club, or Royal Hague, is the oldest golf club in Holland and was founded in 1893 on linksland that was later destroyed during World War II. The club's current course was designed by Harry Colt for a wealthy Dutch golfer in 1938, who then sold the layout to the homeless golf club in the late 1940s.

Despite its location two miles from the North Sea, Royal Hague is a dramatic big dune course that has a strong seaside feeling with mighty fairways that crash and tumble constantly and feature little shaping or man-made design outside the typically understated green sites. Some holes are almost dizzying in their scale, plunging and rising with dramatic proportions. Giving the layout its teeth are a number of heroic drives over ravines and gullies, plus fierce back tees on holes such as the 6th, 7th, 8th, 13th and 16th.

Course highlights include the short 7th, which is a terrific hole blind over a hill, then down to a delicious green nestled beside a large dune. The tumbling and rising 9th is another fine hole, as is the more subtle 11th and the wild 15th with its green beside a hill and beyond a frontal mound. The side-hill 16th across a ravine and then a small knoll, and the tree-lined par five finisher are also dynamic golf holes.

A well-preserved classic Colt layout, most of the original features here are retained, although all eighteen greens were recently renovated by Kyle Phillips after almost 70 years of wear and tear.

Utrechtse Golf Club – De Pan

COURSE OPENED 1928
DESIGNER Harry S. Colt

The Utrechtse Golf Club was formed back in 1894 and moved to an attractive forest outside Utrecht in the 1920s, with Englishman Harry Colt responsible for the design of its new golf course. The Colt creation, De Pan, was completed in 1928 and remains one of the game's true hidden gems.

Heavily treed and laid out over wonderfully undulating sandy terrain, the best holes at De Pan are covered in the same magnificent heather that typifies heathland golf in Britain and are among the most unusual on the European mainland. Examples include the par three 15th, with its narrow green cut into the side of a dune, and the long, rolling 6th hole, played over a rise and then around a large hill that obscures much of the green and a knoll that eats into its right side. Best of all, however, is the utterly original 10th hole, which is a gorgeous short four played through a small saddle gap between two big hills. Elsewhere the 4th green, the second half of the 5th and the short par four 7th, played over a dune and then around another, are also great fun. The 11th is another fine long hole, while the closing stretch from the 15th is particularly attractive, the drivable par four 17th a real standout routed through and then across a healthy cover of heather before the small rise into its excellent green site.

The second oldest golf club in Holland and one of the nation's most private, the course at De Pan is pure Colt and pure class.

OPPOSITE **Another view of the Kennemer Golf & Country Club, this time from the 14th fairway.**

Noordwijkse Golf Club

COURSE OPENED 1972

DESIGNER Frank Pennink

Noordwijkse's short 3rd hole introduces golfers to the woodland portion of the property.

OPPOSITE Played over a rise and then right into this charming green site, the 15th is an attractive two-shot hole.

Founded in 1915, the Noordwijkse Golf Club was based out of a nine-hole links until 1971, when its land was acquired by local authorities in Noordwijk for a housing project. Forced to move, the club then shifted a little north of the town and into a duneland property close to the North Sea that had enough room for a full eighteen-hole layout. While the new site is blessed with mostly ideal golfing terrain, it does also include dense woodland areas that are unfortunately over-planted and interfere badly with several holes, especially on the less consistent front nine.

The modern Noordwijkse was designed by Frank Pennink, apparently with the assistance of club secretary Paul de Jong, and is a difficult links, with most challenges provided by the enduring winds and dangerous bumpy linkscape. Pennink's routing takes you to all points of the compass, with holes laid out across some fairly dramatic sandhills. Sensibly on such an exposed site, the holes are not over-designed, most greens are small, flat and generally flanked by single traps. Aside from the native rough areas and tall pines, from the tee there is an absence of driving hazards with the only fairway bunkers coming on the 18th and seemingly built to protect the 17th tee.

The holes cut through the trees are the links' clear weakness, as over the years they have become terribly narrow, almost to the point of being claustrophobic. The ground is mostly very good for golf, however, and were the 4th through 7th and the front of the 11th cut back, the club would uncover some fine holes, especially the difficult 5th and the narrowing 4th hole, which has an out-of-bounds area running down the left side of a falling fairway that demands a left-sided drive.

Within the open and exposed duneland the standout holes include rolling par fives at the 2nd and 11th and the short par four 8th, played over a rise, then down and around some decent-sized dunes. Strong links holes like the 10th, 13th and 14th are also good, while the 15th and 16th are both mid-length par fours built on superbly pitching golf land that feature excellent green sites. The disparity between the quality of holes is perhaps best illustrated on the par threes, as the 17th is a tremendous long shot into a dune ledge and vastly superior to the previous short holes, which are all among the trees and disappointing despite some interesting land.

While there is no doubt that the setting here is conducive to good golf, the course would be greatly improved with some serious clearing of its heavily wooded areas. As it stands, there is still much to admire about Noordwijkse and its challenging links, though the current layout is a long way from fulfilling its true potential.

Rest of Europe

Hamburger
Circolo Golf Bogogno
Eichenheim
Falsterbo

Golf on continental Europe has a long and often checkered history. The first course was created more than 150 years ago but the game has only recently started to grow with any real momentum. Pioneering course designers such as Willie Park Jr, Harry Colt and Tom Simpson were the first to introduce quality design to the mainland and worked hard to spread the appeal of the game through their courses, but the turmoil of major conflict and decades of resistance to anything British have left the region hurting for worthwhile golf.

Although there are some tremendous courses on offer in France, Holland and parts of the Iberian Peninsula, golf on the European mainland is largely disappointing. This is especially true of modern courses, which are generally American in style but built with smaller budgets and rarely of the standard one would travel any distance to play. Beyond those layouts reviewed in this book, other European courses of note include Belgium's best classics, Ravenstein (Royal Golf Club de Belgique) and Spa (Les Fagnes) by Simpson and Royal Zoute by Colt, which have all been dated by technology and are well below the class of course found in Britain, but still worth a look.

Aside from Colt's incredible Falkenstein course, a few holes at Frankfurter and decent efforts at Sporting Club Berlin (Faldo) and the lavishly Americanized South Course at the nearby Seddiner See, the remainder of golf-hungry Germany is poor. In neighboring Austria the game is not hugely popular but the players are enthusiastic and courses like the immaculate Fontana near Vienna, and Eichenheim in the stunning mountain town of Kitzbühel are likely to entice new players into the game. Like Austria, Switzerland has some stunning sites but little to recommend beyond the views of Crans-sur-Sierre and a very enjoyable members' course at the Geneva Golf Club.

In Sweden, where the game has grown most significantly, the courses are crowded from sunrise to sunset during their short season and layouts of note include Falsterbo, Ljunghusen, Svartinge, the gorgeous lakeside Ullna course and the short Stockholm Golf Club, which has lost several holes but still retains much of its original Colt charm. The oldest club in Scandinavia, Denmark's Kobenhavns (Royal Copenhagen) Golf Club, is also one of the most memorable, built within the vast windswept grounds of a historic castle alive with roe deer that prance around gracefully as you golf.

The Italian lakes district north of Milan has developed into a popular golf destination and Villa D'Este, Biella and the adjacent Circolo Bogogno and Castelconturbia courses do form an enjoyable foursome. The charming Roma Acquasanta course, which is a few miles from the center of Rome and overlooks an ancient aqueduct, is an interesting layout, while the Is Arenas course and the million-dollar views of Pevero on the island of Sardinia are also enjoyable. Throughout the rest of Europe, golf is still relatively new but slowly starting to become more mainstream and there is great potential here, particularly in the eastern nations.

With the open borders and open markets of the new Europe making travel easier on the continent, more and more golfers are turning the obligatory European holiday into a combined golf and sightseeing tour. While the mainland is not a genuine threat to the British Isles yet, there have been some incredible golf sites developed in recent decades, and advances made in construction and design mean there is hope that the future will bring some great golf to this wonderful part of the world.

Hamburger Golf Club – Falkenstein

COURSE OPENED 1930
DESIGNER Harry S. Colt
with Charles H. Alison
and John Morrison

The final third of the par five 2nd hole.

Having firmly established himself as Britain's preeminent golf course architect prior to the First World War, Harry Colt and his partners were keen to help drive the game's development onto the European mainland once hostilities had ceased. By 1928, prosperity was returning to Germany and the Hamburger Golf Club looked to expand its facilities by moving away from Hamburg and into a pine- and birch-covered forest in nearby Falkenstein. With ideal golf ground and a remarkable resemblance to the best in Surrey's Heathland, Colt was the obvious choice for designer and was brought in to suggest plans for the new course.

Given the topography and the designer, Falkenstein was always going to have a classic British appearance, but Colt did some of his best and most original work here, routing a string of tremendous holes across a series of hills and ridges covered in the same glorious heather that made his courses in London so distinctive. Interestingly, for a brief period following the Allied victory in World War II the course was taken over by the British army, which golfed here and must have been delighted to discover this little slice of English heathland in northern Germany.

Despite the turmoil of the war years and subsequent decades of hardship, Falkenstein has changed little and remains a very true account of Colt's golf philosophies. Aside from a couple of traps early in the round, his bunkering style is well preserved with rugged hazards protecting key driving areas and terrific greens that are often raised and feature just enough movement without being overdone.

The course starts with a fairly soft opening hole that climbs into a small incline, the outward nine then skirting beside a large ridge until you reach the audacious 6th, which plays over one hill and then rises substantially into another. The back nine tends to occupy the most dramatic portion of the property and features standout holes like the 17th and the beautiful 12th and 13th holes, the latter with an unusual central bunker sitting on a ledge and forcing you to either lay back for a tricky uphill approach or really flirt with danger to get close to the green.

Although the par threes are less distinguished here than at Colt's best courses in London, the longer holes are superb and more than make up for any shortcomings. Best of all is the wonderfully natural 17th, a cracking par five that technology has turned into a two-shotter and remarkably improved. From the tee, its crested fairway falls to the left, kicking an ideal drive with a touch of draw farther toward the target but leaving those who over-cook the shot either in sand or with a longer second angled toward further bunkers. With a gorgeous green nestled in a bowl and framed by another heather-covered hill, this is one of those rare holes that is both attractive and architecturally outstanding.

Falkenstein is a little short by modern standards but its par of 70 is well protected and the fact that it remains a strong test more than 75 years after being built speaks volumes for both the suitability of the property and the genius of Colt's design. The club also deserves a great deal of credit for faithfully preserving its best features and maintaining the integrity of the initial layout. Germany's premier golf club, Hamburger is blessed with one of the few genuinely world-class golf experiences available on the European mainland.

Circolo Golf Bogogno – Bonora Course

COURSE OPENED 1996/2000
DESIGNER Robert von Hagge
with Rick Baril

View of the 17th hole on the del Conte Course.

OPPOSITE Bending around a pond but artistically framed by the von Hagge bunker shapes, the opening hole on the Bonora Course is a challenging uphill par five.

Established with the opening of its first Robert von Hagge course in 1996, Circolo Golf Bogogno is an impressive 36-hole golf and residential estate set in a sheltered wooded valley in the northern Italian lakes district. Both its Bonora and del Conte courses are made up of nine holes from the original eighteen and another nine completed by von Hagge in 2000.

While the del Conte Course enjoys excellent views of the distant Alps, the Bonora Course is superior for its more consistent test and the use of natural streams and ponds to create a number of fine resort-style golf holes. The bunkering throughout is both attractive and artistic, although not always used strategically as traps are often placed on the outside of fairways that bend around hazards which themselves offer better angles of attack into the greens. A feature of von Hagge's work is the use of unnatural looking mounding, but here the shapes around green and bunker edges, in particular, look less artificial, as the fescues and native grasses give a rugged appearance and help them blend in with their surrounds.

An early example of both his strategy and style is the eye-catching par five opening hole, which bends right around a stream and then heads gradually up to a nicely bunkered green with sand down the left side. Back in the fairway, the left-hand traps are almost superfluous but make a big visual statement from the tee. Other quality moments include the last half of the long 3rd hole, the narrow 4th and 8th, and pretty holes like the 11th, the par three 13th across a murky pond and the dramatic 17th bending gently left around a stream that cuts across the fairway and feeds a pond hard-up against the right side of its slender green. The Cape-style 17th around a lake on the del Conte Course is also memorable both for the quality of the hole and the glamorous Monte Rosa backdrop.

A feature of both courses that works particularly well is the deliberately unkempt appearance of the hazards and periphery areas. Both courses have plenty of ponds and streams and the water is deliberately dirty, murky and brown to offset the lush greens and bright whites of the golf course. Reeds, weeds, vines and thorns are all used to add to the messy surroundings and provide an authentic Italian flavor. The housing is also a class act as the villas are well spread and the complete lack of neat garden beds and pristine lakes gives this a natural and utterly Italian feel and makes it one of Europe's most pleasant golf and residential combinations.

The modern golf estate has never seemed so antique as it does here at Bogogno and it is easy to become swept away in its rustic charms. Although golf is unlikely ever to be your primary reason for visiting Italy, if it is, make sure that Circolo Golf Bogogno is your first port of call.

Eichenheim Golf Club

COURSE OPENED 2000
DESIGNER Kyle Phillips

The historic medieval village of Kitzbühel, high in the Austrian Alps, is home to the Kyle Phillips-designed Eichenheim course, which is one of the finest mountain tracks on the continent and a clear standout in golf-starved Austria.

Built on heavily undulating countryside, the course overlooks the surrounding Alpine area and enjoys magnificent views of the distant mountain peaks and its deciduous forests, natural creeks and attractive canyons. Compromised in some regards by problems obtaining all of the necessary land required to build the course, Phillips' routing is well balanced and manages to squeeze in enough good golf to make the layout enjoyable. Most memorable are the holes aligned to use the snow-capped peaks and Alpine valleys as a backdrop, the short par four 7th being the highlight as it rises and turns to face one of the region's most gigantic mountains.

The Phillips design style for this particular project is distinctly American, with large artistic bunkering employed to attract the eye and greens built with steps and tiers and surrounded by mounding. The course does get hilly in places, which makes it tough to walk, but you will need somewhere to store the camera, so taking a cart is certainly not frowned upon.

One of the most beautiful countries on earth, Austria as a golf destination is a new concept. While most of the older courses here mix average golf with great scenery, Eichenheim is the first, and hopefully not the last, to get the quality of the golf close to the standard of the scenery.

Falsterbo Golf Club

COURSE OPENED 1930
DESIGNER Dr Gunnar Bauer

One of Sweden's oldest golf clubs, Falsterbo was founded in 1909 in a small village on the tip of a scenic peninsula south of Malmö. Members originally golfed on a nine-hole layout designed by Copenhagen Golf Club's professional Robert Turnball on a thin strip of linksland around the area's lighthouse. In 1930 the course was extended to eighteen holes by a local medical practitioner, who kept Turnball's excellent 7th and 14th holes, but otherwise fashioned an entirely new links on the low-set, bumpy terrain.

Occupying one of Europe's windiest golf locations, the flat ground is totally exposed to the elements and located within a native reserve frequented by bird watchers who flock to the area in their thousands during autumn to witness the bird migrations. Protected from the water by a moderate dune ridge, the layout features several marsh areas left by the receding sea and boasts a number of decent holes, starting with the medium-length par four 4th played along the wetlands to its peninsula green. The partially hidden one-shot 8th and demanding driving holes at 9 and 12 across hazards are also solid. As is the finishing stretch, starting with the long par three 14th, which heads toward the lighthouse and over a huge bunker that hides its receptive green complex. Both the 16th and 17th are classic right-bending par fours that reward those driving close to the inside sand traps, while the 18th is a reachable par five along the dunes where a wild slice could actually end up in the Baltic Sea.

Although a recent greens and bunker restoration program by Peter Nordwall and Peter Chamberlain has successfully addressed areas of concern here, course conditioning still remains very hit or miss. The links, however, is a stern test and for all its quirk, Falsterbo is quite a memorable experience.

OPPOSITE Rugged bunkers surround the par four 7th green at Falsterbo.

North & South America

OPPOSITE Even excluding the golfing powerhouse that is the United States, there is much to admire about golf on the North American continent. Pictured here is the par five 9th hole at the exclusive Oviinbyrd Course in Canada.

Canada

The second-largest country in the world, Canada is a land of immense geographical diversity and its countryside, and its golf courses, are blessed with some of the finest scenery on earth. That golf was introduced here before the United States may surprise some, but it was driven by the massive immigration of Scots to Canadian shores during the late 19th century and was first formalized in 1873 when a group of frustrated expats formed the (Royal) Montreal Golf Club, the first in North America. Golf clubs then propagated with great speed and, like in many countries, its best courses were created prior to World War II, and mostly by legendary local designer Stanley Thompson.

Known as the 'Toronto Terror,' Thompson started out as a caddy before becoming Canada's most prominent golfing figure, designing or remodeling more than 140 courses worldwide. His best were in Canada and though he was given some glorious golf sites here, his work in the Rockies at Banff and Jasper is the stuff of legend, while Capilano was a brilliant result from a difficult site and St George's remains one of the finest parkland courses on the continent. His pièce de résistance, however, is the isolated and wonderful Highlands Links course in the Cape Breton Highlands National Park.

Quality golf in Canada is concentrated in its more temperate southern regions and scattered from the spectacular Rockies in the west through golf-rich Ontario and into Nova Scotia in the east. The largest collection of good courses is in Ontario, the area from Toronto to Hamilton being a Canadian Sandbelt of sorts and dotted with older layouts of real class, mostly either designed or in some part shaped by Thompson. Unfortunately, aside from the likes of Bigwin Island, Glen Abbey, Redtail, Beacon Hall and the few courses featured within these pages, most of the modern golf here is frustrating.

Elsewhere, Greywolf in the Rockies, Taboo and Oviinbyrd in the popular Muskoka district and the Links at Crowbush Cove on Prince Edward Island are among the better efforts, but the majority of new courses are American in style and disappointing, as budgets tend to be smaller than in the United States, the golf seasons shorter and grass-growing conditions less favorable. Talented local architect Ron Whitman has managed to build two very fine layouts near Edmonton. The Wolf Creek course from 1984 is a man-made dune structure of considerable believability and quality, while his newer Blackhawk layout has wonderful ambience and interesting strategic design elements. Also noteworthy is the golf on Vancouver Island, which includes Royal Colwood, Bear Mountain and the terribly sporty Victoria Golf Club which, like La Phare at Biarritz in France, is short, narrow, cramped and split by a road but does boast a couple of absolute gems.

Though once a British colony, economically and culturally Canada has developed more in parallel with its southern neighbor, and there is now a heavy American influence on golf development and design. That said, Canadians are fiercely patriotic and, in fairness, their most beloved classic courses are very distinctive. Golf can be a mixed bag here, however, so choose your itinerary carefully, as the best layouts are terrific, but the country's landscape is so beautiful that sightseeing, rather than golf, is sometimes a better option.

OPPOSITE Stanley Thompson's legendary Devil's Cauldron hole (the 4th) at Banff Springs in the Canadian Rockies.

Highlands Links – Cape Breton Highlands National Park

COURSE OPENED 1939
DESIGNER Stanley Thompson

'Nature must always be the architect's model.'

STANLEY THOMPSON

OPPOSITE Crossing part of a lake and featuring a clever green with a diagonal ridge, the short 3rd is one of the many highlight holes at Highlands Links.

Unlike most of the classic courses in North America, the idea to bring golfers to the remote eastern province of Nova Scotia was formed during the Depression years of the 1930s, the National Park Services of Canada hoping to stimulate tourism interest in Cape Breton Island by building a world-class golf course within its stunning Highlands National Park. Course architect Stanley Thompson spent weeks studying aerial photographs of the park and scouring a property boasting an abundance of breathtaking ocean, river and mountain views to find his ideal layout. Despite clear instructions, much of the land he selected for his holes actually sat outside the boundaries of the National Park, but Thompson convinced authorities to forcibly acquire land from more than twenty landowners and then eased their pain by ensuring all were well compensated and offered jobs during the construction process.

Thompson's elaborate plans for Highlands included an out-and-back routing with extraordinary variety. Starting beside the Atlantic shoreline, the course crosses a lake tributary and river mouth marshland before following the Clyburn River through a hardwood forest and finally heading back toward the coastline and ending within an undulating woodland. Beyond the mix of landscapes, the sequence of holes here is also unconventional, as are some of the long and tiring walks between greens and tees, but building Highlands Links was an epic achievement and the journey through the course reflects this.

After a bumpy and bunkerless opener, the 2nd is the first of Highlands' great holes. Also bunkerless, its downhill approach ends with a steep back-to-front

green that is set beyond a small swale and angled in from all sides. The shape and challenge of this target is remarkable, as is the delightfully natural short par three 5th green, which is a shallow half-pipe cut from the left by a big slope off the surrounding hillside. Following the 5th is a par five adjacent to the river mouth, which is a nice driving hole but shaded by other excellent three-shotters like the short and bumpy 16th, one of those seemingly innocuous holes that continue to bemuse even the most regular players. Other moments of note include the short par four 4th, its narrow green sitting atop a steep knob, the semi-blind 9th, par four 13th and wonderfully original par fives at the 7th and 15th. The finishing holes are also impressive, and notorious for the shallow and crumpled target at the short 17th and an immense putting surface full of savage contours on the strategic two-shot 18th. Cleverly shaped green sites like these are a real highlight throughout the course, with the likes of 2, 4, 5, 7, 16 and 18 particularly memorable.

Despite a seaside location and some of the bumpiest land found anywhere outside the British Isles, Highlands Links is not a true links, although the design style and introduced marram grasses do give it an authentic feel. Unfortunately, the course does suffer from a short season and an unnecessary lushness, courtesy of its new irrigation system, but it has put the Cape Breton region, and in many ways Canada, on the golfing map. A tribute to Thompson's design genius, Highlands Links is a genuine masterpiece and remains one of the finest and most remote outposts in golf.

St George's Golf and Country Club

COURSE OPENED 1929
DESIGNERS Stanley Thompson,
Robbie Robinson

One of the restored bunkers protecting
the difficult 2nd green.

A privileged members-only golf and country club, St George's actually started life in 1929 as a public course built within one of Canada's first golf developments close to downtown Toronto. With a growing reputation for producing fine golf courses on fine golf land, Stanley Thompson was selected as course designer and offered first pick of the 2,000-acre site for his holes. His choice of beautiful rolling woodland was inspired, as was his use of the natural ravines and gullies that run through the property, Thompson routing holes along, across and often through them with tremendous variety.

With a more strategic bent than many of Thompson's other famous works, St George's places a great premium on accuracy from the tee, its tight greens difficult to hit when out of position but often enticing enough to encourage golfers to gamble on a heroic recovery. The round begins with a beautifully bunkered uphill par four that is followed by the tough 2nd, one of several terrific driving holes that demand a precise drive down the dangerous side to set up a decent angle into the target. The 4th and 5th feature major undulation and reward those who take an aggressive line down the right with a relatively flat lie, while the cross-gully 6th and semi-dell 8th are both fun par threes.

Back nine highlights include the subtle rolls and ridges of the 10th fairway and the notorious par four 12th, with massive bunkers down the left side of a right-sloping fairway and a green sitting on a ledge that is more difficult to hit the farther right you stray. Also memorable is the 14th, where you must drive long and straight to reach the

OPPOSITE Thompson's tremendous
cross-gully par three 6th hole.

downslope or face crossing the diagonal creek from a hanging lie. The finish is rightly acclaimed as one of Canada's best. A tough par three at 16 is followed by the impossibly difficult 17th, originally conceived as a par five and still featuring its tiny three-shot green, and the strong, slow-rising 18th played through mature trees and striking greenside bunkers.

St George's has been altered many times over the years, most significantly prior to the 1968 Canadian Open, when the club was convinced it faced becoming redundant and hired Thompson protégé Robbie Robinson to lengthen the layout. Controversially, he stretched the 4th and 15th holes into par fives by shifting both greens back and on top of steep hills. He also moved the 9th green and sadly replaced the flatter but still interesting 3rd green with a shallow and severe target quite out of context with Thompson's general philosophies on green shaping.

Decades of further alteration and general decay were mercifully reversed in 2003 and 2004 by the careful work of Ian Andrew and Doug Carrick, who were able to faithfully restore the look and feel of St George's through an extensive bunker restoration program. This involved using early aerial photographs and maps to reshape existing traps back into the Thompson form and return those that had been removed. Archived pictures and old course reviews confirm how good St George's original layout was. Now, thanks to this successful touch-up job, it is once again the premier parkland course in Canada.

Toronto Golf Club

COURSE OPENED 1912

DESIGNER Harry S. Colt

The strong par four 15th rises into this excellent green complex.

OPPOSITE Toronto Golf Club's picture-perfect 9th hole.

The third oldest golf club in North America, Toronto Golf Club was founded in 1876 and moved to its present location beside the Etobicoke River in 1909, when its existing property was swallowed up by the expanding Toronto city limits. The new locale was ideal, only a short distance from the city and full of the sort of natural pitch and fall needed to create interesting golf holes.

Blessed with such a suitable site and armed with a generous budget, British architect Harry Colt was able to build a real monument for the membership, his course opening in 1912 to almost immediate acclaim. As Canada's first great layout, Toronto's influence spread far beyond the mere appreciation of its members. One of the club's young caddies, Stanley Thompson, would grow up studying Colt's ideas both here and at his nearby Hamilton course, and go on to become a design legend in Canada.

Much has changed in the decades since the course first opened. Trees have grown and caddies are no longer part of the club fabric, but thankfully the membership has remained a diligent and dedicated custodian of Colt's timeless architecture. An entry road did force a minor shift in the first fairway many years back, and the bunkering on the par three 14th is clearly not original, but otherwise the course is largely unaltered and sensible tree management and careful restoration programs ensure it will remain very much in line with the Colt vision well into the future.

Beyond the good holes and interesting green sites that Colt is renowned for, his greatest achievement at Toronto was a brilliant routing that makes full use of all of the property's natural features and movement. After a flattish start he grabs your attention with a superb Redan at the par three 4th, its shallow putting surface hidden beyond a ridge and small gully and sloping away from play. The crested landing area and plateau green of the 5th are also fabulous, as is the one-shot 7th, which plays diagonally across a substantial chasm with a bunker waiting to catch those who succumb to the fear of pushing one into the abyss. Played between a trickling creek and a high, fescue-covered hill, the 9th is Toronto's most attractive hole, while its most adventurous is the par five 13th, which heads through a saddle and is then blind over a large crest. The finish from the heavily tilted 15th is special as well, particularly the second shot from atop the 16th fairway and the tough par three 17th. Though many dislike the short 18th, it does feature an attractive pitch from a hog's-back across a deep hollow into the big, sloping green, a hole unlikely to terrorize you but a fun finish, nonetheless, to a wonderful round.

Despite being too short for today's young stars, Toronto's par of 70 is no pushover and provides a much more comprehensive examination of your skills than the more difficult, but more one-dimensional, modern courses in the Toronto area. Along with St George's and Highlands Links, this is the most internationally significant Canadian golf course, and while the club's long history is impressive, it is the quality of Colt's routing and the influence his layout had on future design here that makes this charming club so special.

Capilano Golf & Country Club

COURSE OPENED 1938

DESIGNER Stanley Thompson

The reachable par five 3rd.

OPPOSITE The par three 14th at Capilano drops 25 feet over an entrance road to a terrific green that is bunkered on one side and falls away to a creek on the other.

Situated on Vancouver's north shore, the Capilano Golf & Country Club lies within a prime residential estate developed in the 1920s and 30s by Ireland's Guinness Brewery Family. Blessed with terrific views over the city's harbor, the course is a credit to designer Stanley Thompson, who was able to choose his preferred golf land from the 6,000-acre mountainside property but still had the difficult job of routing holes up, down and across the severely sloping ground.

The first six holes plunge more than 200 feet downhill from the clubhouse and Thompson cleverly laid out the remaining holes in such a way that you rarely sense there is a noticeable uphill gradient to any of them, except for the treacherous par three 9th. He was also seemingly able to use every natural feature on the site within his design, including the valleys and gullies, small ridges or the narrow creekside basin area.

Beyond an inspired routing, Capilano is best recommended for its brilliant greens, which blend almost seamlessly with the surroundings and are largely full of wicked tilts either forward or sideways. Hitting the right areas is absolutely vital, as downhill and cross-slope putts at Capilano in the peak of summer are among the most difficult in Canada. Even the small number of blandish holes at 2, 5 and 10, for instance, are rescued by really good green sites while others, like 1, 3 and 12, with landing areas or turn points dated by technology, are

still fascinating for their terrific targets. The 12th is now a fairly basic drive across corner traps but the short valley approach is into an immense plateau putting surface that has a steep false front to catch the timid and a severely downhill and breaking putt awaiting those who are too strong.

Generally speaking, Capilano has been lovingly preserved by its appreciative membership, although some of the newer bunkers are less visually impressive than the classically shaped originals. Changes to the 6th green and the softening of the contours on the tempting 14th have also been unfortunate. A mid-length drop-shot par three with a small target abutting a creek, the 14th still provides a great lesson on how to make the overused plunging par three effective. Just like the 11th hole, which heads over water into a massively back-to-front-sloping green, every pin placement here brings about a different challenge, with the same dilemma of how hard to press and just where to bail out.

The other par threes are also very good, while the par fives, except for the 18th, are short by today's standards yet frustratingly difficult to birdie. That leaves the par fours and, like most Thompson tracks, Capilano is very much a second shot course. You can usually drive anywhere within the fairways and still have workable angles into the pins. An exception is a hole like 13, where your drive flirts with a dangerous gully and has to be

precise in order to set up a decent shot over the valley and into its shallow green. Although Thompson's collection of two-shot holes is more varied at St George's and Jasper, this group includes some of his finest green complexes. Targets at 2, 3, 12, 13, 15 and 17 are all wonderful, many slanting toward a single flanking trap, meaning that hitting away from sand is often followed by a slippery downhill chip or putt.

From the mighty 13th the run home is first-class, with some superb architecture on awkward land and a great variety of challenges. The long and open par three 16th is an excellent test, as is the fabulous finishing hole, which ends beneath the clubhouse, its tricky green sitting on a shelf above the fairway and beyond a small ridge. Ignoring the beautiful scenery and a number of fine holes that dot the landscape, the overwhelming sense here is of a remarkable routing achievement on a fairly difficult site. Capilano is an exceptional golf club and its course is not only the best on Canada's west coast but among the best few in any of its provinces.

ABOVE Surrounded by cedars and protected by a pond that its large target leans toward, the 11th is another of Capilano's fine par threes.

OPPOSITE Looking toward the mountains and back down the finishing fairway from behind the elevated 18th green.

Jasper Park Lodge Golf Club

COURSE OPENED 1925

DESIGNER Stanley Thompson

Thompson's testing 240-yard 4th hole.

OPPOSITE Framed by the distant
mountains and played alongside a glacial
lake, the short par four 14th is one of
the most attractive holes at Jasper Park.

The first of Stanley Thompson's two alpine classics, the Jasper Park Lodge golf course was built in a large lakeside valley and framed by some of Alberta's most magnificent mountain ranges. Unlike his Banff Springs site, where the mountains directly overlook the course, here they provide a more distant backdrop, although with peaks soaring up to 11,000 feet the setting is no less impressive.

With the densely covered hills and ridges cleared in advance by a large construction team, Thompson was able to make full use of the property's natural elevation changes, building a great variety of holes to create a true golfing adventure. Using Mother Nature's generous gifts as inspiration, he aligned many holes with the surrounding mountain ranges and even shaped some of his features to mimic their distant peaks. Notoriously, he also left mounding in the shape of a curvaceous woman on the 9th hole following a dispute with the owners, Thompson only agreeing to finish the hole once he had been paid.

Labeled Cleopatra, the 9th is one of five fabulous par threes that include the long 4th and the difficult pitching wedge 15th, its tiny target sitting on a small knob and falling harshly on all sides. Miss the green here and you will do very well to limit the damage to a bogey. With the exception of the tumbling 13th, its sunken green hidden beyond a small ridge, the par fives are all reachable but tricky to birdie. The par fours meanwhile are an eclectic mix of styles, with better holes including the fine cross-hill 3rd, which bends up into a small basin, and the brutal, bunkerless 8th hole that plays through two mounds and against the slope before rising toward a skinny hillside green.

Further highlights include the 14th, which demands a careful lay-up through pine trees and along a lake followed by a short-iron approach into a super-small plateau green. The finishing holes are also very strong, particularly the sweeping and dipping 18th, its wonderfully bunkered and contoured green site an appropriately grand finish for such a tremendous course.

Thompson clearly understood his target market and, like at his other resort courses, built Jasper with more width and forgiveness than at his private clubs. He also left most greens open at the front to allow players of all abilities to handle the test. Despite being of only modest length and set amid the rarefied air of the Rockies, which further shortens holes, the par of 71 here is surprisingly well defended, chiefly through a combination of constantly changing elevation and some clever architecture, like the tendency to site bunkers back from greens but with flashed up faces to deceive golfers into believing they are greenside.

When it opened, Jasper Park was an immediate success and its quality prompted the great Dr Alister MacKenzie to declare in 1928 that, 'Canada has taken the lead in golf course architecture and produced eighteen holes that within the whole scope of my experience and knowledge are not surpassed.' Although the course has had maintenance issues since, a recent restoration program has successfully reclaimed some of the lost characteristics of Thompson's original design and ensured that the Jasper layout is once again among the finest mountain courses in the world.

Hamilton Golf & Country Club – Ancaster

COURSE OPENED 1916
DESIGNER Harry S. Colt

'If you have the money to spend, there is no reason why you should not have one of the finest golf courses in America.'

HARRY COLT TO THE HAMILTON
GOLF & COUNTRY CLUB

OPPOSITE The attractive uphill opening hole on the South Nine at Hamilton (10th hole on the Championship Course).

The Hamilton Golf & Country Club was born in 1894 when golfing enthusiasts established a twelve-hole layout within the town of Hamilton, just outside of Toronto. Member dissatisfaction with a subsequent eighteen-hole course prompted a move to nearby Ancaster in 1914, with British architect Harry Colt called in to provide the design. While Colt squeezed a great layout out of subtle landforms at the nearby Toronto Golf Club, at Ancaster he created an outstanding course on a dramatic property full of significant elevation change and broad undulations.

Unlike Toronto and those Colt designed in London's Heathland, Hamilton cannot claim to have totally and faithfully maintained its layout in the purest traditions of the designer. This is in part owing to continual expansion, but also because the club seeks to host regular championship events, which often force unnecessary change upon established courses. The original bunkers, for instance, were rugged, deep, generally grass-faced and deliberately kept untidy, typical of Colt's approach to bunkering. Over the years, and especially in recent times, the club has lost this classic feel by first adding traps with a sharper, more modern look and then renovating most of the originals in this same style. The result is a slightly disjointed-looking golf course, especially to Colt fans who may recognize the holes but probably not the unusual bunker mix.

Hamilton's strength is its routing. While Colt famously planned most courses around his par threes, here the longer holes steal the show, despite 6, 8 and 13 all being fine one-shotters. Featuring a two-tier fairway and creek crossing, the narrow 3rd is the first standout, followed soon after by the brilliant 5th with its drivable green set on a small rise beyond right-side bunkers and angled away to ensure that bombers who overcompensate and pull their drive have little chance of getting the pitch close.

On the back nine an attractive dipping and rising 10th hole and tough, left-bending 11th are equally impressive, as is the stirring finishing hole, its fairway cut by a snaking creek and rising majestically into a basin green set beneath the colossal clubhouse. A bend in this naturally winding creek was strangely straightened on the preceding hole to allow weaker hitters to negotiate it more easily from the tee. Another frustrating modification is the penal front left greenside bunker added to the quirky dogleg 7th hole, whose rippled fairway falls away from the target and was clearly conceived by the designer to reward those who can punch a drive down its narrow left side. Of the other changes, the most positive was the shifting of the green at the long par three 13th onto a rise beyond a series of side-slopes, a clear improvement on Colt's less dramatic original.

Over the years Colt's course has been stretched more than 500 yards and its par reduced by three, primarily to ensure the layout provides a difficult test for major events. With its dramatic elevation change, sloping greens and tremendous variety, Hamilton is certainly a course that forces more thought from the good players than simply which wedge to hit. While most of the routing remains unaltered, there is no doubt that if the club were able to better balance what are genuine improvements with what should never have been touched, Hamilton would be back among the best two or three courses in Canada.

The Fairmont Banff Springs Golf Course

COURSE OPENED 1928

DESIGNER Stanley Thompson

The distinctive bunkering of the 14th (formerly the 18th) at Banff Springs.

OPPOSITE What was once the fabulous opening hole is now the 15th, with the drive still an exhilarating shot from an elevated tee across the river.

OVERLEAF Banff's breathtaking scenery is on display as you approach the strategically bunkered 5th green.

High in the Rocky Mountains of Alberta, the Banff Springs golf course is a Stanley Thompson design that lies in a valley beneath both the majestic Fairmont 'Castle in the Clouds' hotel and the magnificent Banff mountain range. Having successfully built the Jasper Park golf course for a Canadian rail company, Thompson was approached by a rival company to completely overhaul its existing course at Banff, which dated back to 1911 and had been tweaked by Donald Ross in the years prior.

Recognizing the potential in the glorious alpine scenery, the designer blasted parts of the surrounding mountain range, cleared land alongside the glacial Bow River, routed holes toward distant peaks and shifted the course back toward the stunning hotel to create a smorgasbord for the senses. In the process he spent more money, about $1 million, on the construction of Banff Springs than had ever been spent on any golf course previously and, when completed, had successfully put Banff on the map as a world-class golf destination.

Unfortunately, in the decades subsequent to its opening the golf course has changed considerably, mostly during the 1980s, when a new clubhouse was built to capitalize on increased visitor play. Its location and the hotel's desire to add an additional nine holes, forced the configuration of Thompson's holes to be altered. The first fairway and green, formerly the 5th, were also borrowed for the new nine, leaving a fairly bland opening hole complete with some unsightly mounding, which Thompson certainly would not have approved. His original opener, now the 15th, heads straight over Spray River from an elevated tee overlooking the mountains and was a terrific starting hole.

The strength of Banff Springs is the par threes and the series of tough par fours through the early part of the inward nine, the holes Thompson had actually designed to form the closing stretch. The Devil's Cauldron (4th) is the most celebrated of all Banff's holes, plummeting some 70 feet over a small glacial pond to a bowl-shaped green that was built from the imposing mountain backdrop and leans slightly back toward the water. This gorgeous par three is a genuine classic, although tee shots into the valley 2nd and the long one-shot 10th, played across a bend in Bow River, are just as exciting to play. The open-fronted 13th is also a nice par three, with a green that becomes progressively harder to hit the farther back the pin is pushed and the more ambitious one becomes. Of the longer holes, the left-bending 5th and wide-open 6th into a small plateau green are both solid, but the real standouts are the riverside 12th and the boldly bunkered 14th, which was designed as the 18th and fittingly finishes in the shadows of the grand hotel.

Despite the present layout differing considerably from Thompson's original vision, there is still plenty to recommend at Banff Springs. The flow of the course has undoubtedly been hurt by the configuration change, but good golf holes remain good golf holes regardless of when they appear in a round, and there are certainly more than enough here to make the trip worthwhile.

The National Golf Club of Canada

COURSE OPENED 1976
DESIGNERS George Fazio,
Tom Fazio

The long and testing 13th hole.

OPPOSITE No place to miss on the
National's gorgeous penultimate hole.

One of the stiffest tests in North America, the National Golf Club of Canada is an exclusive club that was established in 1976 on the site of a former golf course. Designed as a golfer's golf club, the founding membership purchased additional acreage around the course to allow designers George and Tom Fazio to stretch the layout to championship length and meet their ambition of housing Canada's toughest course.

The existing layout had enough natural ground movement for good golf, as well as several large ravines. The Fazios then incorporated numerous water hazards and built severe driving zones, small greens and added several forced carries to ensure that the new course was utterly unforgiving. While most will be overwhelmed by such a challenge, many good players, who equate quality with difficulty, actually rate this as Canada's top track.

Less taxing than the back nine, the more enjoyable outward side opens with a lovely rolling par four that moves right and rises gently into a false-front green. The downhill approach into the 3rd is also quite nice, with a back left pond pressed hard against a left-sloping green site. The 4th is an incredibly narrow par five smacked between trees and a creek that must be crossed before reaching the small and heavily bunkered target, while the 5th, with its tiny green, is the first of four difficult par threes. The front side

standout, however, is the long and dramatic par four 7th, which heads over and then left around a killer ravine. There is plenty of room to the right of the hole but temptation invariably draws you closer to danger on both strokes.

On the back nine the real eye opener is the absurdly narrow 13th hole, its sliver of fairway snaking between a pond and a large hill that appears steep enough to spear tee balls all the way across the fairway and into the water. An uphill approach over sand and a further pond into a shallow shelf of green is almost as tough. The tee shot on 14 is also severe, as is the tight drive on 17 between trees and a hazard, but the pièce de résistance is the almost Cape-style finishing hole, which is long and drops 40 feet from the tee to a narrow lakeside fairway and then rises 40 feet again into what feels like one of the smallest targets on earth.

Although it may seem wrong to focus solely on difficulty, the National was built to be the toughest course in Canada, and there are few more relentlessly demanding parkland layouts anywhere. Even fun holes to play like the 3rd, 4th, 7th, 13th and 17th are extremely brutal, with the smallest error on any generally resulting in the need to reload. It is unfortunate that the quality of such holes is often overshadowed by the inherent difficulty of the overall experience, although one fancies that is just how the club likes it.

Oviinbyrd Golf Course

COURSE OPENED 2005
DESIGNER Thomas McBroom

The golfing highlight of Ontario's rapidly developing Muskoka region is Oviinbyrd, an ultra-exclusive club servicing less than two hundred members who enjoy exceptional facilities and immaculate golf in the area's serene rock-strewn hills. Thomas McBroom's design makes good use of the site's natural wetland areas and incorporates dramatic rock formations, which dot many of the fairways and provide both strategic driving hazards and an enjoyable visual from the tees.

After a fairly gentle start, the course shifts into gear from the 7th with a fine seven-hole stretch that includes a beautiful short hole, the 8th, played over muddy wetlands into the base of a rocky hill, and a heroic par five played around an attractive lake at the 9th. Also good is the 10th, a short par four that bends around water and gives the bold drive across the hazard a chance to kick up toward the green but is progressively more difficult to approach the farther left, and more safely, you play. Later in the round the course suffers a little from overkill, with both the long, plunging par three 14th and the all-carry tee shot on the 15th a touch severe, while the lakeside par five 18th is a sadly unremarkable end for a course of this calibre.

Well built and with a peaceful, unhurried atmosphere, Oviinbyrd is a very fine experience and one of Canada's premier modern layouts.

Greywolf Golf Course

COURSE OPENED 1999
DESIGNER Doug Carrick

Situated just two hours from Banff Springs and built within a similarly impressive Alpine setting, Greywolf is a breathtaking modern course located at the base of a ski resort in the Purcell Mountains. Boasting almost constant 360-degree mountain panoramas, the course is also home to one of the most thrilling holes in all of Canada, the 6th, which is so dramatic that all eighteen holes were actually planned around it. Played across a massive canyon to a shallow target suspended precariously at the end of a rocky ledge and falling sharply on all sides, the hole is like a mountain version of the famous 7th hole at the National Golf Club (Old Course) in Australia.

Aside from the stunning beauty of the 6th and the overwhelming challenge of the uphill opening hole, other moments sure to impress here include the 7th, the short par four 11th, the par three 12th, the last half of the 14th and the strategic right-bending 16th. The real highlight, however, is unquestionably the 6th hole, and although the architecture does not quite reach the heights of Banff Springs, the overall quality of golf at Greywolf is very good and, in truth, probably a little overshadowed by the beauty of the property.

OPPOSITE The stunning signature 6th hole at Greywolf, a modern resort-style facility in the Canadian Rockies.

The Summit Golf & Country Club

COURSE OPENED 1912
DESIGNERS George Cumming, George Lyon,
Stanley Thompson

The underrated Summit Golf & Country Club was first laid out by Toronto professional George Cumming and leading amateur George Lyon in 1912 and then enhanced significantly in 1919 by a young Stanley Thompson. While Thompson implemented many of his own ideas and made substantial changes, he also sensibly left the good Cumming and Lyon design elements untouched, today's course existing successfully as a tribute to the talent of all three men.

Heavily treed and full of large rolling hills covered in native grasses, the best land here is very attractive, with only long transitional holes at 6 and 16 occupying dull ground. Some of the formations actually seem a little extreme for golf but are cleverly used within a number of unique holes, such as the pushed-up green cut into a steep side-slope on the short 2nd and the superbly undulating 12th hole, which bends along a bumpy ridge and around a large basin into a small fall-away green. Add beautiful valley holes like 1, 8, 14 and 18, the cunning open and bunkerless short fours at 3 and 4 and a number of elevated tees that provide wonderful vistas over the landscape, and you have yourself a very fine golf course.

Unfortunately, in recent years an excellent short par four adjacent to a busy road had to be closed because of safety concerns and, although the resultant shuffling of holes has been well handled, the walk from the 7th green along this gem to the 8th tee is most upsetting. The Summit, however, is still well worth a look for those golfing around the Toronto area.

Devil's Pulpit Golf Association – Devil's Paintbrush

COURSE OPENED 1992
DESIGNERS Dr Michael Hurdzan, Dana Fry

Founded by the brains behind the hugely successful Trivial Pursuit board game, the Devil's Pulpit Golf Association boasts two wild courses in the rolling countryside of Ontario's Niagara Escarpment. Less than five miles separate the original Devil's Pulpit course from the slightly newer Devil's Paintbrush but, although they share the same extravagant designers, the two tracks could hardly be more different. While the Pulpit is a massively over-shaped parkland course, the Paintbrush project was an ambitious attempt at creating a quasi-links by shaping windswept prairie land into seaside formations.

The prominent features at Paintbrush are almost too numerous to mention, especially as many will leave you grimacing. The huge hill fronting the par five 2nd green is pretty cool but does force play out to the right as it is simply an impossible target to hit from a direct angle. Other interesting features include the hidden 5th green, an enormous five-foot step in the 6th green, an old ruined farmhouse on the 8th fairway, the impossibly tough par three 13th hole and two double greens – 2 & 9 and 11 & 14, the latter complete with a big tree in its middle. The finishing two holes are probably the sanest on the course, even though you drive over a rock wall and toward hidden pot bunkers on the 17th and have to aim almost at the clubhouse roof from the 18th tee.

It would be easy to dismiss Hurdzan and Fry's work here as mere folly, but despite oversized and over-contoured greens, random bunkering, bogus ancient rock walls and the mix of sleeper, sod and grass-faced bunkers, the Paintbrush's bold design is remarkably appealing and great fun to play.

OPPOSITE Lakes and linksy hazards are both prominent on the two-shot 15th at the Devil's Paintbrush.

South & Central America

Teeth of the Dog

Mid Ocean

Cabo del Sol

Querencia

South and Central America is an enormous region that represents a considerable portion of the globe's population and much of its ecological diversity. In golfing terms, however, most of the area is third world, with the game only found in small pockets and mostly among the high-end tourist resorts of Mexico and the Caribbean.

Not surprisingly, courses throughout the region have a heavy American influence, with big-name signature designers prolific and the experience generally more about lavish facilities and lush playing surfaces than natural, strategic golf design. Despite growing at a respectable rate, golf remains a minority sport throughout South America, with its best courses commendable but unlikely to stir the passions of seasoned golf travelers. Most of the modern layouts are overtly manufactured, often at the expense of the land's natural features, while the better classics, like Los Leones in Chile and Olivos in Argentina, tend not to have been as well preserved as they might be in other parts of the world. Dr MacKenzie's Red Course (Colorada) at the Jockey Club in Buenos Aires remains the most significant course on the continent, and is an interesting study in what a great designer can achieve, without substantial earthworks, on pancake-flat land. Although his routing is modest at best, the better holes work very well and his tiny greens at 10 and 17 are among the more sinister creations in the game.

In Central America the tropical isles that make up the Caribbean, as well as Bermuda in the mid-Atlantic, are popular playgrounds for American tourists and home to a number of luxurious hotel and golf resort destinations. Royal Westmoreland and the Green Monkey course on the island of Barbados and Tryall, Rose Hall and White Witch in Jamaica are all interesting creations with some appealing design aspects, but well below the quality of gems like Bermuda's Mid Ocean and Pete Dye's Teeth of the Dog course at the Casa de Campo resort in the Dominican Republic. Teeth of the Dog remains the most famous Caribbean creation, its success spawning similar seaside development across Central America, though sadly only a few genuinely worthwhile tracks, including Dye's wild Dye Fore course, also at Casa de Campo.

Golf tourism in Mexico is gathering real momentum as the government starts to recognize the financial potential of the sport and encourages its growth. No longer marketed as a budget destination, the country is now aggressively targeting wealthier travelers and has become one of the most popular international destinations for American golfers, despite only having a few hundred courses. Popular regions like Puerto Vallarta and Los Cabos offer the highest-profile and most expensive golf although, apart from the two courses at Cabo del Sol and Fazio's fine Querencia, neither region has fully realized the potential of its spectacular sun-soaked coastlines.

The romance of the Caribbean and the growing attraction of certain parts of Mexico will ensure that development continues to be strong throughout this part of the world, but for serious golfers wanting more than a nice place to lie on a towel, the following four courses are the pick of this huge region, and the only ones that we can confidently recommend.

OPPOSITE Cactus and coastline characterize the experience of seaside golf in Mexico. Pictured is the 18th hole on the Ocean Course at Cabo del Sol.

Casa de Campo Resort – Teeth of the Dog

COURSE OPENED 1971
DESIGNER Pete Dye

'Almost by accident, I saw before me the most beautiful seaside location for a golf course. Little did I realize that my wonderful discovery would be the start of a lifelong devotion to this Caribbean country and its warm, gracious people.'

PETE DYE ON TEETH OF THE DOG

OPPOSITE Long, strong and across the Caribbean Sea, the gorgeous one-shot 7th hole.

Built on land described by designer Pete Dye as the greatest piece of earth he'd ever seen, the Teeth of the Dog golf course is the showpiece of Casa de Campo, a 7,000-acre resort and housing estate built on the southern Coral Coast of the Dominican Republic. Opening in 1971, Teeth of the Dog has become the Caribbean's most popular golf destination, thanks largely to the long stretch of magnificent coastline it occupies and Dye's three extraordinary short holes built right on the edge of the Caribbean Sea.

Constructed entirely by hand using local laborers, building the course was an arduous process, but Dye claims the design was relatively simple as 'God made seven holes' and he only had to come up with another eleven. Exposed to constant, variable winds and in many ways an archetypal modern resort course, the layout Dye devised has a classic routing with holes set out in clockwise and anti-clockwise loops on either side of a central clubhouse. The seven holes that occupy the prime coastal land grab most headlines, although inland there is a healthy smattering of strategic risk/reward options and some very interesting golf holes mostly defended by heavy-lipped bunkers flanking fast, slightly raised greens.

Among the early holes the standout is the 2nd, a terrific driving test along a rocky wasteland with the green cleverly angled to favor those who can drive beside the hazard.

The short 5th is the first of the ocean holes, its tiny target resting almost entirely within the sea and the wind either pushing you offshore or forcing you to start your ball over the waves. The next par three is the 7th, a thrilling long shot played over the surf and in the same direction as the 5th, this time to a fine green ringed by impressive sand traps. Either side of this classic are brutal par fours that strangely favor those who drive away from the seawall but offer ample opportunity to rack up a large number, the 8th green being the most extreme on the course, with several pin positions virtually inaccessible to all but the highest-spinning professionals. The course then turns inland at the 9th, returning for a three-hole encore starting at the superb 15th. Like the 17th, this Cape-style hole plays along the cliff edge with the ocean lurking on the right to catch anyone slicing away from the heavily treed left side. Sandwiched between these great par fours is the final par three, an exhilarating signature hole played across a rocky cove to a daunting green site that rests atop a ledge.

The success of Teeth of the Dog helped to establish Pete Dye as North America's premier golf course architect and he has remained heavily involved in its evolution, continually tweaking and stretching his famous layout. While the tiger tees, newer bunkers and more severe green contours have been added to increase the challenge for the modern golfer, several hurricanes and a rapidly expanding

residential development have also had an effect on both the landscape and design. The exposed holes along the sea have felt Mother Nature's fury the hardest and been cleared of much foliage over the years, while the huge sandy waste area between tee and green on the 7th had to be grassed and converted into a bank to protect houses and prevent erosion during severe storms. Dye himself has altered and re-contoured nearly all the holes at some point. The lengthening of the short par four 4th and the new bunker across the 18th fairway, built to prevent 300-yard bombs from the tee and to ensure a stiff close to the round, are most notable among the more recent changes.

Although the course is highly recommended, several of the less exciting holes do feel a little underwhelming, this in part due to the illustrious company they keep but also because some lack visual interest from the tee and are only rescued by their tough green complexes. Aside from tricky targets, there is little to recommend on holes such as 1, 3, 11 and 12, while the reachable 14th is a fairly ordinary lakeside par five. What saves 'the Dog,' however, is the tremendous beauty of its setting and the all-world quality of the stunning coastal holes.

ABOVE The shortest of the coastal holes, the 5th plays to a delicious target surrounded by the sea.

OPPOSITE Another of 'the Dog's' glamour holes is the par four 15th, which is reasonably short but particularly brutal on slicers.

The Mid Ocean Club

COURSE OPENED 1921
DESIGNER Charles Blair
Macdonald

*'There is nothing commonplace
about it.'*

CHARLES BLAIR MACDONALD ON
THE MID OCEAN CLUB

The golf course at Mid Ocean is part of a luxury club built within an idyllic estate on the sun-soaked island of Bermuda in the mid-Atlantic Ocean. The original development was started in 1919 when an international shipping company hired American golfing pioneer Charles Blair Macdonald to find land on the island to develop a resort golf course, primarily for their holidaying passengers. Macdonald scoured the small land mass for his site, and selected a clifftop property at Tucker's Point that allowed him to spread the holes across a series of steep coral hills, interspersed with deep inland valleys and full of breathtaking ocean vistas.

Despite its coastal setting and unmistakably British feel, Mid Ocean is not a real links, although the designer did incorporate features and hazards found on the classic seaside courses. As he had done previously at the National Golf Links in New York, here Macdonald built copies of his favorite holes from Britain and Europe, most successfully at the 5th and the terrific 17th, which is a Redan hole but played slightly downhill to a fully visible green site. Slightly less effective are other replicas such as the Short 7th and Biarritz 13th, with its square green and big frontal tier a copy of the fabled French ocean-carry par three that was lost to the sea during the 1940s. As evident in some of his green shaping, he also seemed to have a healthy respect for the Old Course at St Andrews, the contouring at 1, 3, 8, 12, 14, 16, 17 and 18 among the highlights of the round.

Hit the wrong side of any of these huge greens and you end deep in three-putt territory.

Its obvious attractions aside, the Mid Ocean course remains best remembered for its legendary Cape hole, the 5th, which is an architectural masterpiece that has inspired thousands of replications all over the world, especially in North America, where a Cape hole seems an almost obligatory part of every modern golf course. Plunging down and diagonally across a Mangrove Lake, the genius of the hole, like the 16th at Commonwealth in Australia, is not the ever-present threat of water down one side but instead the shape of a green which forces those looking for birdie to drive closer to the lake. Here a steep right-to-left tilt to the putting surface is further complicated by a prominent ridge running through the right half to further shrink the landing area for any approach coming in from the safer side. To some degree technology has slightly spoilt the driving challenge for the good players here, as the back tees are farther left and play more across the water than the original tees, which head diagonally along the lake. Whether this historic par four is superior to the 2nd at North Berwick in Scotland, upon which it was surely based, or the hundreds of subsequent versions of the Cape is debatable, but there remains no doubt that this much-copied hole is an outstanding success and rightly revered.

There are other moments to savor as well including a fine opening hole, difficult

OPPOSITE Mid Ocean's wonderful opening hole, which sweeps left to a green perched above the Atlantic.

approaches into the 8th and 9th, the cross-hill 12th, a terrific closing stretch from the 15th and a diverse set of driving challenges, with no two tees presenting the golfer with the same visual examination. Macdonald also cleverly kept tees and greens close together to ensure it was a manageable walking course despite some steep gradients. There were minor modifications made to the layout in the 1950s by Robert Trent Jones, including back tees on the 5th, but so sound was the original planning that, Trent Jones himself acknowledges these changes were insignificant.

Mid Ocean does have a couple of problem spots, including scattered housing and a public access road dissecting the property, which together with the widely varying landscapes give the layout a slightly incoherent feel. These issues aside, Mid Ocean was the earliest example of quality golf design in the islands around America and the club remains the region's shining light. Those who dismiss the course as a one-hole wonder will not only miss a great hole but also a truly exceptional golf experience.

OPPOSITE Macdonald's marvelous Cape hole from the original tee. Those who flirt with the water are left with a much easier approach.

Cabo del Sol – The Ocean Course

COURSE OPENED 1994
DESIGNER Jack Nicklaus

'At Cabo del Sol it was apparent that the closer the routing got to the edge of the ocean, with the desert vegetation, the more exciting and unique the course could be.'

JACK NICKLAUS

OPPOSITE The view from the final tee on the Ocean Course, the fairway bending around the shoreline to a wonderful green set before the sea.

Nicklaus Design's most celebrated resort course, the Ocean Course at Cabo del Sol, is part of a massive 1,800-acre residential-resort development that revolutionized the Los Cabos region and helped popularize holiday golf in Mexico. The course is a mixture of sea and desert golf, with each hole cut from a natural desert landscape but those on the exterior touching the blue waters of the Pacific and boasting some of the most exhilarating ocean frontage in all of golf.

From a central clubhouse the course is arranged in a large figure eight, with three holes on each nine occupying the prime coastal area and providing most of the highlights. It is Jack Nicklaus's belief that, 'the strength of an oceanfront golf course is the quality and variety of the inland holes,' and away from the sea at Cabo he managed to design several gems. These include a couple of strong par fives and the difficult par four 10th, which drops significantly from the tee and then features a nasty approach across a rock-strewn valley and into a shallow green guarded by deep bunkers and cacti. The shorter but narrower 14th is no less intimidating as you drive over a deadly *arroyo* that snakes along the left side of the fairway before cutting back in front of the green. There are also a few real brutes, such as the long plunging par three 13th and the uphill 8th, with its approach across a large sandy wasteland and deep frontal bunker one of the most demanding anywhere.

Despite these interesting interior holes, the Nicklaus course at Cabo del Sol is all about the ocean, and it is the coastal stretch of the 5th through 7th and 16th through 18th that draws the masses back here year after year. Although the short 7th does feel a tad artificial, there is no denying the phenomenal quality of the remaining ocean holes. The 5th is a lovely par four that bends around sand and heads toward the sea, while both the 6th and 17th are par threes that are built atop granite outcroppings, the penultimate hole playing straight across a pristine white sandy cove to a clifftop green pressed hard against the surf. The 18th then hugs the coast as it curves along the shoreline, the fairway giving a strategic advantage to those able to drive close to the water as a central or safer left side drive leaves a frightening approach played directly at the Pacific and with little room for error. One of the finest closers in the game, this stunner occupies an amazing piece of land and is among the top few holes in the bulging Nicklaus portfolio.

The Ocean Course has evolved and changed considerably in its relatively short life, with even the famous seaside holes being placed under the knife on more than one occasion. After inexplicably being shifted 40 yards inland, the 16th green has since been moved back against the rocky coastline and lowered by several feet, making the downhill approach, straight at the ocean, even more spectacular. The greens, which opened unusually flat for a

Nicklaus track, have been reshaped and now have more than enough movement to keep things interesting without going overboard. Several fairway traps have also been added or altered to temper technology. The resort's growth has had an impact on the course as well, most notably from places like the 5th tee, where multiple hotel developments have cramped the fairway and damaged the visual.

Jack Nicklaus was very conscious of the opportunity he had to create something special at Cabo and sensibly focused hard on ensuring that the nines were balanced and the inland golf was up to the standard of the seaside holes. One of the most photogenic layouts on earth, Cabo del Sol's Ocean Course is an extremely impressive achievement, with the designer able to extract fine golf holes out of the best parts of the property. The course does have a few indifferent moments and some uninspiring terrain, yet the sensible placement of the most dramatic coastal holes toward the close of the round ensures golfers end their day on a huge high, which is great for generating repeat business and has no doubt helped establish this resort's enormous international profile.

ABOVE Nicklaus's plunging par three 13th hole.

OPPOSITE Part of an extraordinary closing sequence, the 17th is a breathtaking beach-carry par three.

Querencia Golf Club

COURSE OPENED 2000
DESIGNER Tom Fazio

*'At Querencia I feel we never
compromised on creating the best
possible course on a very unique
and special piece of land.'*

TOM FAZIO

OPPOSITE Fazio's short but
dramatic 14th hole.

OVERLEAF A sweeping view of
the 5th at Querencia.

Querencia is a private golf and housing estate built in hills that overlook the coastline on Mexico's Baja Peninsula. Full of rocky canyons and distant views of the Cortez Sea, the Tom Fazio designed golf course is different from the others along the coast, as its dramatic topography and native desert vegetation of flowering bushes, tropical plants and cacti, rather than scenic beach views, provide most of the aesthetic attraction.

Limited play and a mandatory cart policy meant that getting between holes at Querencia would not be an issue, and allowed Fazio to concentrate on producing as many thrills as possible irrespective of any routing problems they caused. Searching the enormous property for the best pieces of land, he routed most holes atop or through a series of impressive valleys and deep rocky ravines, the outrageously dramatic landscape proving the perfect foil for Fazio's natural artistic flair.

There are a number of quality holes throughout the round, including the half-horseshoe 4th hole that plays along a ridge above a massive valley and follows the landform all the way to a green perched on a perilous ledge. The plunging and rising 5th hole and the narrow 7th, its target located on the brink of a deep craggy *arroyo*, are both good holes, as is the short 8th, which heads across the same *arroyo* to a slightly over-shaped but attractive green site. Although the front nine shades the back, the standout hole is probably the

200-yard 11th, which drops into a canyon and comes complete with stunning outlooks over the hills in all directions.

Despite Fazio's design philosophy and hazard placement being more artistic than strategic, the course is tougher than one may expect, especially on wayward drivers as the vegetation off the cut grass is very thick. Many of the tees are steeply elevated and look down upon the boldly contoured fairways, adding both a visual excitement and intimidation factor to the tee shots. Some of the greens are a touch overdone and the odd extreme moment, like the last third of the 9th and the anti-strategic short par four 17th, keep the course off the top rung, but this is an enjoyable desert experience nonetheless.

While the heavily developed Los Cabos area has become a golfing hotspot in recent years, most of the golf along the coast is compromised because holes and homes invariably end up fighting for prime seaside land. Although Querencia does have nice views of the distant sea, its setting is not a distraction, nor are the holes compromised by beach proximity or housing plots. Whether you like Fazio and his cookie-cutter approach to golf course design or not, he deserves credit for extracting dramatic golf holes out of a pretty rough environment. His fans will no doubt love Querencia, but the true mark of its quality is that even his harshest critics are bound to find enough here to admire.

Asia

OPPOSITE Immaculate grooming, lavish clubhouse facilities and superb scenery are common on golf courses throughout Asia, but good design is generally more difficult to find. Pictured right is the par three 4th hole on the Lake Course at China's impressive Spring City Golf & Lake Resort.

Japan

A land of almost ten million players, Japan's golfing history has parallels to that of Australia. Its origins, popularity and architectural timelines are similar and the dominant influence on the game here was also the brief stay of a visiting British golf course designer.

The game was introduced to Japan by foreign nationals, the earliest club established by an English tea merchant on Mt Rokko, high above Kobe, in 1903. The first club to be founded and created by Japanese golfers was the Tokyo Golf Club in 1913, which later decided to engage Harry Colt's firm to design its second course after its first had been sold for development. Reluctant to travel, Colt instead sent his associate Charles H. Alison, who then stayed on to make new design plans for Hirono and Kawana as well as to revise Naruo, Kasumigaseki and Ibaraki. Alison's arrival changed Japanese golf forever and his legacy, like MacKenzie's in Australia, extends beyond leaving fine courses of his own to the subsequent work of those he taught and inspired during his visit.

Golf's popularity gradually increased from Alison's departure in 1931 through to the onset of the Pacific War, which brought the industry to a complete halt. The war years destroyed many courses, while following the conflict others were either converted back to farming ground or left in a permanent state of disrepair. It was not until the occupying forces returned golf land to the community in the early 1950s that attempts were made to restore the classics. The game took off again slowly at first and then with great gusto during the heady days of the 1970s and 80s, when the Japanese economy boomed, golf numbers increased and most of its 2,400 odd courses were built.

Contrary to what many believe, and beyond the elaborate garden beds, water features and communal clubhouse baths, the quality of golf in Japan is actually very high and vastly superior to the rest of Asia. Its best layouts are terrific and the club environments a charming diversion from anything you may have experienced elsewhere. The biggest issue for western golfers here are the greens. As a result of the humid Asian summers many clubs retain a two-target policy with the summer greens generally korai grass, a putting surface most will find utterly unacceptable. Thankfully, a number of the better-managed and more progressive clubs have successfully converted their courses to a single bentgrass surface.

Japan's best layouts tend to be those of a classic vintage, as most modern facilities focus on immaculate presentation, first-class amenities and remarkable levels of service, often at the expense of good golf. The recent slowdown in the Japanese economy has left clubs struggling to fill memberships and timesheets. The good news is that many are now more open to outside play than before and the green fees are less expensive, although you should still expect to pay close to a Pebble Beach-sized fee at the leading clubs here.

Though planning a trip to Japan may seem a little overwhelming, the country is less intimidating than one might imagine, and its incredible culture and countryside make it an outstanding destination. For those who like to combine travel with their passion for golf, the courses featured here, along with the likes of Ono, Karuizawa, Hakone, Phoenix Country Club and the charming and original 1903 Kobe course, are very highly recommended.

OPPOSITE **The 11th hole on the Fuji Course at the Kawana Hotel, one of the premier layouts in the surprisingly strong golf country of Japan.**

Hirono Golf Club

COURSE OPENED 1932

DESIGNER Charles H. Alison

'Almost every hole has some bold natural feature, and for variety of scene and of strokes Hirono is difficult to beat. I can name no superior among British inland courses.'

CHARLES H. ALISON

OPPOSITE The short 5th is the first of Hirono's remarkable par threes.

Japan's most distinguished golf club, Hirono was created by opportunistic golfers from Kobe who approached leading British designer Charles H. Alison while he was working on the Tokyo Golf Club and Kawana's Fuji Course. They had acquired part of a vast estate owned by an ex-feudal warlord and asked that Alison consider its suitability for golf. Well dispersed with lakes, ponds and dams as well as terrific natural ravines, gullies and undulating woodland, the property delighted Alison, who took the job as designer and declared their course would be the best in Japan and one of the finest in existence.

As was his practice, Alison then retreated into his hotel room with notes and contour maps of the property, and after seven days emerged with a design that, sixteen months later, would open to instant acclaim. His strategic layout was routed across a stunning variety of landforms and complemented by greens that were tilted and bunkered to reward bold driving with better angles. He also designed four incredible par threes that, despite changes, remain among the most celebrated sets of short holes in the world. A standout feature of the early course was the bunkering, Alison creating fearsome hazards that were deliberately deep and often part of sprawling complexes. Insistent that the bunkers feel natural, he designed them to be untidy in appearance with the sand splashed up on uneven faces. Regrettably, many have since

been cleaned up and their faces grassed over.

The highlight of Hirono is approach play. While some of the drives no longer present the challenge they once did, approach shots into 2, 4, 10, 11, 14, 16, 18 and each of the par threes are all still demanding. The course starts with a generously wide par five and a string of fine two-shot holes before reaching the 5th, an all-world short hole across a gorgeous fiord to a wonderfully bunkered plateau green. The Devil's Divot 7th hole is another outstanding par three, played diagonally across a deep sandy ditch. Sadly the removal of a central bunker and the tidying of Alison's messy sand scrapes have made the long carry slightly less intimidating. Elsewhere the 10th, 11th and clever side-hill 14th are all very good, as is the par five 15th, its fairway cut by ditches that create distinct landing areas for each shot. The closing stretch is a tough assignment, with a high plateau green on the 16th followed by a long par three and the difficult 18th, which demands an accurate and strong drive across what was once a spectacularly bunkered diagonal gully.

While the strengths of Alison's design remain evident, changes made over the years have unquestionably hurt the course. The most notable alteration is the 90-degree change in direction on the classic cross-dam par three 13th. Once played to a peninsula green with a falloff to the water on one side, its tee was twice shifted 45 degrees when the 12th hole was

extended. Bunkers were also added to now flank the green and distance the target from the water, removing the fear of a bold shot trickling into the dam. Other smaller changes include the slight realignment of the 3rd tee without an adjustment to the fairway bunker and the removal of a greenside trap and addition of small pines to the right of the 9th green. There was also once a sandy waste area short-right of the 14th green, which would barely be in play today but would certainly add to the visual appeal of the hole.

The quality of Hirono's early course is apparent in the club's fine set of black and white photographs taken of all eighteen fairways and greens back in 1933. Proof of how great this course once was, the images should also act as an instructional manual on how Alison wanted his holes set up. The current practice of leaving long choking grass between cut surfaces and bunkers, for instance, not only damages his design intent but also detracts from the enjoyment of the game. Regardless, Hirono is revered in Japan and is still the country's best layout, though one suspects that this was once a true giant of the golfing world.

ABOVE Alison's intimidating bunker shapes guard the fearsome cross-gully 7th hole, known as the Devil's Divot.

OPPOSITE A picture of tranquility, the tee on the 13th hole was originally placed well to the right, with the left side of the green falling toward the water.

Kawana Hotel – Fuji Course

COURSE OPENED 1936
DESIGNER Charles H. Alison

'The scenery resembles that of the French Riviera, but at not a single spot between the Italian and Spanish frontiers can be found so superb a combination of sea, cliffs, trees and mountains.'

CHARLES H. ALISON ON KAWANA

OPPOSITE The view from the back tee on Fuji's famous 15th hole.

The Kawana Hotel was the brainchild of a wealthy businessman named Baron Kishichiro Okura, who was educated in Britain during the early 1900s and returned to Japan to build an English-style luxury retreat on his stunning Izu Peninsula property. Following work on the Tokyo Golf Club, Charles H. Alison holidayed at the Kawana Hotel in late 1930 and was so overwhelmed by its beauty that he convinced the Baron he should build a world-class golf course on his dramatic site.

The land available for Alison's course was on a rocky ledge high above Sagami Bay, with glorious views over the water to Oshima Island and Mount Fuji on clear days. Unlike clifftop courses such as Pebble Beach or Old Head that boast uninterrupted views, here there was dense foliage separating coast from course, significant gradient changes and a wide variance in terrain. The result is an unusual mix of dunes, links and parkland, which is tied together by Alison's brilliant design, exceptional fairway bunkering and a routing that takes full advantage of the landscape's best features and is dotted with a number of outstanding golf holes.

Despite similarities with courses like New South Wales, Turnberry, Mid Ocean and even Pebble Beach, the truth is that Fuji is unlike any of the more famous tracks it is often compared to. The course opens well. From an elevated tee the first hole drops dramatically then rises again toward the ocean and is followed by a par four along the heavily wooded cliffs that falls across fine rolling ground. The 3rd is a short par five which turns sharply right and up a steep hill, demanding those eager to get home in two cut off three deep bunkers on the inside of the dogleg. Fuji really starts to show its class at the superb 7th, a mid-length par four played across a series of ridges that cut the hole and hide a thin strip of fairway full of bumps and humps. The slender green then falls sharply to the right and in any sort of wind is a terrifying target to approach from anywhere other than the middle of the fairway. The next is an excellent par three, while the 9th is a split fairway par four with a redundant right side but a brilliant left valley and another wonderful green.

On the back nine, the long and wide-open par five 11th is tremendous fun as it tumbles down toward a large tiered green framed by the sea and Kawana's distinctive lighthouse. This touch of Turnberry marks the start of a magnificent run of holes that brings you back to the clubhouse along an elevated and undulating plateau. The 13th is a real gem, with its green angled and bunkered to present great difficulty for those approaching from outside a narrow fairway corridor that is hard to identify within the larger landing area. The 14th is another fabulous hole, which doglegs right around a deep bunker, the approach a beautiful shot through a swale and onto the raised green. Next up is the signature hole of the Fuji Course, a breathtaking par five played alongside cliffs and across a big rolling fairway. Plunging down from

a lofty back tee, the aggressive drive needs to flirt with the sea and carry coastal forest to set up a decent line into an obscured green that rests in a depression and is dissected by a small ridge. Despite a number of other terrific moments throughout the round, this extraordinary hole will provide the lasting memory of Kawana for most who play here.

Unfortunately, like many layouts in Japan, the course is wall-to-wall korai grass, which is decent to play approach shots from but simply awful to putt on unless it is prepared in tournament mode. This and the ever-changing landforms are probably the only criticism of a course that thoroughly deserves its reputation as Asia's finest resort layout. Regardless of whether you prefer the less dramatic consistency and superior turf quality of Hirono or the boldness of Fuji holes such as 7, 9, 14, 15 and 17, a day's golf at Kawana is a tremendous adventure and one that won't soon be forgotten.

OPPOSITE Part of a string of fine golf holes, the par four 14th bends to the right and plays onto this elevated green.

Kasumigaseki Country Club – East Course

COURSE OPENED 1929
DESIGNERS Kinya Fujita,
Shiro Akaboshi,
Seiichi Inoue

Terrific twin targets on the par four 6th.

OPPOSITE The right green on the
mid-length 3rd hole at Kasumigaseki East.

First opened in 1929, the 36-hole Kasumigaseki Country Club is significant as not only the proud owner of the richly impressive East Course, but also as the first club to adopt the two-green policy, a peculiar concept unique to Japan that clubs use to spread wear on their greens. Originally designed by Kinya Fujita and Shiro Akaboshi, the course was converted to two-greens in 1937 by Seiichi Inoue after an experiment by British architect Charles H. Alison and a local botanist to cultivate an evergreen bentgrass for the putting surfaces had failed.

Unlike most of the one thousand Japanese courses subsequently built with summer and winter greens, here they were an afterthought, and as a result of land already assigned to golf holes, the dual targets are generally smaller and the complexes more intimate than on other layouts. Strangely, however, there is no course in Japan where multiple targets work better either visually or within the strategy of the hole. Many holes boast two good greens, while only the 4th, 10th and 14th have one side which is clearly inferior.

Kasumigaseki East features a classic routing across parkland that appears quite flat but is not without nice golf undulation, each little break or bump in terrain being well used within the subtle design. From the slightly side-hill aspect of the opening tee shot through to the final valley approach, this is the most consistent test in Japan, with barely an indifferent hole on the course.

The design is surprisingly strategic given 36 greens dot the property, but with both targets often in fairly close proximity the reward for a good drive is an equally short shot or superior angle no matter which green you are playing to.

Very good regardless of its configuration, the East Course with all of its best elements combined is as impressive as the celebrated classics of London's Heathland or Melbourne's Sandbelt. A nice opening drive could be followed by fine approaches into the right green on the 2nd and either green on the 3rd. Left on the par three 4th is a fabulous target of Sandbelt appearance, while the right green on 6, the crested par four 8th and right green on the short 10th, which crosses a deep ravine, are all terrific. From the 10th the layout gets a little back and forth but the holes remain solid and the right greens on 15, 16 and 17 and left green on the finishing hole are all excellent.

Golf in Japan is quite an experience, and the quality of the classic courses is greater than one might expect. It can be dangerous, however, to recommend old clubs here, as holes are generally either good or poor depending on the greens being used. By contrast, most of the better holes at Kasumigaseki East work well into either target, meaning the course can be endorsed with greater confidence. Although short by modern standards and unknown internationally, Kasumigaseki is a true Japanese gem and is a track that anyone with the means to play should.

Naruo Golf Club

COURSE OPENED 1930
DESIGNERS Joe E. Crane, Harry C. Crane,
Charles H. Alison

Among Japan's most famous classic courses, the Naruo Golf Club was initially founded on seaside land in 1920 by British expats but shifted into the untouched hills outside Osaka during 1930. Scottish professional Joe Crane and his brother Harry designed the layout on beautifully rolling ground that includes a pronounced gully dissecting the property, which proved a useful feature on several key holes. When Charles H. Alison made his landmark journey to Japan he spent a week at Naruo with Harry Crane and provided the club with a report on a number of possible course alterations.

One of the features of Naruo is how both the fairway landing zones and greens around the central gully are built at basically the same level, approaches over the ravines therefore seeming more intimidating. Technology has unfortunately hurt several of the better holes, with the small greens at 3, 5 and 6, for instance, all significantly easier to approach now that the long hitter can power a drive down onto the flat valley floor. Less affected are others, like the big-drawing 8th hole, played around a hill and into a lovely basin green site, or the strong par four 10th across a dramatic depression. The three finishing par fours are also very strong, the 17th the standout for a terrific approach played from beyond one ridge and up into a fabulous green atop another.

Although a few holes could do with some extra length, the club is unfortunately now landlocked, the encroaching suburbia even forcing the erection of several safety nets to protect surrounding homes. The other pressing issue confronting the modern Naruo Golf Club is the dense korai grass on its greens, which is terrible to putt on and offers no real challenge to good players missing targets. Despite these problem areas, the land here is interesting and the design mostly very good, thus making a round at Naruo well worth the journey.

Koga Golf Club

COURSE OPENED 1955
DESIGNER Osamu Ueda

Koga is an unheralded but charming seaside golf club built through an undulating pine plantation close to the city of Fukuoka. In a similar mold to Newcastle in Australia and East London in South Africa, Koga boasts a stack of solid holes that are exposed to tricky trade winds and mostly feature small built-up greens guarded by steep banks and rugged bunkering.

The undulation is less pronounced here than at Newcastle or East London, but is constant and well used by Japanese designer Osamu Ueda who ensured short walks between holes and managed to squeeze eighteen alternate greens onto the compact and heavily forested site without making the course feel too confined.

Of the better holes the straightaway par four 3rd is a particular favorite, the deep bunkers short of the plateau green and left of the lay-back zone tightening a hole where every yard gained from the tee eases the challenge of the approach. The 2nd is also a fine hole, across a small ridge and bending into pines, while the approach across a shallow valley on the 8th is another highlight. The back nine continues the theme of gently rising greens and deep surrounding sand trouble; Woodhall Spa would be proud to own the left trap on 16, which is at least ten feet deep and pressed hard against the shallow part of the green. Other good holes include the mini-Calamity 11th and the par five 12th, which tumbles across the best contours on the course and is especially enjoyable if you can draw a drive around the corner and catch a ride down one of the slopes. The 18th is a cracking short par four where the rewards of successfully hitting your driver are enormous, as the pitch in from any sort of distance is diabolical.

Koga does get a touch back and forth in places and its facilities are not lavish, but this tight and terrific little course is a class act and clearly one of Asia's best from this era.

Abiko Golf Club

COURSE OPENED 1930
DESIGNER Rokuro Akaboshi

Opening in 1930, the Abiko Golf Club was designed by Rokuro Akaboshi, who was an eager student of golf design and followed Charles H. Alison closely on his travels through Japan that very year. Like Kasumigaseki East, the course was originally conceived with single greens and had a distinctly British feel, the bunkering being classically shaped, rugged and grass-faced and not unlike those built by Harry Colt, who was the mentor and partner of Akaboshi's teacher, Charles Alison.

Starting superbly, the course opens with a series of attractive and well-built golf holes routed across the most interesting undulation on the site, the first seven holes being among the most enjoyable anywhere in Japan. After two strategically bunkered par fours, the 3rd hole is a fantastic par three across a valley and deep frontal trap. The 5th is also very good, your drive needing to be played up the tighter right side of its falling fairway in order to avoid an awkward stance and horrible angle into the dangerously shallow target. This is followed by a reachable par five with an awesome second shot across a picturesque valley and through tall central trees to an excellent raised green site.

The 7th is then a wonderful long par three, but from here, with the exception of the short 13th, the course loses its way a little. Most of the back nine was flattened and used as rice fields after the Second World War and although some minor undulation was rebuilt, it is not used as well within the design nor is the fairway movement or hole construction quite as effective as the terrific opening stretch.

Tokyo Golf Club

COURSE OPENED 1940
DESIGNER Komyo Ohtani

Founded in 1913, the Tokyo Golf Club is an historic club that shifted twice before settling next door to Kasumigaseki Country Club on the outskirts of Tokyo in 1940. The club's previous home was closer to the city and its Charles H. Alison designed course, considered Japan's first outstanding layout, was seized by the Japanese military during World War II.

It was the man who first brought Alison to the club and then became a disciple of his design philosophies, Komyo Ohtani, who was then responsible for creating the club's new home. Ohtani's course supposedly followed some of the routing ideas from the Alison layout and copied his distinctive design style, most notably at the 2nd and 13th, with their wonderful diagonal cross-bunkers, but also in the excellent shaping of the right green on the 6th, left green on the one-shot 8th and the short par four 14th. The best stretch of holes comes at the finish, from the strategic 16th and the nice dropping par three 17th to the strong par four closing hole with its two terrific, and totally individual, greens.

The major problem with today's course is the loss of some of Ohtani's design intent and the unsatisfactory double greens. Sadly, you never play to the best set of greens here as the good targets alternate and, unlike at Kasumigaseki, there is a major discrepancy in quality. Holes such as 6, 9, 15 and 17, for instance, are fabulous to one green and disappointing to the other. The course is also no longer an exciting driving test and some of the better fairway bunker complexes have become lost within its expanding foliage. Though Tokyo is a fun golf course to play, some shallow and tired bunkering, dated driving zones and mixed greens are ultimately telling.

OPPOSITE Japan's curious two-green system on display here at the 8th hole at Tokyo Golf Club.

Rest of Asia

A mix of extravagant affluence and absolute poverty, Asia may be our most diverse continent culturally but its booming golf industry lacks the sort of quality and range that exists in stronger regions like Britain and North America. Generally speaking, the game is still an elitist pursuit here, confined to poor destinations that cater to wealthy travelers or prosperous regions whose affluent golfers pay excessive fees for their pastime. There is little municipal or affordable golf anywhere in Asia. The established clubs tend to be expensive institutions with little regard for the aspiring golfer and modern development is largely confined to luxury resorts and lavish country clubs.

In terms of participation, golf's growth has been most pronounced in South Korea, where the success of tournament professionals abroad has led to a massive rise of interest in the game. Unlike Japan, however, the domestic marketplace cannot support its two-and-a-half million golfers, and many of the South East Asian resorts in Thailand, Indonesia and Malaysia, built initially to cater to the traveling Japanese, are now focusing on the thriving Korean market. Despite most of its mountainous mainland being unsuitable for golf and the small southern island of Jeju almost at saturation point, the Korean government is determined to more than double the country's two hundred courses by 2015. A rapid increase in wealth combined with inexpensive labor costs has also led to huge growth in China, with golf now part of some superb resort destinations, but unfortunately still inaccessible for the masses.

Asian golfers are generally very brand conscious, and it is no surprise that clubs able to buy championship pedigree or afford to pay the exorbitant appearance fees of big name professionals have the highest profiles. Most local golfers are more interested in a course built by Nicklaus or played by Tiger than one lauded in a book like this. For the discerning visitor therefore, seeking out the region's celebrity layouts is generally a misguided practice. Some tour stops like the Bukit Course at Singapore Island Country Club, Fanling in Hong Kong, Nine Bridges, the World Cup Course at Mission Hills and Beijing's Pine Valley are worth visiting, but most of the others are largely forgettable. The likes of Spring City and Tiger Beach in China, Nicklaus's Legends Course in Malaysia, Pinx and Blackstone on Jeju Island, Nirwana Bali, Ria Bintan and Bill Coore's Klub Rimba Irian in Indonesia are among the few unlikely Asian gems.

The traditional western concept of a day's golf is largely foreign in many parts of Asia, where players can take up to three caddies, rounds can last half a day, and the experience is as much about the culinary delights of the clubhouse as the quality of the golf holes. Although the market does not appreciate good design and the steamy sauna-like climate is unsuited to the growing of decent golf grasses, there are some great sites here and the sumptuous resort facilities, friendly locals and few genuine standouts featured in the following pages are all worth celebrating.

OPPOSITE Indonesia's Ria Bintan Resort is home to one of the better ocean courses in Asia. Pictured is its par three 9th hole, which protrudes out into the South China Sea.

Nirwana Bali Golf Club

COURSE OPENED 1998
DESIGNERS Greg Norman,
Bob Harrison

'At Nirwana we were lucky to get the spectacular clifftop holes but we are most proud of our work in the open inland landscape, particularly the extensive rice fields we built to create the impression that the golf course had been laid out through them.'

BOB HARRISON

OPPOSITE **Nirwana's incredible 7th hole.**

Part of a large coastal resort on the Indonesian island of Bali, the Nirwana Bali golf course was designed by Greg Norman and Bob Harrison in 1998 and is every bit as good as their best work in Australia. Built on a spectacular seaside property, the layout boasts an intriguing mix of landscapes with a series of glamorous coastal holes mixed with an undulating interior surrounded by dense jungle vegetation. Although famous for its ocean-carry par three, the heart of Nirwana is its dynamic inland holes, which feature some of the best design elements on the course and most of the site's interesting ground movement.

From the opening hole, Nirwana weaves through deep valleys and thick forests, across creeks and gullies, over beaches and onto the region's stunning cliffs. Exposed to variable winds, the routing cleverly changes direction regularly and is highlighted by excellent green shaping and strategic fairway bunkering. Driving is rarely cramped, although you often feel the need to play down a tighter side to get a level stance, shorter shot or better angle into the green sites. A number of targets are then pressed hard against wandering creeks and ditches and generally slanted toward danger, forcing those hoping for decent uphill birdie putts to really flirt with the hazards.

The first four holes loop inland from the clubhouse and are a tremendous introduction to both the golf course and to Bali. The opening side-hill drive is actually played across rows of staggered rice paddies and needs to avoid deep inside dogleg bunkers to set up a good shot down toward a green nestled against a jungle backdrop. The 2nd hole is then a lengthy par three alongside a forest to a smallish green sloping sharply toward the trouble. After excellent approach shots into the 3rd, 4th and 5th, the long, dipping par five 6th is the first to catch a glimpse of the sea as it heads toward an attractive target framed by the waters of the Indian Ocean. It is followed by Nirwana's signature, a breathtaking short hole played across the ocean's crashing waves into a wickedly angled green that punishes those cowering away from the water. Farther along the coastline, and fully visible from the tee, is the haunting Hindu sea temple of Tanah Lot, which rests among the surf on its own rocky outcrop. Even without such incredible views, this would still be one of the modern game's finest par threes.

From here the course turns back away from the shore. Heading toward the clubhouse, the 9th is the first of several holes with hazards fronting the putting surface, the fairway sweeping left through trees to a green set just beyond a gully and pressed against the rice fields. The clever mid-length par four 12th is another such hole; it points seaward but bends late through a valley toward a steep back-to-front green beyond an estuary, the wind usually whipping in from the side as you attempt the treacherous approach. The next heads back

along the coastline and is drivable with a favorable wind, though its narrow green is set at the very edge of the cliff, making the gamble extremely dangerous. The last of Nirwana's outstanding par threes, the 14th then plays partly over a volcanic sand beach in the opposite direction to the 7th and with a more receptive elevated green for those bailing away from the sea. Completing the round is a series of solid holes that form an excellent closing set. The 15th is a strong and strategic two-shot hole dominated by sand, while the final three each feature a green guarded by a frontal ditch.

Asia is home to a number of disappointing ocean courses, but Nirwana Bali is a real treat and much better than the one-hole wonder that some reviews imply. Indeed, the variety of holes and landforms incorporated within the design is quite remarkable, and when set up to play firm and fast, this stunning layout is one of the world's great resort golf experiences.

OPPOSITE The 14th is Nirwana's final par three and features a tee shot played across part of a beach.

The Club at Nine Bridges

COURSE OPENED 2001
DESIGNER Ronald Fream

The par four 5th hole.

OPPOSITE One of the highlights of the pristine Nine Bridges layout is this tricky uphill approach into the skyline green on the 8th.

OVERLEAF The second shot into the par five 18th, which gives golfers the chance to end with an eagle putt or splash further into trouble.

The game of golf is exploding in South Korea and in particular on the popular and rapidly developing southern island of Jeju, home to the impressive Club at Nine Bridges. Founded by the grandson of the Samsung visionary, the course takes its name from the eight stone bridges that span the site's lakes and wandering creeks, the ninth bridge being a metaphoric link between the club, its members and the game of golf.

Nine Bridges is located 1,800 feet up Mt Halla and surrounded by national park. The private and idyllic retreat is a pure golf experience existing without any outside distraction or annoying residential component whatsoever. The club cost close to $100 million to build, with a large chunk of the total spent covering all eighteen tees, greens and fairways with bentgrass and growing Kentucky Blue in the roughs to provide contrast and add visual definition. In comparison with other courses in Korea, the most pleasing aspect of Nine Bridges is the fairway shaping, designer Ronald Fream concentrating less on mounding and more on creating realistic movement and natural-looking golf holes.

Set out in two distinct loops, the course begins with the heavily treed and rolling outward nine and closes with the lake-infested back nine, strangely considered by the club to be its Scottish side. The front, or American, half is superior and actually has a distinct British feel, with some nice plateau greens, a Redan-shaped par three and even a Principal's Nose

bunker complex. The more open inward nine is much less impressive and, although the 12th and 16th are decent holes, to compare any of it to Scotland seems a bit of a stretch, so overdone is some of the shaping and so unnecessary some of the water hazards.

The opening nine, on the other hand, is terrific and crosses several natural ravines, which were cleverly incorporated into the long par five 3rd hole and the difficult 4th. It also offers genuine strategic options on a number of other holes. The 5th, for instance, bends right around a large bunker complex and then left around a lake. It is followed by the very British 6th hole, with its nostril-like bunkers in the middle of the fairway forcing either a layback off the tee, a drive into the safer but longer left side, or one down the dangerous right side. Elsewhere, the almost-Redan 2nd hole is nice enough to stand out among a pretty average set of par threes. The opening hole is very good, while the beautiful uphill 8th is a wonderfully simple short par four that appears a relatively trouble-free affair until you reach the horizon green and all its associated slope. Like a number of holes later in the round, you feel the site's elevation here as the island's notorious trade winds can wreak havoc with approach play.

While the deterioration from front nine to back at Nine Bridges is disappointing, this is clearly the best layout in Korea and there is still more than enough quality throughout the course for it to be recommended.

Spring City Golf & Lake Resort – Lake Course

COURSE OPENED 1999
DESIGNER Robert Trent
Jones Jr

'Spring City is destined to become one of the great golf resorts in the Asia Pacific region.'

ROBERT TRENT JONES JR

Located a short distance from the ancient capital of Yunnan Province in southern China, the Spring City Golf & Lake Resort was built on a mountainside almost 7,000 feet above sea level and overlooking the beautiful Yang Zong Hai Lake. With an ideal year-round climate for golf and grass growing, the resort enjoys tranquil views across the still waters of the lake to the surrounding mountain range and is not dissimilar to the setting of Scotland's famous Loch Lomond club, the golf also with a distinct American flavor.

The more impressive of the resort's two courses is the Robert Trent Jones Jr designed Lake Course, which is laid out beneath the elevated clubhouse and drops down the hillside toward the water with three holes touching the lake's edge. The design team shifted more than 4.5 million cubic meters of earth, primarily rock, to construct the course, with most holes built on ledges and terraced down toward the water. Lined by thick native grasses, the course is severe on stray balls and par is well protected by some extreme driving challenges, excessive length and heavily contoured green shapes.

Hardly an ideal start, the opening tee shot is fairly typical of what to expect throughout the round, a dramatic plunging drive to a narrow fairway with an instant reload for those missing on either side. Although the rest of the course is similarly penal, there is no denying the adventurous quality of holes like 2, 3, 4 and 7, which tumbles toward the lake and is a fun hole to play provided you can find the narrow fairway from the tee. The next three holes lie partly within the lake. The short 8th drops sharply to a green backing onto the water and is followed by a beautiful par five right along the lake's edge that is reachable in length, but sadly not in design, as the neck of the green pinches in so tight that only the desperate or deranged would take it on.

Perhaps the biggest highlight is the intimidating long par three 10th, played from a lakeside tee over part of the hazard and up a steep ridge to a seemingly tiny target. Requiring at least your longest iron, anything short or right will crash down the rocky cliff and into the water while a thick, menacing hillside waits on your left. So scary and narrow is the shot here that many actually choose to lay-up. Of the remaining back nine, the beautifully sited 13th green with its lake backdrop and the very fine 18th hole are the standouts. Despite moments of extravagance, the impeccably maintained Lake Course is terrific fun, well constructed and enjoys the most pleasant golf views in China.

Also part of the Spring City Resort is the more user-friendly Mountain Course by Jack Nicklaus Design. Built higher into the hillside and just as immaculately presented, the course is best remembered for its early lake views and its excellent 18th hole, which crosses a deep ravine and ends beneath the wonderful clubhouse.

Tiger Beach Golf Links

COURSE OPENED 2000

DESIGNER Beta Soong

The believability of the Tiger Beach
shaping is apparent here at the 3rd green.

OPPOSITE Bending around a water
hazard, the lengthy par four 10th is one
of Tiger Beach's most difficult holes.

Situated an hour from Qingdao in north-east
China, Tiger Beach is a refreshingly authentic-
looking modern links-style course carefully
crafted by two devout links lovers from Taiwan.
Set along the golden shores of the Yellow Sea,
the course was conceived and designed by Beta
Soong, a financial investor, real estate developer
and avid art and antiques collector with no
previous golf design or construction experience.
The site he selected for his links was a barren and
isolated seaside property with pleasant sea views
and a temperate climate, which was ideal for golf.

Though not strictly linksland because of its
heavy clay base and broader-leafed grasses,
Soong was nevertheless fanatical about creating a
realistic experience complete with pot bunkers,
raised greens, thick off-color roughs and natural-
looking ground movement. His course
superintendent, Brad Chih, did an excellent job
during construction and the strength of Tiger
Beach is the believability of his shaping. Greens
and surrounds are outstanding and protected by
deep bunkers and nice collection areas that lead
weak shots toward the well-placed hazards. The
internal green contours are quite intricate and
offer a range of ground game options, while the
driving zones are generally narrow and the
fairways lined by small jumbled dune ridges not
dissimilar to the softly contoured terrain of its
sister course, Carnoustie in Scotland.

Unfortunately, the rocky water hazards are an
unnecessary blight on the course, and aside from
spoiling the links aspect they do not really help
Soong's design. Both the par five 8th and 14th

reward those who play away from the water,
while the brutal 10th hole has a lake that totally
cuts off the recovery option for a misplaced
drive. The biggest criticism of the layout,
however, is the continual north-south
orientation of a back and forth routing where
virtually every hole is either straight down or
against the constant sea winds.

Lacking the subtle directional shifts that
typify the classic British links, good players
driving well here can really get into a groove
and it is no coincidence that the best holes on
the course, 12 and 13, are those where you
change the direction of play. The difficult 12th
is a long par three with a built-up green played
across the wind for the first time, and the 13th
is a tremendous short par four bending through
some minor protruding dunes into an attractive
target. Elsewhere the individual quality of holes
like 1, 2, 4, 6, 7, 15, 17 and 18, as well as the large
number of terrific green sites, help the course
overcome any routing problems it may have.

One of biggest challenges facing Tiger
Beach stems from the attitude of its mostly
Korean clientele, who seem to associate lush
green grass with quality golf and will not come
to play if the course is too firm. This mindset
unfortunately prevents the hard and fast
conditions that the exceptional shaping of the
layout deserves. Regardless of any frustrations
with the softness of such a bouncy-looking
course, the totally sculptured Tiger Beach
Golf Links is a special find in China and one
of Asia's rare modern gems.

Mission Hills Golf Club – Norman Course

COURSE OPENED 2004

DESIGNERS Greg Norman,
Bob Harrison

Shades of Doonbeg 14 in the tiny 4th green.

OPPOSITE Classical bunker shapes, mountain backdrops and penal rough areas characterize the testing Norman Course at Mission Hills, the 15th hole.

Less than an hour from the Hong Kong border, Mission Hills is an enormous resort and residential development with ten golf courses spread over three sites between the relatively affluent Chinese cities of Shenzhen and Dongguan. Though each course is named after a prominent golf identity, such as Jumbo Ozaki, David Duval, Ernie Els, Annika Sorenstam and even teaching professional David Leadbetter, eight were actually built by a two-man IMG design team. The original World Cup Course and the Norman Course are the exceptions and, not surprisingly, the standouts.

The Jack Nicklaus-designed World Cup Course opened on the resort's Shenzhen site in 1994, with the nine subsequent courses all completed in less than a decade, and the final five, built in the hills of Dongguan, taking just two years to build. The Norman Course was the tenth layout to open at what is now the world's largest golf complex and is one of the most difficult tests in all of Asia. It was created by Greg Norman's Australian design team, headed by Bob Harrison and Harley Kruse, who were offered first choice of the huge and hilly property for their layout. Although some serious grading and earthmoving was required, their chosen land was the most golf-friendly on site. The more open front nine tends to wander atop steep ridges and hug a series of hillsides, while the tighter back nine is mostly set down in two deep valley floors and surrounded by heavily forested mountain slopes that create an attractive backdrop for the golf.

With a distinct lack of the repetitive design found elsewhere at the resort, this is clearly the most attractive and original of the ten courses. It is also unquestionably the toughest, with the narrow fairways bordered by thick native grasses, dense forest vegetation and sharply cut sand-faced bunkers that are deep and punishing throughout the course. Approach play is also tricky, as the greens and fringes are heavily contoured and cut short to allow a variety of recovery shot options. As a set they probably don't work quite as well as some of the other greens by this team but the small crests, false fronts and run-off areas create interesting situations and do blend naturally with their surrounds.

While the course enjoys excellent views, good golf terrain and a number of fine holes such as the 1st, 2nd, 7th and 17th, ultimately what keeps it from more elite company are the few holes that seem excessively difficult. These include a couple on the back nine that are cut through hills and bunkered to force the better player to lay-up but leave the average golfer still needing to pierce two hills with a driver and dissect a very tight fairway to keep the ball in play. There is also the slender kidney-shaped par three 4th, which is remarkably similar to Norman's 14th at Doonbeg and stands out as the only green totally surrounded by trouble, the left side falling into oblivion and probably too severe for the caliber of golfer who plays here.

The Norman Course at Mission Hills may be a bruising examination, but a round here is thoroughly enjoyable and, along with the chance to play the original World Cup Course, is reason enough to visit this fabulous destination.

Ria Bintan Resort – Ocean Course

COURSE OPENED 1999
DESIGNER Gary Player

Pristine, peaceful and unhurried, the Indonesian island of Bintan may seem worlds away from the hustle and bustle of Singapore but is less than an hour by ferry and a popular destination for that country's somewhat fanatical golfers. Easily the best kept and constructed of the island's courses is the Gary Player-designed Ria Bintan Ocean Course.

The layout comes recommended primarily for a glamorous stretch of holes, the 7th through 10th, which play toward and then along the emerald waters of the South China Sea. The green on the short cross-sea 9th actually rests entirely within the ocean and is surrounded by large boulders that complete the dramatic picture. Both the 7th and 8th, with the sea as their backdrop, are good holes, but elsewhere the golf is typically resort-style with a greater emphasis placed on the visual than the strategic aspect of design. An example is the deep, grass-faced bunkers, which make a striking feature from the tee but are poorly designed as their lips face tees rather than targets and allow good players to hit crisp long irons out of the shallow side and directly at the green.

Although the holes away from the beach are fairly nondescript and the bunker inside a bunker beside the 10th green is silly, the Ria Bintan experience is quite enjoyable. The panoramic sea views and blinding white sand beaches are superb and the few ocean holes are good enough to make it worth a side trip for those in nearby Singapore.

Pinx Golf Club

COURSE OPENED 1999
DESIGNER Theodore G. Robinson

Part of a unique luxury hotel and golf retreat, the Pinx Golf Club is an exclusive facility set within pleasant surroundings on South Korea's Jeju Island. With outlooks across the island's blue coastline and a number of holes boasting views of the impressive Mt Halla, this golf course is pure resort fare with lush green playing surfaces, cart paths and an abundance of manufactured water hazards.

The core of the course is quite good, with the greens a standout. Many are actually built up and designed with clever breaks and interesting contours. The best of the attractive complexes are those on the 5th, 9th, 11th, 13th, 14th and 18th. What hurts Pinx, however, is the lack of detail in the fairways, with almost no internal fairway shaping done despite vast amounts of earth being pushed to the sides to create symmetrical mounding. Bunkering is also a problem, the haphazard look and location of the round or sprawling bunker shapes often meaning that bad shots are unlucky to find trouble instead of being lucky to avoid it.

This successful and popular golf club has many positives, especially the clubhouse facilities and the incredible hotel, but serious shaping and construction shortfalls on the course ultimately keep it from being one of Asia's absolute elite.

OPPOSITE The 5th hole at the Pinx Golf Club is an excellent long par three.

Africa

OPPOSITE Africa is an extraordinary continent, though serious golf travel is almost exclusively restricted to South Africa, where British settlers managed to introduce a genuine golf culture. Pictured is the 14th hole at Pezula, one of several modern golf developments to take advantage of the region's dramatic coastline.

South Africa

South Africa is a country of astonishing geographical diversity, from the fertile plains of its high veldt and the subtropical coastline of KwaZulu Natal to the wide, unbroken savannahs of the Eastern Transvaal and the soaring peaks of the Drakensberg Mountain Range. The golf industry here is no less varied. It had modest beginnings back in 1885 when the Cape Golf Club was formed by British General Sir Henry Torrens, who laid out a course in front of his military camp. There is now a golf course in virtually every town in South Africa but, like most of the golfing world, it was not until the 1920s and 30s that quality design first reached these shores. Colonel S.V. Hotchkin and the well-traveled Charles H. Alison made the long journey from Britain to design gems such as Glendower in Geuteng and East London and Humewood along the Eastern Cape. Strangely, the giant of this period, Durban Country Club, was designed by little-known locals who were given a terrific site and managed to create Africa's first world-class golf course.

South Africa is most significant today as the birthplace of multiple major champions such as Bobby Locke, Gary Player, Ernie Els and Retief Goosen, as well as the venue of golf's first million-dollar tournament. This event is still played annually at Sun City, a Vegas-style resort built within a province that was separated from the country during the dark days of apartheid and thus avoided boycotts and sanctions. Golf in post-apartheid South Africa has boomed, with new developments popping up all over the country. While classics such as Durban and Humewood remain the nation's premier layouts, modern golfing highlights include the Leopard Creek/Kruger National Park double, the ambitious 'Links' project at the Fancourt resort and the stunning scenery at Pezula, Oubaii and Atlantic Beach. Disappointments include highly rated estate courses at Pecanwood and Erinvale, the old courses in Cape Town and poor design efforts on beautiful land at Arabella and Fish River Sun.

The strongest golf regions here are Johannesburg, which houses a number of fine private clubs, the increasingly popular Garden Route and the KwaZulu Natal coastline, which includes Durban, its smaller sister course Beachwood and a surprising find called Prince's Grant by Peter Matkovich. For a quirky treat, Umdoni Park south of Durban is worth a look, its wild coastal land sure to please the adventurous golfer who can tolerate the odd bad bounce or uneven lie and put up with a few poor holes in exchange for some really fun stuff.

South Africa is an extraordinary country and a terrific place to visit; the warmth of the hospitality and the standard of accommodation at resorts like Pezula, Fancourt, Sun City and Leopard Creek is truly remarkable. While the quality and diversity of modern golf sites here is also impressive, there is sadly little design variety, as most of the contracts are given to a select few established names. Were the golf courses themselves as interesting as the wildlife, the national parks, the hotels or even the land most are built on, South Africa would be unrivaled anywhere as a golf destination.

OPPOSITE Modern golf with a classic feel at the Atlantic Beach estate near Cape Town. This is the par three 12th hole, which has wonderful views across the sea to the city's famed Table Mountain.

Durban Country Club

COURSE OPENED 1922

DESIGNERS George Waterman,
Laurie Waters

Durban's wicked little 12th hole, which became notorious when the Prince of Wales once missed the green and took 16 strokes to hole out.

OPPOSITE The view from the tee on the magnificent par three 2nd.

South Africa's most internationally recognized golf club, the Durban Country Club was founded in 1920 following the flooding of the Durban Golf Club during the South African Open, and the fear that the city would not host the event again unless another course was built. A new club was formed, and the chosen site for its course was old swampland north of Durban's city center, which was blessed with magnificent sand dunes and located less than 100 meters from the Indian Ocean's golden coastline. George Waterman and Laurie Waters designed the layout and although it has been tweaked several times since, including by Colonel S.V. Hotchkin in 1929, the majority of the course remains basically as first designed.

Durban is a contrasting mix of links and parkland golf, with fairways generally cut through dense tropical vegetation and native bush. Eight holes are routed within the severely undulating dunes and the remaining ten are situated out on the flatlands. The opening five holes run adjacent to the beachside boundary and occupy the site's prime sandhills. The best of these is the par three 2nd, which overlooks the coastline and features a superbly bunkered back-to-front-sloping target. Squeezed between this masterpiece and another wonderful short hole is the world-famous par five 3rd, which heads through a substantial dune valley. Elsewhere on the front side, the 5th and 6th are both excellent strong fours, while the par five 8th is a fantastic challenge that is notorious for its semi-blind approach shot played across a heavy diagonal ridge and into a small crowned green ringed by the thick bush.

The back nine is unfortunately a bit of a mixed bag. The two closing holes are fabulous, but the rest is laid out across a fairly flat and unexciting field with several holes of only moderate architectural interest. The obvious exception is the evil par three 12th, which is a real card wrecker and plays along a steep ridge to a narrow tabletop green that falls sharply on either side. The 17th is a remarkable piece of routing, its approach crossing a deep basin that features some nauseating undulation. Completing the round is a charming, drivable par four with an obscured and falling target that must be approached from a narrowing left section of fairway.

An exciting journey from start to finish, the highlights at Durban generally come on holes where the significant gradient changes are used within the fairways. The massive bumps leading into the elevated 17th green, for instance, and those fronting the par five 8th are some of the largest on the course and the optical intimidation they present golfers has helped protect the layout from becoming redundant in the wake of technological advances. The expansion of the city, however, has had an affect on the club, with the course now wedged between two major coastal roads and the 16th hole realigned to accommodate the widening of a freeway. The 15th also had to be rebuilt in 2002 after flooding had damaged the original hole.

While there is no doubt that Durban deserves its place among the top few courses on the African continent, it is slightly spoilt by the weaker flatland holes farther away from the shoreline. Its best holes are very special, however, and although there is a major disparity between these and the less impressive moments, there is much to admire about the Durban Country Club and its delightful course.

Humewood Golf Club

COURSE OPENED 1931
DESIGNER Colonel S.V.
Hotchkin

The wonderful crosswind par three
6th hole.

OPPOSITE Humewood's 18th green
and elegant clubhouse.

The Humewood Golf Club was born in 1929 when members of the Port Elizabeth Golf Club approached Colonel S.V. Hotchkin to design a second golf course for their town. The proposed site for the new layout was a compact tract of coastal land adjacent to Algoa Bay, a famously windy coast that had, over the years, receded to present golfers with a perfect linkscape full of bumps, humps, ripples and swales.

Africa's only true links, Humewood has a very traditional feel, with a distinguished set of holes that you will almost swear were transplanted straight from the British Isles. Hotchkin's holes are primarily oriented east and west and either play directly into or against the fierce offshore winds that lash the bay. Lined by thick coastal shrub and underbrush, the fairways are reasonably generous but feel quite tight, while the bunkering is a mix of deep revetted greenside traps and softer, simpler shapes through the fairway.

Wind is a key feature of the challenge at Humewood, and although the prevailing westerly typically helps on each of the par fives, it hurts on all four of the long par fours. The course starts with a series of understated but clever links moments before reaching the first of its two classics, the par three 6th, which is one of Africa's finest holes. Often little more than a wedge, it plays across the wind to a narrow crowned green that falls sharply and is heavily trapped on all sides. The other short

holes are also very good, as are the birdieable par fives, but the remaining highlight is undoubtedly the long two-shot 13th, which generally plays into the westerly and features a dramatic, almost lunar, landscape not dissimilar to that at Royal St George's. As with a number of holes on the back nine, you will struggle to find flat lies on this fairway, the approach usually played with a wood or long-iron across a climbing, corrugated fairway and into a terrific tabletop target resting beyond a large mound.

Other attractions of the course include difficult tee shots on the 4th, 7th and 11th, the short but hidden par four 16th, a charming plateau green on the 5th, and the classic obscured approach over a series of small ridges into the 10th green. The generous but bumpy opening hole is also very good, while the heavily undulating finishing hole, set in the shadows of the elegant colonial-style clubhouse, is a splendid close to the round.

As genuine as links golf outside Britain gets and a superb test of your golfing capabilities, Humewood comes highly recommended, not simply because it is a links but because it is a fine links and the continent of Africa hurts for good golf. Were it in Britain it would not rate as high as it does here, but this is a rare jewel in South Africa and ought to be one of the first courses confirmed on the golf itinerary for anyone making the trip to this intriguing country.

Fancourt Resort – The Links at Fancourt

COURSE OPENED 2000
DESIGNERS Gary Player,
Phil Jacobs

'The Links at Fancourt is without a doubt the most fascinating project in our portfolio of over 200 courses around the world. To take such a terrible piece of ground and create this incredible landscape was an accomplishment I'll never forget.'

GARY PLAYER

OPPOSITE The 216-meter par three 2nd plays across an immense artificial landscape toward a dangerous green framed by the distant Outeniqua Mountains.

Located along South Africa's popular Garden Route, the Fancourt Estate had existed for more than 100 years before it was transformed into a golf destination in the 1980s when Gary Player designed the first of his four courses here. Following a string of financial failures, the estate was purchased a decade later by Dr Hasso Plattner, the German founder of software giant SAP. Plattner had ambitious expansion plans for the resort, which included the addition of a 'links' course to be built on an adjacent airstrip with no natural features and a heavy clay base.

As far from genuine linksland as you could find, Plattner and his designers, Player and Phil Jacobs, dumped 700,000 cubic meters of soil onto the flat site and then pushed it around to build their own massive dunescape. The aim was to create a unique links-like experience complete with lumpy fairways, pot bunkers and thick off-color native grasses. Daunting from tee to green, the course is extremely long, with the well-bunkered fairways set between ragged dune ridges that rise up to 20 feet high and the majority of targets shaped to present intriguing ground versus aerial options.

The severity of the challenge presented by the Links is evident from the demanding opening hole, which is tight from the tee and, like the adjacent 18th fairway, occupies the naturally higher ground. Feature holes down on the main paddock include the downhill par three 2nd hole, the brutal par four 3rd, dotted with deep traps and a burn guarding the front of its small green, and the short par four 6th. On the back nine, the bumpy 10th rises to a wicked plateau green, while the 12th is a murderously long par four that ends with a narrow target sitting atop a crest and falling into a hidden pond on one side and steeply down into a deep hollow on the other. The 15th is the postcard hole, a difficult dogleg left around wetlands that extend all the way to the green and even wrap around the back and right side of the target.

The most obvious sore point with the Links is the unnaturalness of playing corridors, which are often softly rolling and lacking in the awkward stances and odd bounces that typify a traditional links, but surrounded by heavy and messy dunes. These are certainly not the most realistic dune creations in golf, but of all the manufactured links-style courses worldwide this is clearly the most intimidating.

Purists who don't think they will like this artificial links probably won't. It is simply too easy to pick fault here with penal ponds, cart paths, long walks between holes, lush green surfaces and some extreme design all conspiring to damage its authenticity. The course is conceptually compelling, however, and you have to give the design team credit for building a number of good holes amid all the earthmoving. Had the effort been made to make the dunes look as realistic as those at a place like Kingsbarns, or more shaping been used within the holes, it would have been even more impressive. As it stands, The Links at Fancourt is a considerable achievement and is a marvelous modern golf course with an already awesome international reputation.

Leopard Creek Country Club

COURSE OPENED 1996
DESIGNER Gary Player

'With its proximity to the Kruger National Park, I can't imagine a golfer having a more African Safari experience than at Leopard Creek.'

GARY PLAYER

A private club with a small invitation-only membership, Leopard Creek was the brainchild of billionaire business entrepreneur Johann Rupert. Incorporating a prestige residential component, the 890-acre development is located on the southern perimeter of the world-famous Kruger National Park near Malelane in Mpumalanga, and is bordered to the north and west by Crocodile River. A quality high-end golf experience that will seduce most visitors with its pristine playing surfaces, luxury thatched roof clubhouse and dramatic design, Leopard Creek is much more than just glitz and glamour with some exceptional resort golf in a uniquely African environment.

Originally designed by Gary Player, the course was radically overhauled a few years after opening following advice from one of its members and residents, Jack Nicklaus. Where Player had typically built up his greens, tees and bunkers, Nicklaus suggested they be lowered to look more natural. Aside from flat waterside greens on the front nine par threes, which are a touch featureless, his changes are impressive and a major improvement to the layout. Around the same time, the club also removed a wall behind the 13th green to open up the views over Crocodile River and into the vastness of Kruger, which was a real masterstroke as it allows golfers to watch the wildlife while they wait to putt.

The most surprising aspect of Leopard Creek, apart from its captivating setting, is how strategic some of the two-shot holes are. Both the 4th and the tempting 6th are very good, as are signature holes like the twinned 9th and 18th, which share a crocodile infested pond and demand thrilling all-carry approach shots into their greens. The dogleg 13th across and then along a diagonal creek toward the National Park is a fine risk/reward hole for the average handicapper, while the left-bending 1st hole and the narrow 17th both have nice chase-in green entrances. The 8th green, with the front left side of its kidney shape falling away sharply, is yet another treat. From a negative perspective, the 180-degree teeing area at the par three 16th is a little over the top and the turf could do without the two adult giraffes strutting around the property, but otherwise the club's owner has done well to show restraint here.

Leopard Creek is by no means simply an expensive resort but rather a quality American-style target golf course in superb settings that is full of exciting shots to play. The fact that Africa's incredible wildlife roams within your general vicinity as you play adds to the allure of a round here. Indeed, it is the entire Leopard Creek experience that is highly recommended. From the immaculate golf course and old-world clubhouse to the brilliant on-site hotel and life-changing experience of an early morning journey through the Kruger National Park, this is quite a golf destination.

OPPOSITE In the shadows of the luxurious Leopard Creek clubhouse, golfers approach the 9th green (left) and 18th green (right) across a dangerous pond inhabited by crocodiles.

Sun City Resort – Gary Player Country Club

COURSE OPENED 1979
DESIGNER Gary Player

The 15th green on the Gary Player course is just one of the many small clover-shaped targets on this difficult track.

OPPOSITE Ending in front of its unique clubhouse is the par five 18th on the Lost City course.

Built within a former volcanic crater, Sun City is a landmark luxury resort and casino made famous in the golfing world by the twelve-man Million Dollar Challenge held on the Gary Player Country Club course every December. The resort is bordered by the Pilanesberg National Park, which became a national park in 1979 following the largest game-resettlement project in the history of South Africa. The park is now thriving with wildlife including Africa's famous Big Five: lion, leopard, elephant, buffalo and rhinoceros.

Named after its designer, the Gary Player Country Club is the resort's centerpiece and has been significantly revamped and strengthened since opening, especially in recent years when a staggering number of back tees have been added and each of the bunkers deepened and enlarged. Built primarily over flat terrain and surrounded by dense *bushveld*, the course is notorious for its tiny greens. Many are clover-shaped and feature wings to allow tournament pins to be tucked behind bunkers on tiny pieces of green. Coupled with choking kikuyu grass in the roughs and fringe areas, which makes recovery play both difficult and monotonous, this is one incredibly punishing test.

Most holes play between bunkers from the tee, then onto small slippery greens ringed by sand or fronted by ponds. After a relentless start the central holes offer the best chances at birdie. The par five 9th features an island green and is a fun hole to play if long enough from the tee to be tempted to have a go at the green in two, while the 10th is another reachable three-shot hole with a

microscopic green surrounded by thick rough. The finishing holes are also quite good. The 16th is the standout par three, while the lengthened 17th had its green pushed into the water and, despite trees and sticky rough along the lake edge detracting a little from the risk/reward possibilities of the tee shot, is much improved. A tough dogleg over water to a really tight green, the 18th is a good closer and an appropriate end to such a ruthless challenge.

The Player design is not overly strategic or clever but instead relies on its relentlessness and quality grooming to impress. In many ways the excessive difficulty is disappointing, however, as the course is now one of the world's longest, the greens among the world's smallest and, for mere mortals, a number of holes have simply become too hard.

Opening in 1993, Sun City's second course, the Lost City Country Club, was also designed by Gary Player's company and is considered the resort's poorer cousin, even though many scribes prefer its greater playability. With more width and elevated tees, the course is most significant for a crocodile-carry par three and the adjacent finishing holes, the long par four 9th and reachable par five 18th both heading along a cascading lake with the Flintstone-esque clubhouse as their backdrop.

Though neither course at Sun City is outstanding, for all its tournament history the Gary Player Country Club does warrant a look, especially for those who can afford to stay in the resort's five-star Palace of the Lost City Hotel.

East London Golf Club

COURSE OPENED 1923
DESIGNERS George Peck, Colonel S.V. Hotchkin

One of South Africa's oldest golf clubs, East London's current course is a charming layout built among thick native bush on fabulous coastal duneland along the Eastern Cape. Reminiscent of other heavily wooded seaside courses such as Newcastle in Australia, it was designed by George Peck and Colonel S.V. Hotchkin and opened shortly after the First World War.

The strength of their course is its front nine, which tumbles wildly across beautifully rolling ridges, the unconventional routing heading into and around the dunes, plunging down valleys and over hills to hidden targets. There are probably a few too many short par fours for the modern golfer's liking, but those early on are genuinely fun to play and only offer up birdies to players taking an aggressive line from the tee. Holes like 1, 3, 4 and 5 are all terrific, while the 9th is a cracking hole that heads over a large crest and then down and left through a pronounced bush-lined valley. On the back nine the 12th is a standout and follows a similar shape, rising toward the coast and offering players great views of the nearby Indian Ocean. Elsewhere the short 17th is a fabulous par three, and although most of the other closing holes are fairly ordinary they fail to tarnish a tremendous day's golf.

In terms of topography and quality, East London is a real roller coaster and is the sort of high-class, unpretentious golf course that South Africa desperately needs more of.

Atlantic Beach Golf Club

COURSE OPENED 2000
DESIGNER Mark Muller

Atlantic Beach is a unique and heavily developed golf and residential estate north of Cape Town that is built on rolling sandy terrain and enjoys superb views across Table Bay to the city's famed Table Mountain. While most new developments are compromised by the building of golf on unsuitable ground, here the golf land is pure, the holes routed over a series of small dunes and cut through corridors of thick indigenous coastal shrub known as fynbos. Unfortunately, this fynbos is protected and off-fairway areas are actually treated as lateral hazards and out-of-bounds for stray golfers. As many fairways are narrow, driving under the typically windy conditions is therefore very demanding. The 4th hole, for instance, is a particularly nasty experience as it is played over a scrubby dune to a hidden fairway with out-of-bounds down both sides.

Though the fairway grass is not as keen as a fine fescue, the course does play firm and bouncy like a links, and holes alter character with every wind change. Charmingly, the par five 15th is almost drivable downwind, while the unusual half punchbowl 17th could be played successfully with a putter. Equally memorable are the short 5th and 12th holes for their Table Mountain backdrops and the 10th, a brilliant driving hole across a valley to a crested fairway that flirts with a disused sand quarry. There are also a number of sporty greens, including the half-hidden 9th and 17th and the severely tilted 6th and 15th.

While the unfortunate dune restrictions and invasive housing prevent Atlantic Beach from reaching loftier heights, of the modern estate courses in Africa this is definitely one of the best.

OPPOSITE Sprawling sand traps protect the 18th fairway on the solid Atlantic Beach layout.

Pezula Golf Club

COURSE OPENED 2000
DESIGNERS Ronald Fream, David Dale

Located in the heart of South Africa's Garden Route, the Pezula Golf Club is situated atop a massive bluff overlooking both the stunning African coastline and the entrance to the Kynsna lagoon. Despite enjoying one of the most spectacular sites in the country and being covered in an indigenous coastal fynbos, the golf course is distinctly American in style, with heavily contoured greens, eye-catching bunker shapes and an integrated housing component, which regrettably occupies several key scenic and golfing locales.

After an unusual opening par five that forces you to lay-up off the tee, the front nine loops away from the sea and features several holes hugging the edge of a clifftop that looks down upon the quaint town of Kynsna. Better holes include the almost Cape-style 2nd and the par three 3rd, although most of the highlights are reserved for the back nine, which plays along the coastal side of the property, heading out toward and then briefly along the Indian Ocean. The steeply sinking 12th and 13th both enjoy stunning views, although those on the 13th are spoilt by housing built along the fairway and between the green and sea. The next hole is a short four that drops toward the rocky coastline and features the most glamorous backdrop of all, though unfortunately its green is ringed by sand eliminating aggressive options from the tee.

Hamstrung by housing, Ronald Fream's design is mostly sound, except for the odd extreme green and the occasional misplaced risk/reward fairway bunker. His work at Pezula, however, was always going to be upstaged by the views, especially the extraordinary outlook beyond the 14th green.

Oubaai Golf Club

COURSE OPENED 2005
DESIGNER Ernie Els with Nicklaus Design

Less than six miles from the city of George, Oubaai is an up-market golf development built on an elevated headland high above the ocean. Although its final three holes jut out toward the sea, most of the golf is inland of the wonderful clubhouse and bordered by a deep river valley and surrounded by the Outeniqua Mountain Range.

Oubaai's design team included champion golfer Ernie Els, who thankfully had a strong input, particularly on the green-shaping, which is the strength of the layout. A fan of Melbourne's Sandbelt, Els conceived of greens with a similarly simple approach. Small to medium in size, they are firm and slick, yet not overly contoured and generally tilted in context with the preceding fairway. Several nice short par fours with strategic bunkering and a terrific par three across a deep ravine are part of a very solid outward half, and although the course loses its way a little from the 11th, the views on the finishing few holes do help rescue the back nine. One of the biggest question marks over Oubaai is how future housing will affect the course. While most homes will be on the low side of the property and built into valleys, a great many are planned for inside the layout and could damage the visual enjoyment of a round here.

Oubaai is the first course that Els designed in his homeland, and one suspects also the first in which he was actively involved during the design process. With clever green sites, attractive chipping areas and several fine holes, this is a pretty handy modern course and a very good design start for the popular South African.

Ratings & Rankings

OPPOSITE Ireland's Old Head is one of the
world's most spectacular golf courses. Pictured is
the view from the 18th tee looking back down the
17th fairway and along the coast.

Ratings
& Rankings

Best Holes

Best Courses

'Golf, a single journey or a series of adventures?'

OPPOSITE **One of the best and most breathtaking par threes in golf, the 7th hole at Nirwana Bali.**

Although ranking lists make fascinating reading, none are really able to provide an accurate or 'official' rank of quality, because the definitive description of great golf has still not been written. Is quality golf a single coherent journey or a series of adventures? Do low-profile links or elevated clifftop sites make more exciting golf venues? Are natural courses or man-made masterpieces most worthy of our admiration? The answer in each instance comes down to personal preferences, as no golf course is perfect and every golfer, including those on ranking panels, seeks subjective pleasure in every round he or she plays.

About the only thing ranking lists successfully achieve is the stirring of healthy debate. After all, how does one really compare St Andrews to Sun City or Turnberry to Teeth of the Dog, when it is barely the same game played at each venue? While the majority of magazines try to assign numeric values to the elements that they believe typically make up a golf course, variations in interpretation and the individual tastes and critical ability of some of their panellists may ultimately hurt the credibility of the final result.

The biggest misconception in golf is to equate difficulty with quality, a belief not helped by panels continually elevating tough tournament venues to the tops of their lists. The most contentious area of course analysis, however, is conditioning or presentation. Unfortunately, how a course is groomed is often given as much weight as how the holes are actually designed and built, which is a nonsense considering judges only see a course once or twice and are in no position to accurately assess its typical turf standards. Focusing on turf quality can also distort reality, and I would hate to turn golfers off wonderfully original layouts like the Berkshire, Highlands Links or Paraparaumu Beach because their perfectly playable fairways do not offer the same lush lies available at nearby resorts.

Although every attempt has been made to ensure that the reviews in this book are written dispassionately, there remain elements of bias in even the most balanced golf course critique. There are also large variances in analytical methodology. My view that judging the quality of a course involves considering the individual strength of all eighteen holes and then factoring in the more general elements of setting, construction, conditioning and overall design, for instance, differs considerably from the more mathematical method of assigning scores to criteria like shot values, resistance to scoring, design variety and memorability which the magazines employ to compile their ranking lists.

Ultimately, the only truly accurate rankings are an individual's own, so while they are unlikely to meet with universal agreement, in order to provide an insight into my own personal preferences, and given the inevitability of the 'Which is best?' question, here are what I regard as the best, hardest and most dramatic golf courses and golf holes on the planet.

Darius Oliver

Best Holes – Par Threes

Best Par Threes – Classic

Royal Troon 8th
Royal Melbourne (West) 5th
Royal County Down 7th
St Andrews (Old) 11th
Royal Portrush (Dunluce) 14th
Kingston Heath 15th
Royal County Down 4th
Muirfield 13th
Gleneagles (Kings) 5th
Rye 7th
New South Wales 6th
Swinley Forest 4th
Highlands Links 5th
Humewood 6th
Royal Worlington & Newmarket 5th
Yarra Yarra 11th
The Berkshire (Red) 16th
North Berwick 15th
Ono 17th
Banff Springs 4th
Biarritz (La Phare) 14th
Durban 2nd
Hirono 5th

The Berkshire (Red) 10th
Moortown 10th
Woodhall Spa 12th
Vale do Lobo (Royal) 16th
Saunton (East) 5th *England*
Royal Aberdeen 3rd
Royal West Norfolk 4th
Stoke Park Club 7th *England*
Royal Dornoch 2nd
Cruden Bay 4th
Western Gailes 7th
Turnberry 15th
Kasumigaseki (East) 10th
County Sligo 16th
West Sussex 5th
Royal Birkdale 12th
Morfontaine (Valliere) 4th
Royal Melbourne (West) 7th
El Saler 17th
Newcastle 7th
Jockey Club (Colorada) 17th
Muirfield 4th
Jasper Park 15th
Royal Dornoch 6th

Abiko 7th
Toronto 4th
Royal Aberdeen 17th
Sunningdale (Old) 4th
Metropolitan 2nd
Hillside 10th
North Berwick 4th
The Addington 13th *England*
Kennemer 15th
Sunningdale (New) 5th
Ballybunion (Old) 15th
Silloth on Solway 9th
West Sussex 8th
Hirono 7th
Kingston Heath 10th
Royal Melbourne (West) 16th
Morfontaine (Valliere) 9th
Portmarnock 15th
Woodlands 17th
Carnoustie 8th
Commonwealth 9th
Titirangi 11th
Mid Ocean 17th
Royal Aberdeen 8th

Best Par Threes – Modern

Nirwana Bali 7th
The National (Old) 7th
Barnbougle Dunes 7th
Teeth of the Dog 5th
Doonbeg 9th
Peninsula (North) 2nd
Teeth of the Dog 7th
Cabo del Sol (Ocean) 17th
Greywolf 6th
Oitavos 14th
Doonbeg 14th
Teeth of the Dog 16th
Cape Kidnappers 13th
The Dunes 17th
Thirteenth Beach (Beach) 16th
Querencia 11th
Ellerston 6th
Port Royal 16th *Bermuda*
Waterville 17th
The National (Moonah) 5th
Enniscrone 17th
St Andrews Beach (Gunnamatta) 6th
Fancourt (Montague) 17th

Kingston Heath 15th

Royal Dornoch 2nd

Ballybunion (Old) 15th

Teeth of the Dog 16th

Best Set of Par Threes

Swinley Forest
Rye
Teeth of the Dog
The Berkshire (Red)
Royal Melbourne (West)
Royal County Down
Cabo del Sol (Ocean)
Muirfield
Hirono
Kingston Heath
Royal Portrush (Dunluce)
Morfontaine (27 Holes)
Royal Aberdeen
West Sussex
Thirteenth Beach (Beach)
Paraparaumu Beach
Jasper Park
New South Wales
Nirwana Bali
Turnberry (Ailsa)
Royal Dornoch
Ono
Yarra Yarra

Hardest Par Threes

Carnoustie 16th
The National (Ocean) 9th
Doonbeg 14th
Cruden Bay 15th
Royal Portrush (Dunluce) 14th
Royal Troon 8th
St Andrews (Old) 11th
Spring City (Lake) 10th
Rye 7th
Turnberry (Ailsa) 6th
Rye 14th
Royal County Down 4th
Teeth of the Dog 16th
Tralee 13th
West Sussex 6th
Woodhall Spa 12th
Royal West Norfolk 4th
Kennemer 15th
Moonah Links (Open) 17th
Saunton (East) 5th *England*
Thirteenth Beach (Beach) 16th
St Andrews Beach (Gunnamatta) 16th

Most Spectacular Par Threes

Doonbeg 14th
Nirwana Bali 7th
The National (Old) 7th
Banff Springs 4th
Royal Portrush (Dunluce) 14th
Cabo del Sol (Ocean) 17th
Vale do Lobo (Royal) 16th
New South Wales 6th
Greywolf 6th
Teeth of the Dog 16th
Teeth of the Dog 5th
Narooma 3rd *Australia*
Teeth of the Dog 7th
Doonbeg 9th
Port Royal 16th *Bermuda*
Banff Springs 10th
Ria Bintan (Ocean) 9th
Cape Kidnappers 13th
Cruden Bay 4th
Ballybunion (Old) 15th
Royal Troon 8th
Old Head 3rd

Kauri Cliffs 14th
Kingsbarns 15th
Royal County Down 4th
Old Head 16th
Spring City (Lake) 10th
Tralee 13th
Barnbougle Dunes 5th
Ballybunion (Cashen) 16th
Nirwana Bali 14th
Tralee 16th
Oubaai 6th
Joondalup (Quarry) 3rd
Kauri Cliffs 7th
Hirono 5th
Old Head 7th
St Enodoc 15th
Praia D'El Rey 14th
Durban 2nd
Spring City (Lake) 8th
Barnbougle Dunes 7th
Ellerston 6th
Querencia 14th
Oitavos 14th

Rye 7th

Doonbeg 14th

Banff Springs 4th

Spring City (Lake) 10th

Best Holes – Par Fours

Best Par Fours – Classic (under 340m)

North Berwick 13th
Royal Adelaide 3rd
Lahinch 13th
Ballybunion (Old) 6th
Royal Dornoch 5th
Royal Melbourne (West) 10th
St Enodoc 4th
Tenby 3rd
New South Wales 14th
Kawana (Fuji) 7th
Royal County Down 6th
Kingston Heath 3rd
Pennard 7th
De Pan 10th
Woodlands 4th
County Louth 14th
Royal Hague 7th
Royal Aberdeen 5th
Royal Melbourne (East) 1st
El Saler 8th
Commonwealth 17th

Muirfield 3rd
Machrihanish 3rd
St Andrews (Old) 12th
Paraparaumu Beach 8th
St Andrews (Old) 18th
North Berwick 18th
Machrihanish 6th
Kennemer 10th
Hamburger (Falkenstein) 13th
Royal Troon 7th
Cruden Bay 3rd
The Island 14th
Kingston Heath 9th
Hamilton 5th
Durban 18th
Sunningdale (Old) 11th
Woodlands 7th
Koga 3rd
Royal Cinque Ports 6th
St George's Hill 4th
Royal Portrush (Dunluce) 8th
Portmarnock 14th
Royal Liverpool 2nd
Ganton 3rd

Best Par Fours – Modern (under 340m)

Barnbougle Dunes 4th
Praia D'El Rey 4th
Barnbougle Dunes 15th
Carne 11th
Kingsbarns 6th
St Andrews Beach (Gunnamatta) 2nd
Enniscrone 12th
Cabo del Sol (Ocean) 14th
Wolf Creek (South) 8th
Enniscrone 13th
Waterville 16th
Doonbeg 5th
Barnbougle Dunes 12th
Club Pelican 12th
Loch Lomond 14th
Eichenheim 7th
Kennedy Bay 7th
Teeth of the Dog 15th
Portsea 13th
Prince de Provence 2nd
Castelconturbia (Yellow) 7th
Peninsula (South) 7th

Best Par Fours – Classic (over 340m)

Royal County Down 9th
Royal Melbourne (West) 6th
St Andrews (Old) 17th
Ballybunion (Old) 11th
Hamburger (Falkenstein) 17th*
St George's Hill 10th
Royal County Down 3rd
Royal Melbourne (West) 17th
Royal Dornoch 14th
Royal County Down 2nd
Swinley Forest 12th
North Berwick 2nd
Paraparaumu Beach 13th
Morfontaine 8th
Machrihanish 5th
Murcar 7th
Sunningdale (Old) 7th
Royal Worlington & Newmarket 3rd
Royal County Down 13th
Newcastle 5th
Highlands Links 2nd
St George's Hill 17th

North Berwick 13th

Kennemer 10th

Praia D'El Rey 4th

*Falkenstein 17th   * Par 5 on scorecard*

Machrihanish 1st
Silloth on Solway 4th
Gleneagles (Kings) 13th
County Sligo 17th
Ballybunion (Old) 17th
Royal Portrush (Dunluce) 5th
Humewood 13th
Ballybunion (Old) 9th
Mid Ocean 5th
Royal Aberdeen 1st
West Sussex 16th
Commonwealth 16th
Murcar 3rd
Prestwick 17th
Royal Birkdale 9th
Turnberry (Ailsa) 16th
New South Wales 15th
Royal Dornoch 17th
The Berkshire (Red) 8th
Royal Melbourne (East) 18th
Kawana (Fuji) 14th
Durban 17th
Carnoustie 2nd
Paraparaumu Beach 17th

Portstewart (Strand) 1st
Royal Aberdeen 9th
Yarra Yarra 5th
Royal West Norfolk 3rd
Commonwealth 11th
Nefyn & District 13th
East London 9th
Abiko 5th
Carnoustie 15th
New South Wales 7th
Lahinch 3rd
St Enodoc 3rd
Woking 11th
Royal Aberdeen 4th
Royal Portrush (Dunluce) 4th
Royal Porthcawl 3rd
Kennemer 9th
West Sussex 4th
Metropolitan 5th
St Enodoc 6th
Muirfield 6th
Rye 4th
Royal Adelaide 11th
Royal Canberra 16th

Best Par Fours – Modern (over 340m)

Carne 8th
Cabo del Sol (Ocean) 18th
The National (Moonah) 3rd
The National (Moonah) 11th
Golf du Médoc (Châteaux) 4th
St Andrews Beach (Gunnamatta) 18th
Mission Hills (World Cup) 4th
Doonbeg 15th
Cape Kidnappers 17th
Atlantic Beach 10th
Carne 17th
Barnbougle Dunes 17th
The National 7th *Canada*
The National (Moonah) 10th
Cape Kidnappers 1st
Golf du Médoc (Châteaux) 13th
Praia D'El Rey 15th
Valderrama 10th
Loch Lomond 18th
Dye Fore 4th
Teeth of the Dog 17th

Cape Kidnappers 12th
Spring City (Mountain) 18th
Ellerston 16th
Nirwana Bali 9th
Cabo del Sol (Ocean) 16th
The National (Moonah) 16th
Prince de Provence 7th
Valderrama 2nd
Teeth of the Dog 2nd
The National (Moonah) 4th
Kennedy Bay 15th
Cape Kidnappers 7th
Portstewart (Strand) 5th
Kauri Cliffs 17th
Doonbeg 18th
Cabo del Sol (Ocean) 10th
Greywolf 16th
Ellerston 7th
Spring City (Lake) 13th
Circolo Golf Bogogno (del Conte) 17th
Les Bordes 6th
Oviinbyrd 12th
Les Bordes 18th
Fancourt (Links) 10th

Mid Ocean 5th

Royal Adelaide 11th

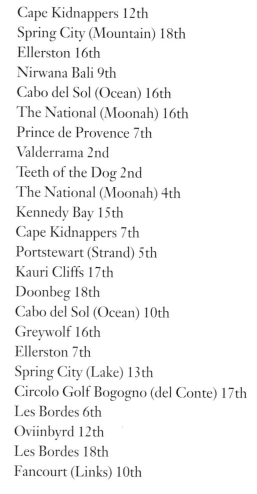

The National (Moonah) 11th

Greywolf 16th

Best Holes – Par Fours

Best Set of Par Fours

Ballybunion (Old)
St Andrews (Old)
Royal Melbourne (West)
Royal Dornoch
Royal County Down
The National (Moonah)
St George's Hill
Royal St George's
Carnoustie
Royal Aberdeen
Kingston Heath
Machrihanish
Sunningdale (New)
Prestwick
St George's
Royal Adelaide
Morfontaine
Muirfield
Carne
Commonwealth
North Berwick
Cape Kidnappers
Ellerston

Hardest Par Fours

St Andrews (Old) 17th
Royal Dornoch 14th
Royal Lytham & St Annes 15th
The National 13th *Canada*
Rye 4th
Royal St George's 15th
The National (Ocean) 18th
The National 18th *Canada*
Royal Troon 11th
Carnoustie 17th
Fancourt (Links) 3rd
Muirfield 1st
Royal County Down 9th
Turnberry (Ailsa) 9th
The European Club 7th
Ellerston 16th
Carnoustie 15th
Les Bordes 18th
The National (Old) 3rd
Prestwick 13th
Old Head 4th
Teeth of the Dog 8th
Sanctuary Cove (Pines) 10th *Australia*

Tralee 12th
Teeth of the Dog 12th
Royal Lytham & St Annes 18th
Rye 13th
Carnoustie 18th
Old Head 14th
Royal West Norfolk 3rd
Muirfield 18th
Royal County Down 3rd
The Addington 8th *England*
The National (Moonah) 16th
Ellerston 8th
Royal Johannesburg (East) 11th
Royal Lytham & St Annes 17th
Valderrama 18th
St Andrews Beach (Gunnamatta) 13th
St George's 14th
Ballybunion (Old) 6th
Prestwick 17th
Valderrama 2nd
Highlands Links 2nd
Royal County Down 8th
Ellerston 7th

Most Spectacular Par Fours

Royal County Down 9th
Ballybunion (Old) 11th
Pezula 14th
Cabo del Sol (Ocean) 18th
New South Wales 14th
Kauri Cliffs 17th
Machrihanish 1st
Sperone 11th
Cabo del Sol (Ocean) 16th
Praia D'El Rey 15th
Ballybunion (Old) 17th
Teeth of the Dog 15th
Carne 11th
Sperone 13th
Royal Portrush (Dunluce) 5th
North Berwick 2nd
Cape Kidnappers 12th
Crans-sur-Sierre 7th
Gulf Harbour 16th
North Berwick 14th
Ballybunion (Old) 7th
The Cut (Port Bouvard) 12th
Eichenheim 7th

St George's Hill 1st

The National (Canada) 13th

Muirfield 18th

Pezula 14th

Best Holes – Par Fives

Best Par Fives – Classic

New South Wales 5th
St Andrews (Old) 14th
Carnoustie 6th
Royal Melbourne (West) 4th
The Addington 16th *England*
Royal Aberdeen 2nd
Cruden Bay 6th
Royal Liverpool 8th
Kawana (Fuji) 15th
Royal St George's 4th
Royal Cinque Ports 3rd
Morfontaine (Valliere) 5th
Highlands Links 16th
The Addington 12th *England*
Royal Cinque Ports 16th
Royal County Down 1st
Silloth on Solway 13th
Royal West Norfolk 8th
Carnoustie 14th
St Enodoc 1st
Abiko 6th
Hillside 11th
Durban 8th

Best Par Fives – Modern

The National (Moonah) 7th
Waterville 18th
Doonbeg 1st
The European Club 3rd
The National (Moonah) 15th
Valderrama 4th
Golf du Médoc (Châteaux) 14th
The K Club (Palmer) 7th
Bigwin Island 18th
The National (Moonah) 2nd
The National (Ocean) 17th
St Andrews Beach (Gunnamatta) 17th
Ellerston 9th
Circolo Golf Bogogno (Bonora) 1st
Kingsbarns 12th
Thirteenth Beach (Beach) 11th
Carne 10th
Nirwana Bali 6th
Ballybunion (Cashen) 15th
Valderrama 17th
Sperone 16th
Noordwijkse 11th
Waterville 11th

Best Set of Par Fives

The National (Moonah)
Highlands Links
Kawana (Fuji)
Woodhall Spa
Muirfield
Silloth on Solway
Royal Cinque Ports
Durban
The Addington *England*
Ellerston
Valderrama
Kingston Heath
Lahinch
Victoria *Australia*
Yarra Yarra
Carnoustie

Most Spectacular Par Fives

New South Wales 5th
Old Head 12th
Bigwin Island 18th
Kawana (Fuji) 15th
Old Head 17th
Sperone 16th
Doonbeg 1st
The National (Ocean) 1st
Ballybunion (Cashen) 15th
Spring City (Lake) 9th
Prince's Grant 15th
St Enodoc 1st
Kauri Cliffs 15th
The National (Old) 8th
Ballybunion (Cashen) 17th
The Addington 12th *England*
Waterville 18th
The National (Ocean) 17th
Kingsbarns 12th
Pezula 12th
Kawana (Fuji) 11th
Pennard 16th

New South Wales 5th

The European Club 3rd

Valderrama 17th

Kawana (Fuji) 15th

Best Holes – Miscellaneous

Best Opening Hole

Machrihanish
Royal Aberdeen
Portstewart (Strand)
St George's Hill
Royal County Down
Doonbeg
Carne
Kingsbarns
Royal West Norfolk
St Enodoc
Portmarnock
Chiberta
Royal Melbourne (East)
The European Club
Highlands Links
Kingston Heath
Cape Kidnappers
The National *Canada*
Nefyn & District
St George's
The National (Ocean)
Nirwana Bali
St Andrews (Old)

The Berkshire (Blue)
Elie
Metropolitan
Humewood
Circolo Golf Bogogno (Bonora)
Kawana (Fuji)
Royal Liverpool
Golf du Médoc (Châteaux)
Woodlands
Brora
Mission Hills (Norman)
Portsea
Royal Porthcawl
Ellerston
Nine Bridges
Mid Ocean
Paraparaumu Beach
Blairgowrie (Rosemount) *Scotland*
Kennemer
Chantilly (Vineuil)
Eichenheim
Jasper Park
Noordwijkse
Hirono

Best Closing Hole

Cabo del Sol (Ocean)
Royal Melbourne (East)
Waterville
Royal Dornoch
St Andrews Beach (Gunnamatta)
El Saler
Kingsbarns
Royal Lytham & St Annes
Chantilly (Longères)
Royal Porthcawl
Spring City Resort (Mountain)
Hamilton (South)
St Andrews (Old)
Jasper Park
Carnoustie
St Enodoc
Highlands Links
Hirono
Capilano
Ganton
North Berwick
Royal Melbourne (West)
Muirfield

Bigwin Island
Ellerston
St George's
Notts
Royal Sydney
Kasumigaseki (East)
Commonwealth
Durban
Golf du Médoc (Châteaux)
The Summit
Mid Ocean
Victoria *Australia*
Atlantic Beach
The National (Moonah)
Koga
Peninsula (North)
Royal Troon
Chantilly (Vineuil)
Doonbeg
Humewood
Royal Adelaide
Barnbougle Dunes
Les Bordes

Machrihanish 1st

Circolo Golf Bogogno (Bonora) 1st

Royal Porthcawl 18th

Mid Ocean 18th

Best Opening Stretch
(Holes 1 – 3)

Royal County Down
Royal Aberdeen
St Enodoc
The National (Moonah)
St George's Hill
Royal Melbourne (East)
Royal Dornoch
St Andrews (Old)
Machrihanish
Tenby
Royal Melbourne (West)
St Andrews Beach (Gunnamatta)
Royal Porthcawl
Durban
The European Club
Metropolitan
Highlands Links
Royal Birkdale
Silloth on Solway
Carnoustie
Kingston Heath

Best Closing Stretch
(Holes 16 – 18)

St Andrews (Old)
Cabo del Sol (Ocean)
Royal Melbourne (West)
Carnoustie
Commonwealth
Waterville
Royal Melbourne (East)
County Sligo
Teeth of the Dog
Highlands Links
Ganton
Royal Dornoch
Brora
St Enodoc
Turnberry (Ailsa)
The National (Moonah)
El Saler
Mid Ocean
Carne
Pennard
Chantilly (Vineuil)

Hardest Opening Hole

Machrihanish
Muirfield
Royal Liverpool
Tenby
Saunton (East) *England*
Enniscrone
Highlands Links
Greywolf
Silloth on Solway
Spring City (Lake)
Royal Birkdale
Royal St George's
Wentworth (West)
The National (Old)
The Berkshire (Blue)
Joondalup (Quarry)

Hardest Closing Hole

The National *Canada*
Les Bordes
The National (Ocean)
Mission Hills (Olazabal)
Royal Lytham & St Annes
Sun City (Gary Player)
Carnoustie
Royal St George's
Muirfield
Spring City (Mountain)
Royal Portrush (Dunluce)
Valderrama
St Enodoc
Kingsbarns
Teeth of the Dog
Cabo del Sol (Ocean)
Doonbeg
Moonah Links (Open)
Cape Kidnappers
Loch Lomond

Royal Aberdeen 3rd

St Andrews (Old) 18th

The National (Old) 1st

Les Bordes 18th

Best Holes – Miscellaneous

Best Stretch (Any Three Holes)

Royal Melbourne (West) 4-6
Royal County Down 2-4
Royal County Down 7-9
North Berwick 13-15
New South Wales 5-7
Ballybunion (Old) 9-11
Royal Dornoch 4-6
St Andrews (Old) 14-16
New South Wales 14-16
Teeth of the Dog 15-17
Ballybunion (Old) 6-8
Newcastle 5-7
West Sussex 4-6
Morfontaine (Valliere) 3-5
Royal Troon 7-9
Royal Portrush (Dunluce) 4-6
St Andrews (Old) 11-13
Morfontaine 7-9
Machrihanish 5-7
The National (Moonah) 2-4
Abiko 5-7
Royal Worlington & Newmarket 3-5

Kawana (Fuji) 13-15
Royal Cinque Ports 15-17
Cruden Bay 4-6
St Enodoc 4-6
North Berwick 2-4
Royal Aberdeen 3-5
Hirono 3-5
Royal Aberdeen 8-10
Doonbeg 13-15
Rye 5-7
Royal Portrush (Dunluce) 12-14
Lahinch 3-5
Nirwana Bali 5-7
Silloth on Solway 3-5
Ballybunion (Old) 15-17
Teeth of the Dog 5-7
Carnoustie 13-15
Carne 15-17
Jasper Park 13-15
St George's Hill 8-10
Westward Ho! 4-6
Kawana (Fuji) 7-9
Praia D'El Rey 13-15

Sunningdale (Old) 5-7
Sunningdale (New) 7-9
El Saler 6-8
Ellerston 6-8
Woking 12-14
Cape Kidnappers 11-13
Carne 8-10
Barnbougle Dunes 3-5
Kasumigaseki (East) 8-10
The Berkshire (Red) 8-10
Cape Kidnappers 5-7
Golf du Médoc (Châteaux) 12-14
Naruo 3-5
Nirwana Bali 12-14
Barnbougle Dunes 13-15
Royal Liverpool 11-13
Cabo del Sol (Ocean) 6-8
Sperone 11-13
The National (Moonah) 9-11
Royal Melbourne (West) 10-12
Spring City (Lake) 8-10
The Addington 7-9 *England*
Silloth on Solway 12-14

New South Wales 6th

Teeth of the Dog 5th

Barnbougle Dunes 15th

All-Star Holes

All-Star Eighteen – Classic Holes

Hole	All-Star	Apologies
1	Machrihanish	Royal Aberdeen, Portstewart (Strand)
2	Royal County Down	North Berwick, Durban
3	Royal Adelaide	Royal County Down, Tenby
4	Royal Melbourne (West)	Royal County Down, Swinley Forest
5	New South Wales	Royal Dornoch, Royal Melbourne (West)
6	Royal Melbourne (West)	Carnoustie, New South Wales
7	Royal County Down	Sunningdale (Old), Rye, Kawana (Fuji)
8	Royal Troon	Morfontaine, Royal Liverpool
9	Royal County Down	Ballybunion (Old), Royal Birkdale
10	St George's Hill	Royal Melbourne (West), The Berkshire (Red)
11	Ballybunion (Old)	St Andrews (Old), Yarra Yarra
12	Swinley Forest	Woodhall Spa, St Andrews (Old)
13	North Berwick	Paraparaumu Beach, Muirfield
14	Royal Dornoch	Royal Portrush (Dunluce), New South Wales
15	Kingston Heath	Kawana (Fuji), North Berwick
16	West Sussex	Commonwealth, The Berkshire (Red)
17	St Andrews (Old)	Royal Melbourne (West), Hamburger (Falkenstein)
18	Royal Melbourne (East)	Royal Dornoch, Chantilly (Longères)

All-Star Eighteen – Modern Holes

Hole	All-Star	Apologies
1	Doonbeg	Carne, Kingsbarns
2	St Andrews Beach (Gunnamatta)	Peninsula (North), The National (Moonah)
3	The National (Moonah)	The European Club, St Andrews Beach (Gunnamatta)
4	Barnbougle Dunes	Praia D'El Rey, Golf du Médoc (Châteaux)
5	Teeth of the Dog	Doonbeg, Portstewart (Strand)
6	Kingbarns	Greywolf, Oubaai
7	Nirwana Bali	The National (Old), Barnbougle Dunes, The National (Moonah)
8	Carne	Wolf Creek (South), Nine Bridges
9	Doonbeg	Ellerston, Ria Bintan (Ocean)
10	Atlantic Beach	The National (Moonah), Valderrama
11	Carne	The National (Moonah), Querencia
12	Enniscrone	Kingsbarns, Thirteenth Beach (Beach)
13	Golf du Médoc (Châteaux)	Cape Kidnappers, Spring City (Lake)
14	Oitavos	Doonbeg, Cabo del Sol (Ocean)
15	Barnbougle Dunes	Praia D'El Rey, Doonbeg
16	Teeth of the Dog	Ellerston, Thirteenth Beach (Beach)
17	Cabo del Sol (Ocean)	Carne, Cape Kidnappers
18	Cabo del Sol (Ocean)	Waterville, St Andrews Beach (Gunnamatta)

All-Star Eighteen – Underrated Holes

Hole	All-Star	Apologies
1	Royal West Norfolk	Chiberta, Cape Kidnappers
2	Highlands Links	Nirwana Bali, Royal Aberdeen
3	Tenby	Murcar, Kingston Heath
4	Silloth on Solway	Mission Hills (World Cup)
5	Morfontaine (Valliere)	Newcastle, Highlands Links
6	Ballybunion (Old)	Cruden Bay
7	Murcar	Western Gailes, Pennard
8	El Saler	Paraparaumu Beach
9	Kingston Heath	Westward Ho!
10	De Pan	Kasumigaseki (East)
11	Hillside	Kawana (Fuji)
12	Woodhall Spa	The Addington *England*
13	Lahinch	Humewood
14	Biarritz (La Phare)	County Louth
15	Kennemer	Turnberry (Ailsa)
16	The Addington *England*	Royal Cinque Ports, Brora
17	St George's Hill	County Sligo, El Saler
18	El Saler	Hirono, Spring City (Mountain)

All-Star Eighteen – Hardest Holes

Hole	All-Star	Apologies
1	Muirfield	Machrihanish
2	Royal County Down	Valderrama
3	Fancourt (Links)	The National (Old)
4	Rye	Old Head
5	Saunton (East) *England*	Kauri Cliffs
6	Turnberry (Ailsa)	West Sussex
7	The European Club	Rye
8	Teeth of the Dog	Ballybunion (Cashen)
9	The National (Ocean)	Turnberry (Ailsa)
10	Sanctuary Cove (Pines)	Spring City (Lake)
11	Royal Troon	Royal Johannesburg (East)
12	Woodhall Spa	Teeth of the Dog
13	The National *Canada*	Prestwick
14	Royal Dornoch	Royal Portrush (Dunluce)
15	Royal St George's	Royal Lytham & St Annes
16	Carnoustie	Teeth of the Dog
17	St Andrews (Old)	Royal Lytham & St Annes
18	The National *Canada*	Les Bordes

PLANET GOLF | RATINGS & RANKINGS 381

Best Courses

Best Courses in Africa

Durban
Humewood
Fancourt (Links)
Leopard Creek
Sun City (Gary Player)
Atlantic Beach
East London
The River Club
Oubaai
Royal Johannesburg (East)
Pezula
Prince's Grant
Glendower
Fancourt (Montague)
Beachwood
Zimbali
Sun City (Lost City)
George
Wild Coast
Champagne Sports Resort
Houghton
Morningside Farm
Umdoni Park

Best Courses in Asia

Hirono
Kawana (Fuji)
Nirwana Bali
Kasumigaseki (East)
Nine Bridges
Spring City (Lake)
Naruo
Koga
Tiger Beach
Mission Hills (Norman)
Abiko
Tokyo
Ono
Hong Kong GC (Fanling)
Mission Hills (World Cup)
Ria Bintan (Ocean)
Pinx
Phoenix
Pine Valley
Singapore Island (Bukit)
Mission Hills (Faldo)
Blue Canyon (Canyon)
Blackstone

Best Courses in Australasia

Royal Melbourne (West)
New South Wales
Kingston Heath
The National (Moonah)
Barnbougle Dunes
Royal Adelaide
Victoria
Ellerston
Royal Melbourne (East)
Paraparaumu Beach
Commonwealth
Cape Kidnappers
Peninsula (North)
Woodlands
Newcastle
St Andrews Beach (Gunnamatta)
Metropolitan
The Dunes
Kauri Cliffs
Kooyonga
Yarra Yarra
Portsea
Thirteenth Beach (Beach)

Best Courses in Europe

Morfontaine
Valderrama
Hamburger (Falkenstein)
Kennemer
Chantilly (Championship)
Praia D'El Rey
Prince de Provence
El Saler
De Pan
Les Bordes
Golf du Médoc (Châteaux)
Noordwijkse
Chiberta
Hardelot (Les Pins)
Circolo Golf Bogogno (Bonora)
Falsterbo
Sperone
Royal Hague
Troia
Sotogrande (Old)
Eichenheim
Fontainebleau
Oitavos

Durban 2nd

Hirono 13th

Royal Melbourne (West) 5th

Chantilly (Longères) 18th

Best Courses in Great Britain & Ireland

Royal County Down
Royal Dornoch
Ballybunion (Old)
St Andrews (Old)
Royal Portrush (Dunluce)
Royal Aberdeen
North Berwick
St George's Hill
Royal St George's
Lahinch
Prestwick
Carnoustie
Swinley Forest
Machrihanish
Sunningdale (New)
Rye
Turnberry (Ailsa)
Muirfield
Sunningdale (Old)
Carne
Gleneagles (Kings)
Royal Porthcawl

Best Courses in North & South America

Highlands Links
Teeth of the Dog
St George's
Cabo del Sol (Ocean)
Mid Ocean
Toronto
Jasper Park
Hamilton
Capilano
Banff Springs
The National
Querencia
The Summit
Wolf Creek
Oviinbyrd
Devil's Paintbrush
Dye Fore
Sandy Lane (Green Monkey)
Blackhawk
Cabo del Sol (Desert)
Cataraqui

Best Golf Resort – Golf

Highlands Links
Turnberry (Ailsa)
Teeth of the Dog
Gleneagles (Kings)
Barnbougle Dunes
Cabo del Sol (Ocean)
Kawana (Fuji)
Mid Ocean
Jasper Park
Doonbeg
Nirwana Bali
Banff Springs
Praia D'El Rey
Nine Bridges
Kauri Cliffs
Fancourt (Links)
El Saler
Les Bordes
Spring City (Lake)
Leopard Creek
Sun City (Gary Player)
Atlantic Beach

Best Golf Resort – Hotel

Pinx (Podo)
Gleneagles
Sun City (The Palace of the Lost City)
Fairmont Banff Springs
Pezula
Kauri Cliffs
Nirwana Bali
Les Bordes
Royal County Down (Slieve Donard)
Leopard Creek (Malelane Sun)
Turnberry
Highlands Links (Keltic Lodge)
Cabo del Sol
Fairmont Jasper Park Lodge
Nine Bridges
The K Club
Spring City
Fancourt Resort
Mission Hills
Mid Ocean
Atlantic Beach
Kawana Hotel
Laguna Whitsundays

Lahinch 3rd

Cabo del Sol (Ocean) 18th

Gleneagles (Kings) 5th

Fairmont Banff Springs

Best Courses

Best Front Nine

Royal County Down
Royal Melbourne (West)
Royal Portrush (Dunluce)
Royal Aberdeen
Machrihanish
West Sussex
Royal Dornoch
Lahinch
Rye
Turnberry (Ailsa)
Ballybunion (Old)
The National (Moonah)
St Andrews (Old)
Highlands Links
St George's Hill
Carnoustie
Morfontaine
Royal Worlington & Newmarket
Durban
Royal St George's
Sunningdale (New)
St Enodoc
Newcastle
Hirono
Ellerston
Barnbougle Dunes
Nirwana Bali
Portstewart (Strand)
Abiko
Royal Liverpool
Cruden Bay
Teeth of the Dog
Prestwick
Morfontaine (Valliere)
Kasumigaseki (East)
Nine Bridges
Royal Porthcawl
New South Wales
Paraparaumu Beach
St George's
Toronto
The European Club
Ganton
Royal Melbourne (East)
Royal Troon
Carne

Best Back Nine

St Andrews (Old)
Carnoustie
North Berwick
Ballybunion (Old)
Royal Melbourne (West)
County Sligo
New South Wales
Waterville
Cabo del Sol (Ocean)
Victoria *Australia*
Carne
Woking
Kingston Heath
Royal Dornoch
Cape Kidnappers
St George's Hill
Hamburger (Falkenstein)
St George's
Royal Melbourne (East)
Barnbougle Dunes
Ganton
Kennemer
Jasper Park

Best Coastal Courses

Royal County Down
Royal Dornoch
Ballybunion (Old)
St Andrews (Old)
Royal Portrush (Dunluce)
New South Wales
Royal Aberdeen
North Berwick
Royal St George's
Lahinch
Prestwick
Carnoustie
Machrihanish
The National (Moonah)
Rye
Highlands Links
Turnberry (Ailsa)
Muirfield
Teeth of the Dog
Carne
Barnbougle Dunes
Royal Porthcawl
St Enodoc

Royal County Down 4th

Nine Bridges 8th

Carnoustie 18th

Royal Portrush (Dunluce) 14th

Cabo del Sol (Ocean)
Kawana (Fuji)
Kingbarns
Royal Birkdale
Cruden Bay
Mid Ocean
County Sligo
Doonbeg
Nirwana Bali
Paraparaumu Beach
Durban
Waterville
Cape Kidnappers
Royal Liverpool
Royal West Norfolk
Royal Troon
Kennemer
Humewood
The European Club
Newcastle
Praia D'El Rey
St Andrews Beach (Gunnamatta)
Kauri Cliffs

Best Inland Courses

Royal Melbourne (West)
St George's Hill
Swinley Forest
Morfontaine
Sunningdale (New)
Kingston Heath
Sunningdale (Old)
Gleneagles (Kings)
West Sussex
Hirono
St George's
Royal Adelaide
Woodhall Spa
Victoria *Australia*
Ellerston
The Berkshire (Red)
Royal Melbourne (East)
Valderrama
Toronto
Hamburger (Falkenstein)
Woking
Loch Lomond
Ganton

Best Views

Old Head
Royal County Down
New South Wales
Sperone
Cape Kidnappers
The National (Old)
Nefyn & District
Kauri Cliffs
Banff Springs
Cabo del Sol (Ocean)
Teeth of the Dog
Doonbeg
Praia D'El Rey
St Enodoc
Turnberry (Ailsa)
Nirwana Bali
Pezula
Kawana (Fuji)
Barnbougle Dunes
Loch Lomond
Ballybunion (Old/Cashen)
County Sligo
The National (Moonah/Ocean)

Spring City (Lake)
Royal Portrush (Dunluce)
Ria Bintan (Ocean)
Ullna
Tralee
The Cut (Port Bouvard)
North Berwick
Crans-sur-Sierre
Highlands Links
Lahinch
Eichenheim
Cruden Bay
Clearwater Bay *Hong Kong*
Kingsbarns
Laguna Whitsundays
Pennard
Monte Carlo
Royal Porthcawl
Pevero
Royal Dornoch
Carne
Greywolf
Port Royal *Bermuda*
Jasper Park

Paraparauma Beach 13th

Sunningdale (New) 5th

Sperone 11th

Greywolf 6th

Best Courses – Miscellaneous

Hardest Courses

Sun City (Gary Player)
Royal County Down
Carnoustie
Moonah Links (Open)
Muirfield
Royal Dornoch
Valderrama
Royal St George's
The National *Canada*
Cape Kidnappers
Rye
Ballybunion (Cashen)
Royal Lytham & St Annes
Ellerston
Teeth of the Dog
Woodhall Spa
Ganton
Mission Hills (Norman)
Doonbeg
The National (Ocean)
Dye Fore
Troia

Best Greens

Royal Melbourne (East/West)
Royal Dornoch
Morfontaine (27 Holes)
Royal St George's
Machrihanish
Woking
St Andrews (Old)
Rye
Royal Portrush (Dunluce)
Kingston Heath
Muirfield
Prestwick
Highlands Links
North Berwick
The National (Moonah)
Royal County Down
Victoria *Australia*
County Sligo
Swinley Forest
Teeth of the Dog
Ellerston
Sunningdale (Old/New)
Hirono

Killer Greens

St Andrews (Old) 11th
Prestwick 15th
Morfontaine (Valliere) 3rd
St Andrews (Old) 14th
Royal Dornoch 14th
Royal St George's 15th
Prestwick 13th
Bintan Lagoon (Nicklaus) 13th
Jockey Club (Colorada) 17th
Rye 14th
North Berwick 16th
Victoria 7th *Canada*
Teeth of the Dog 8th
Machrihanish 12th
Westward Ho! 9th
Royal Troon 8th
Highlands Links 2nd
Royal St George's 9th
Rye 7th
Pennard 7th
Kingston Heath 15th
Royal Dornoch 6th
St Andrews (Old) 17th

Machrihanish 13th
Royal Melbourne (West) 6th
Jockey Club (Colorada) 10th
Machrihanish 5th
Royal Dornoch 5th
Royal St George's 10th
Royal Melbourne (West) 7th
Cape Kidnappers 8th
St Andrews (Old) 2nd
Morfontaine 9th
Barnbougle Dunes 10th
Morfontaine (Valliere) 4th
Morfontaine 10th
Naruo 14th
Morfontaine 11th
Kingston Heath 3rd

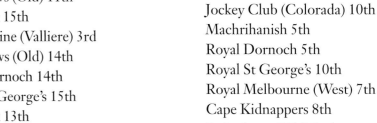

Sun City (Gary Player) 9th   *Royal St George's 6th*   *Morfontaine (Valliere) 3rd*   *St Andrews (Old) 2nd*

Best Bunkering

Royal Melbourne (East/West)
Royal County Down
Kingston Heath
St Andrews (Old)
Carnoustie
Muirfield
Royal Dornoch
The National (Moonah)
Woodhall Spa
Barnbougle Dunes
Victoria *Australia*
Ganton
St George's Hill
Morfontaine
West Sussex
Royal Liverpool
Hirono
Commonwealth
County Sligo
Ellerston
Sunningdale (New)
Royal West Norfolk
Royal Aberdeen

Royal Troon
Cape Kidnappers
Royal Golf des Fagnes (Spa)
St George's
Kasumigaseki (East)
Yarra Yarra
Paraparaumu Beach
Golf du Médoc (Châteaux)
St Germaine
Alwoodley
The Berkshire (Red/Blue)
Koga
Woodlands
Jasper Park
Kawana (Fuji)
Prestwick
Royal Porthcawl
Mission Hills (Norman)
The European Club
Nirwana Bali
Peninsula (North)

Killer Bunkers

St Andrews (Old) 17th
Woodhall Spa 12th
St Andrews (Old) 11th
Woodhall Spa 5th
Muirfield 17th
St Enodoc 6th
Royal Troon 8th
Westward Ho! 4th
Ganton 16th
St Andrews (Old) 14th
Koga 16th
Muirfield 13th
Royal West Norfolk 4th
Prestwick 17th
The National (Ocean) 4th
Little Aston 18th
Walton Heath (Old) 16th
Royal Melbourne (West) 10th
Royal St George's 4th

Best Conditioning

Ellerston
Metropolitan
Royal Melbourne (East/West)
Valderrama
Nine Bridges
The Capital
Kingston Heath
Spring City
The National (Moonah)
Kingsbarns
Sandy Lane (Green Monkey)
The Grove
Les Bordes
Prince de Provence
The National *Canada*
Royal County Down
Cabo del Sol (Ocean/Desert)
Fancourt Resort (Links)
Phoenix
Victoria *Australia*
Querencia

Royal Melbourne (East) 1st

The Berkshire (Blue) 13th

Royal West Norfolk 4th

Nine Bridges 15th

Acknowledgements

Although PLANET GOLF aims to document and celebrate the wonderful golf courses and golf holes that make our game so special, a tremendous note of recognition must also go to the millions of golfers worldwide who support the sport and make the game such a terrific social and recreational activity. Without golfers there would be no golf courses, and without the passionate golfer, no venues of exceptional quality. This book is, therefore, dedicated to anyone who shares our passion for great golf.

A book of this scale is simply not possible to put together alone. Needless to say, there are countless people to thank. We'll start with the most obvious. To Richard Launder, we thank you for your unwavering support and faith in the concept throughout this long process. Our gratitude also to Andrew Cunningham for an expert design and for putting up with all the chopping and changing, Emma Wilson and Neil Conning for their editing assistance and Margaret Kaplan, Michael Jacobs, Steve Tager, Mark LaRiviere and the crew at Abrams for their energy and expertise in helping bring PLANET GOLF to the golfing public.

Most thanks, however, should be reserved for the greater golf industry, who so warmly welcomed us on our travels. To the countless secretaries, managers, professionals and club personnel who have assisted us through this project we offer our most grateful appreciation. In particular, we wish to extend a special word of acknowledgement to friends who have gone beyond the call of duty to help arrange rounds, hotels, transfers or simply to ensure our travels were safe and comfortable. These include Sho Abiro, Ian Andrew, Noriaki Aoki, Archie Baird, Nuno Bastos, Mike Chadsey, T.D. Clagett, Ben Cowan-Dewar, Dolph Cox, Noel Cronin, Jean Dulout, John Duncan, Jim Fraser, Gilles Gagnon, Lori Grant, David Harris, Barbara Heimlich, Tony Hitchcock, Junn Ikada, Jim Ironside, Young-Sam Kang, Tatsuo Kato, Mr N. Kawamata, Michael Y.H. Kim, James Laidler, Fanny Lee, Seon K. Lee, Young-Duk Lee, Nick Leefe, David LeStrange, Pat Maguire, Rory Mathews, Rob McDannold, Jim McKenna, Norman McLean, Stuart McLean, Bryan Mewett, Dee Nakamoto, Masa Nishijima, Yasuhiko Oe, Jamie Ortiz-Patiño, Ken Payet, Col. Ian Pearce, Joe Pinnington, Mauro Repossini, John Robinson, Pat Ruddy, Mark Sajatovich, Richard Sattler, Fintan Scannell, Mamoru Seto, Colin Simpson, Peter Smith, Greg Tallman, Adrian Tan, Bill Taylor, John Terry-Lloyd, Randall Thompson, Ian Valentine, Richard Wax, Dermot Whelan, Winky Wong, Holly Wood, Martin Yates, Arthur Yeo, and Edward Zhu.

Our deepest gratitude also goes to Greg Norman for his Foreword contribution and to the various golf designers and developers who provided comments for the book and helped with access to their courses. The Bernard Darwin quotes were reprinted with permission of A P Watt Ltd on behalf of Paul Ashton, Ursula Mommens and Philip Trevelyan. Every effort has been made to contact all the other copyright holders and should there be any omissions they will be corrected in future editions. Thanks also to www.drivetravel.com.au for assistance with our travels.

Finally, our love and eternal thanks to our families. To Darius' family, Leeanne, Persia, Indy and Chantilly, who made coming home after each trip the best part of the whole project. And from David, thanks for the smiling faces of Lynn, Danielle, Jessica and Joanna, who were a joy to see upon returning home, plus a warm thank you to Tim for taking care of his mother.

We are truly fortunate to have met so many wonderful people over the past four years and to have shared our passion with such a wide variety of personalties. PLANET GOLF has been a remarkable journey, and to all who shared our travels: we are forever in your debt.

Darius Oliver

David Scaletti

'This book is dedicated to all for whom the game of golf is a passion, and not just a pastime.'

OPPOSITE The Old Course at St Andrews is the spiritual home of the game for all passionate golfers. Here, David Scaletti captures the 5th green as the setting sun meets the gathering clouds.

PREVIOUS PAGES The 13th green, Ellerston Golf Course, Australia.

Index

Editor: Emma Wilson
Designer: Andrew Cunningham
Production Manager: Andrew Cunningham

Library of Congress Cataloging-in-Publication Data

Oliver, Darius.
  Planet golf : the definitive reference to great golf courses outside the United States of America / by Darius Oliver ; photography by David Scaletti.
    p. cm.
  Includes index.
  ISBN-13: 978-0-8109-9403-4 (hardcover)
  ISBN-10: 0-8109-9403-8
  1. Golf courses—Guidebooks. I. Title.
  GV975.O45 2007
  796.352'068—dc22
                          2007015628

Produced in China by Australian Book Connection
10 9 8 7 6 5 4 3 2 1

Prepress by Splitting Image Colour Studios Pty Ltd

HNA
harry n. abrams, inc.
a subsidiary of La Martinière Groupe

115 West 18th Street
New York, NY 10011
www.hnabooks.com

For more information on the courses featured in this book,
or the general golf planet, please visit

www.planetgolf.com.au

PRELIM IMAGES
Page ii: Praia D'El Rey, Portugal – 14th hole
Page iii: Kingston Heath, Australia – 15th hole, Royal Porthcawl, Wales – 18th hole, Nine Bridges, South Korea – 5th hole